Writing for
Publication

Related Titles of Interest

Using Technology in Learner-Centered Education: Proven Strategies
for Teaching and Learning
David G. Brown, Gordon McCray, Craig Runde, and Heidi Schweizer
ISBN: 0-205-35580-3

Instructing and Mentoring the African American College Student:
Strategies for Success in Higher Education
Louis B. Gallien Jr. and Marshalita S. Peterson
ISBN: 0-205-38917-1

Emblems of Quality in Higher Education:
Developing and Sustaining High-Quality Programs
Jennifer Grant Haworth and Clifton F. Conrad
ISBN: 0-205-19546-6

Grant Writing in Higher Education: A Step-by-Step Guide
Kenneth T. Henson
ISBN: 0-205-38919-8

Learner-Centered Assessment on College Campuses:
Shifting the Focus from Teaching to Learning
Mary E. Huba and Jann E. Freed
ISBN: 0-205-28738-7

Revitalizing General Education in a Time of Scarcity:
A Navigational Chart for Administrators and Faculty
Sandra L. Kanter, Zelda F. Gamson, and Howard B. London
ISBN: 0-205-26257-0

The Adjunct Professor's Guide to Success: Surviving and
Thriving in the College Classroom
Richard E. Lyons, Marcella L. Kysilka, and George E. Pawlas
ISBN: 0-205-28774-3

Success Strategies for Adjunct Faculty
Richard E. Lyons
ISBN: 0-205-36017-3

Teaching College in an Age of Accountability
Richard E. Lyons, Meggin McIntosh, and Marcella L. Kysilka
ISBN: 0-205-35315-0

An Introduction to Interactive Multimedia
Stephen J. Misovich, Jerome Katrichis, David Demers,
and William B. Sanders
ISBN: 0-205-34373-2

Teaching Tips for College and University Instructors:
A Practical Guide
David Royse
ISBN: 0-205-29839-7

Creating Learning-Centered Courses for the World Wide Web
William B. Sanders
ISBN: 0-205-31513-5

Designing and Teaching an On-Line Course:
Spinning Your Web Classroom
Heidi Schweizer
ISBN: 0-205-30321-8

Shaping the College Curriculum: Academic Plans in Action
Joan S. Stark and Lisa R. Lattuca
ISBN: 0-205-16706-3

Faculty of Color in Academe: Bittersweet Success
Caroline Sotello, Viernes Turner, and Samuel L. Myers Jr.
ISBN: 0-205-27849-3

The Effective, Efficient Professor: Teaching, Scholarship, and Service
Phillip C. Wankat
ISBN: 0-205-33711-2

The Student Guide to Successful Online Learning:
A Handbook of Tips, Strategies, and Techniques
Ken W. White and Jason D. Baker
ISBN: 0-205-34104-7

The Online Teaching Guide: A Handbook of Attitudes,
Strategies, and Techniques for the Virtual Classroom
Ken W. White and Bob H. Weight
ISBN: 0-205-29531-2

For further information on these and other related titles, contact:
College Division

ALLYN AND BACON, INC.
75 Arlington Street, Suite 300
Boston, MA 02116
www.ablongman.com

WRITING FOR PUBLICATION

Road to Academic Advancement

Kenneth T. Henson
The Citadel

Boston   New York   San Francisco
Mexico City   Montreal   Toronto   London   Madrid   Munich   Paris
Hong Kong   Singapore   Tokyo   Cape Town   Sydney

Executive Editor and Publisher: Stephen D. Dragin
Senior Editorial Assistant: Barbara Strickland
Marketing Manager: Jennifer Armstrong
Editorial-Production Service: Omegatype Typography, Inc.
Composition Buyer: Linda Cox
Manufacturing Buyer: Andrew Turso
Cover Administrator: Rebecca Krzyzaniak
Electronic Composition: Omegatype Typography, Inc.

For related titles and support materials, visit our online catalog at www.ablongman.com.

Library of Congress Cataloging-in-Publication Data

Henson, Kenneth T.
   Writing for publication : road to academic advancement / Kenneth T. Henson.
      p. cm.
   Includes bibliographical references.
   ISBN 0-205-43319-7 (alk. paper)
      1. Authorship. 2. Academic writing. 3. Scholarly publishing. I. Title.

PN146.H38 2005
808'.02—dc22

                                                                    2004052673

Printed in the United States of America

10 9 8 7 6 5 4 3 2   09 08

College professors are the most fortunate people I know. To be sure, over the past decades our job has changed. We spend too much time on nonacademic tasks, and the paperwork load increases daily. Yet, what could be more exciting than confronting the unknown, stretching the mental limits, and introducing young people to the secrets within our disciplines?

Have you ever thought how different your own life would be if you lived, say, a couple of hundred miles from the nearest college campus? Although at times we all might long for more bucolic surroundings, most of us would immediately miss the environment where time is still taken to pursue truth, and our clients and colleagues are dedicated to learning.

Through more than two decades of conducting workshops on campuses from coast to coast, meeting literally thousands of professors, I have concluded that my profession is dominated by good people, people who spend their lives helping others improve their lot in life. There are few greater callings. It is to these honorable people that I humbly dedicate this book.

CONTENTS

Illustrations   xvii

Preface   xix

About the Author   xxi

1   Why Write?   1

Reasons to Write   3
A Time and Place for Everything   10
When Is the Best Time to Write?   11
Tooling Up for the Job   13
The Best Place to Write   14
Perennial Excuses   19
Taking Inventory   20
A Final Word   21
Recapping the Major Points   22
References   22

2   Finding Topics   24

The Dissertation: A Source of Topics   25
Grants as a Source of Topics   27
Your Job as a Source of Topics   27
Other Occupations as Sources of Writing Topics   28
Reference Books as a Source of Topics   29
Forecasting the Future   30
    Using Speakers to Predict Future Topics   30
    Using Journal Editors to Predict Future Topics   31
    Using Professional Association Yearbook Editors
        to Predict Future Topics   31
Recapping the Major Points   32
References   32

3   Getting Started   33

The Right Title   34
   Choosing Titles for Nonfiction Journal Articles   36
Writing the First Sentence   37
Paragraphing   39
Go Ahead and Write   40
Profile: Arnold and Jeanne Cheyney   40
Recapping the Major Points   41
References   42

4   About Style   43

Writing Clearly   46
   Write Concisely   46
   Write Positively   48
   Treat Genders Fairly   52
Recapping the Major Points   58
References   58

5   Organizing Articles   59

Organizing Nonfiction Articles   61
   Organizing Skill No. 1: Establishing Credibility   61
   Organizing Skill No. 2: Achieving Substance   61
   Organizing Skill No. 3: Paragraphing   67
   Organizing Skill No. 4: Using Flowcharts to Organize   69
Putting It Together   70
Recapping the Major Points   70
References   70

6   Using Journals, Libraries, Surveys, and Action Research   71

Using Journals   72
   Physical Characteristics   72
   Article Length   72
   Reading Level   73
   Guidelines for Authors   73
   Call for Manuscripts   75
   Coming Themes   75
   Reviewers' Guidelines and Rating Scales   75
Using Libraries   78
   Identifying Topics   78
   Identifying Target Journals   79
   Using Your Own Expertise   80

Using Surveys   81
Using Action Research   87
Recapping the Major Points   87
References   88

7   **Common Errors in Writing for Journals   89**

The Nature of Writing   90
Mistakes and Recommendations   90
    Mistake: Lack of Familiarity with the Journal and Its Readers   90
    Mistake: Wrong Style   93
    Mistake: Failure to Check for Grammatical Errors   94
    Mistake: Failure to Include Substance   95
    Mistake: Failure to Write Simply and Clearly   97
    Recommendation: Select Your Target Journals in Advance   99
    Recommendation: Identify Coming Themes   99
    Recommendation: Find a Good Title   99
    Recommendation: Focus on the Opening Paragraph   99
    Recommendation: Avoid Provincialism   100
    Recommendation: Review Your Manuscript   101
Recapping the Major Points   106
References   106

8   **Communicating with Journal Editors   108**

The Author–Editor Relationship   109
    The Telephone   109
    The Query Letter   111
    The Cover Letter   115
Guest Editing   116
Recapping the Major Points   117
Reference   117

9   **Questions Writers Ask   118**

Why Do You Write?   119
What Suggestions Can You Give to Aspiring Writers?   120
Have You a Favorite Success Story?   120
How Do You Handle Rejection?   122
What Distinguishes Highly Successful Writers
    from Less Successful Writers?   123
Is It O.K. to Send a Manuscript to Multiple Publishers?   124
Are There Advantages in Collaborating?   125
Should I Collaborate Long Distance?   126

Should I Write Articles before Writing Short Stories or Books?   126
What Is a Refereed Journal?   127
Is It Wise to Use Vanity Publishers?   128
What About Self-Publishing?   128
If Asked, Should I Pay a Journal Publishing Expenses?   129
Should I Be a Specialist or a Generalist?   129
Questions Regarding Copyright   130
How Can Authors Learn to Use the Library More Effectively?   132
Are Colloquialisms and Clichés Acceptable?   133
Should I Use Tables and Graphs in My Articles?   134
What Should I Do When an Editor Keeps Holding
   My Manuscript?   134
Whose Name Comes First?   134
Who Is Listed First If the Collaborators Are Professors
   and Graduate Students?   135
If I Furnish My Dissertation or Thesis for a Collaborator to Shape
   into a Manuscript, Is That an Equitable Exchange?   135
If I Share a Book Idea with a Publisher, How Can I Be Sure It Won't
   Be Turned Over to a More Experienced Author?   136
What Does It Mean When an Editor Asks the Author to Rewrite
   and Resubmit a Manuscript? Should I Do That?   136
Should I Use a Computer?   137
What Should I List on My Résumé as Publications?   138
Do You Recommend Using Support Groups?   138
Recapping the Major Points   139
Reference   139

10 Getting Book Contracts   140

Choosing the Right Book to Write   141
Writing Professional Books   141
Writing Books for University Presses   142
Developing a Prospectus   143
   Content Outline   143
   Sample Chapters   145
   Book Description   146
   Market Description   148
   Description of the Competition   148
   Author Description   149
Selecting a Publisher   149
   Send Query Letters   152
Negotiating the Contract   152
Recapping the Major Points   153
References   155

11 Planning for Success   156

Managing Each Manuscript   158
 Step 1: Identify Topic Areas   159
 Step 2: Identify Two Sets of Journals—Specialized and General   160
 Step 3: Assign Priorities to the Journals You Listed   160
 Step 4: Refine Your Journal List   161
Profile: Bonnidell Clouse   161
Develop a Tracking System   163
Getting Mileage   164
 Maintain a Current Résumé   166
 Write Book Chapters   166
 Apply to Daily Work   166
Recapping the Major Points   167
Reference   168

12 Grant Proposal Writing   169

Make Your Proposal Timely   171
Learn How to Develop Fresh Ideas   171
Identify and Use Your Assets   172
Gather the Necessary Materials   173
Match Your Strengths with the Funders' Goals   174
 Deadlines   175
 A Format for Proposals   175
Foundation Proposals   176
 Guideline 1: Match Your Expertise with the Needs
 of Various Audiences   179
 Guideline 2: Add a Unique Angle   179
 Guideline 3: Make a Convincing Commitment   180
 Guideline 4: Be Flexible   181
 Guideline 5: Use Every Opportunity to Gather Information
 about Available Money   182
 Guideline 6: Make Your Request Economically Responsible   183
 Guideline 7: Make the Proposal Easy to Read   183
 Guideline 8: Follow the RFP Guidelines Precisely   184
 Guideline 9: Develop a Project Evaluation Process   185
 Guideline 10: Test the Budget against the Narrative   185
Recapping the Major Points   186
Reference   187

13 Parts of a Proposal   188

Transmittal Letter   189
Title Page   190

Abstract   193
Table of Contents   194
Purposes, Goals, and Objectives   194
Timetable   195
Evaluation   197
Budget   198
   Be Reasonable   198
   Make In-Kind Contributions   198
Checklist   199
Summary   200
Recapping the Major Points   201

14 Three Winning Proposals   202

Prelude   203
Proposal One: Project ESCAPE   203
   Purpose of the Proposal   203
   Putting the Funder's Goals First   205
   Unique Features   205
Using the Literature   206
   Dealing with Disagreement   207
   Using Modules   207
   Disseminating the Grant   209
   Lessons Learned from Project ESCAPE   211
Proposal Two: The Summer Physics Institute   211
   The Role of Passion   211
   Choosing Language   213
   Unique Features   213
   Lessons Learned from the Summer Physics
      Institute Grant   216
Proposal Three: A Million-Dollar Technology Proposal   216
   Using Relationships with Potential Funders   216
   Using Your Strengths   218
   Using the Literature   218
   Lessons Learned from the Technology Grant   219
Summary   220
Recapping the Major Points   220

15 Using Technology to Write Grants   222

Surfing the Internet   223
Using the Internet to Validate   223
Sources Available on the Internet   226

The Federal Register   *227*
The Catalog of Federal Domestic Assistance   *228*
The Commerce Business Daily   *228*
National Data Book of Foundations   *228*
MedWeb   *228*
GrantsNet   *228*
U.S. Department of Education   *228*
National Science Foundation   *228*
Summary   229
Recapping the Major Points   229

16 Using Writing to Gain a Tenure-Track Position and Tenure   230

The Rise of Non Tenure-Track Faculty   231
What the Change in Status of Non Tenure-Track Faculty
    Means to You   231
Align Your Grants and Articles with Your Department's
    Goals   232
Action Research   233
Preparing for the Interview   235
Recapping the Major Points   236
Final Note   236
References   236

Appendixes

A   Preferences of Journals in Various Disciplines   237
B   Sample Call for Manuscripts   258
C   Sample Announcement of Coming Themes and Requests
    for Manuscripts   261
D   Attending Writing Workshops   264
E   University Presses   266
F   Sample Proposal for Funding   270
G   Sample Proposal Rating Form   280
H   Profile of an Article   283

Glossary   *291*

Name Index   *295*

Subject Index   *297*

ILLUSTRATIONS

Figure 1.1   Sample article conceived and outlined while waiting
               for my son
Figure 4.1   Editing exercise
Figure 4.2   Effect of close editing
Figure 4.3   Writing positively
Figure 4.4   Advanced editing exercise
Figure 4.5   Good editing is a step-by-step process
Figure 4.6   Treating genders equally
Figure 4.7   Eliminating sexism through pluralizing
               and restructuring
Figure 4.8   Replacing long expressions with fewer words
Figure 4.9   Writers should use small words
Figure 4.10   Additional editing practice
Figure 4.11   Sample student article
Figure 5.1   Establishing credibility
Figure 5.2   Communicating visually through structure
Figure 5.3   Paragraphing exercise
Figure 5.4   Using flowcharts to show organization
Figure 6.1   Graph for estimating readability—extended
Figure 6.2   Rating scales raise the quality of manuscript evaluations and
               simplify the evaluators' work
Figure 6.3   Systematic research method
Figure 6.4   Sample survey questionnaire
Figure 6.5   Articles produced by periodically readministering the survey
               to editors
Figure 6.6   Sample questionnaire cover letter
Figure 6.7   Revised questionnaire cover letter
Figure 7.1   Part One: Sample article style A
               Part Two: Sample article style B
Figure 7.2   Referencing the work of others
Figure 7.3   Expanding application beyond one geographical region
Figure 7.4   Expanding the relevance of information
Figure 8.1   A poorly received query letter
Figure 8.2   Another poorly received query letter
Figure 8.3   Sample of a successful query letter
Figure 8.4   Sample cover letter
Figure 9.1   Statement of ASA policy on multiple submission

Figure 9.2   Refereeing occurs in degrees
Figure 10.1   Sample chapter outline for a how-to book
Figure 10.2   More detailed content outline for a how-to book
Figure 10.3   Contents section that both entertains and informs
Figure 10.4   Detailed chapter outlines for textbooks
Figure 10.5   Content comparison chart
Figure 10.6   Charts of publishers
Figure 10.7   Sample query letter to book publishers
Figure 11.1   Journal profile
Figure 11.2   Sample individual manuscript tracking form
Figure 11.3   Sample of multiple tracking system
Figure 12.1   Sample entry from the *Federal Register*
Figure 12.2   Matching strengths with the funders' goals
               and practices
Figure 12.3   Sample evaluation of problem or needs statement
Figure 12.4   A model proposal letter
Figure 12.5   Sample proposal abstract
Figure 13.1   Sample transmittal letter
Figure 13.2   Sample title page
Figure 13.3   Sample proposal abstract
Figure 13.4   Sample table of contents
Figure 13.5   Sample timetable
Figure 14.1   Sample flowchart
Figure 15.1   Programs for functional area of small business—sample
Figure 15.2   Federal Register
Figure 16.1   Items that adjunct faculty want most from their institutions

PREFACE

There are many genres of writing, but all can be grouped into two types, fiction and nonfiction. People who read fiction insist on being entertained. Those who read nonfiction often enjoy some entertainment, but they demand to be informed. I know this because I have been speaking to and writing for nonfiction audiences for over a decade, and my audiences always arrive with a definite purpose—to learn how to write for publication. I have only one choice; I must either meet this expectation or get out of the business. As a nonfiction writer, I face the same choice—either make good on my promises or stop writing.

In my years of speaking and administering large organizations, I have learned that people are complex, and the ways of grouping and identifying them are unlimited. One possible segmentation would be to view all people either as successes or failures. But the truth is that in some ways we are all successes, and in other ways we are all failures. The trick is to experience more of the first than of the second. The purpose of this book is to help you do just that.

In this book you will find a system that has worked for thousands of people. Yet, to work for you it will require your trust in its ability to do just that. More important, it will require trust in your own ability to develop the skills needed to succeed at the level you wish to succeed. Oscar Wilde said, "We are all in the gutter, but some of us are looking up at the stars."

The sad news is that most people are content to stay in the gutter; some even take comfort in knowing that as long as they stay at the bottom they are safe from falling. The good news is that, by using this book and that often overlooked resource, "yourself," you can raise yourself to the heights that you choose.

This book is prescriptive, and I make no apology for that. Furthermore, like this preface, it is written in first and second person. I chose this style because I find it the clearest and most direct way to communicate. Robert Louis Stevenson has said that, "The job of the writer is not just to write but to write what you mean; not to affect your reader but to affect your reader precisely as you wish." My goal is to help you set and reach your personal and professional goals through writing for publication.

ACKNOWLEDGMENTS

Behind every successful project is a person with vision. My appreciation to Steve Dragin, executive editor at Allyn and Bacon, for his vision and his ability to turn that vision into reality. Success is always welcomed; it is even better when reached while working with people you enjoy.

A special thanks to the many professors and deans who have provided me with opportunities to take my writing workshops to over two hundred campuses from coast to coast. Thanks, too, to Donovan Walling, Phi Delta Kappa's special publications editor, for publishing my 1998 monograph, *A Brief Guide to Writing for Professional Publication* (second edition, 2005).

I would like to thank the reviewers of this book for their helpful comments: Patricia K. Lowry, Jacksonville State University; Robert J. McDermott, University of South Florida; Michael C. Reinschmidt, California State University at Chico; and Edward F. Vacha, Gonzaga University.

Finally, I want to acknowledge Barbara Strickland, Senior Editorial Assistant to Steve Dragin, for her guidance and patience throughout the development of this book.

ABOUT THE AUTHOR

Kenneth T. Henson is Distinguished Professor of Education at The Citadel. He has conducted over two hundred workshops on writing for publication.

His more than two hundred articles in national, refereed journals include articles in *Writers' Digest, The Writer,* and many other journals, including ten articles in the Phi Delta Kappan. His thirty books include *Constructivist Methods for Teaching in Diverse Middle-Level Classrooms* (Allyn & Bacon, 2004), *Grant Writing in Higher Education* (Allyn and Bacon, 2004), *Teaching Today: An Introduction to Education, 7th ed.,* coauthored (Prentice-Hall, 2005), *Managing Secondary and Middle Level Classrooms,* coauthored (Corwin Press, 2005), and *Curriculum Planning: Integrating Multiculturalism, Constructivism, and Education Reform, 2nd ed.* (McGraw-Hill, 2001; reprinted by Waveland Press, 2003).

Writing for Publication

1

WHY WRITE?

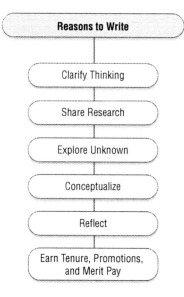

I had flown so little at the time that, just the idea of crossing the Atlantic in a plane was exhilarating. As we descended, my thoughts were distracted by the beautiful patchwork quilt design made by the old stone fences on the British landscape, a sight that would become familiar to me over the coming year. The charm of the landscape and its ancient structures made the whole experience seem like a dream, but the jolt of the plane touching down on the runway roused me to the realization that this was no dream: my Fulbright appointment was real. For the coming year, the "mother country"—with its cosmopolitan life of London, the venerable museums, the castles and stately homes—would be my home.

I'm a planner by nature, and in the months since I learned of this award I'd had time to rehearse this year in my mind, and over the coming year my Fulbright "to do" list would not shorten but would actually grow, although I diligently used every weekend to shorten the list. Some of the unforeseen opportunities would be far grander than my planned activities: fashion shows at Harrods, the Chelsea flower show, Covent Gardens, an invitation to the Queen's garden party, and the purchase of a 1947 Mark VI Bentley which I would ship from South Hampton to Newark as a keepsake, a reminder of the reality of this year-long fairy tale. And there would be repeated requests from the American Embassy to speak to British audiences. Through these engagements, I would learn to appreciate some unique British qualities, such as their insistence on doing things the proper way, or not at all.

But all of these experiences could wait; for now I had other cultures to explore. Between our touchdown at Heathrow and my initial work assignment, I had exactly thirty days to do as I pleased, and I was determined to use these days well. Dropping off some luggage at my new home, I picked up the keys to my Triumph and we were on our way to the White Cliffs of Dover. By nightfall we would be in France.

The drive from Calais to Paris was beautiful. The small road was lined with evenly spaced trees that evoked the paintings of van Gogh, and the rural hamlets with their plain facades appeared to be from an earlier century. Paris left us looking forward to the spring when we could return to see her at her best. Pisa, the Riviera, Nice, and Monte Carlo were on our immediate "to do" list. Rome met and exceeded our expectations, as I drove the Appian Way to the Catacombs. The expanse of the ruins, particularly the height of the columns, left me awestruck. But there was more to see: Salzberg, Vienna, and Geneva, where we shared a table with a Swiss native who fluently spoke six languages.

Copenhagen has more charm than most people can imagine. The tulips of Holland and Denmark were so lovely and the fields so large that I felt gluttonous for seeing so many of them at once. A table overlooking the Olympic ski run at Oslo, the Viking ships, and the Kon Tiki were all icing on the cake. An Olson liner would take us from Oslo to Newcastle, but once again we would pass through England without seeing a sunset, and on to Scotland to check out the castles and heather.

All this, and my assignment literally had not begun. The year in England would give me a sense of what history means to a people who live among buildings that date back to Norman times. But the most unexpected benefit— even more than returning with a Mark VI Bentley and a prized collection of brass rubbings that my wife and I had made in Westminster Abbey—was the way we had learned to look at our own country and ourselves.

Writing, like traveling and living abroad, offers unlimited benefits. Like travel, it brings unpredictable opportunities, and writing also broadens and deepens one's perception. Now that I have lived abroad, the world news takes on a special significance. Like travel, writing brings clarity and increases our level of awareness. Just as traveling makes us aware of subtleties in the language and customs of the places we go, writing for publication brings increased appreciation and ability to communicate.

I started with a travel story because of the similarities that exist between traveling and writing and also to show that many benefits can accrue from writing for publication. My own writing for publication was surely a large factor, perhaps the decisive one, in the selection of my application for the Fulbright program. My writing has also been the decisive variable allowing me to work at a number of major universities, including three years of teaching on weekends in the Bahamas. Writing has given me opportunities to learn about my own country as well, as I now travel out of state one day a month to present a one-day workshop on writing for publication. I have no doubt that writing for publication can serve any educator in equally enjoyable and enriching ways.

REASONS TO WRITE

People can be placed in two groups: the talkers and the doers. Some people enjoy just sitting around talking about writing, telling why they don't write for publication. One person said that he doesn't write for publication because "there are just too many mediocre books and articles out there, and I don't want to associate with mediocrity." Others talk a lot about the writing they plan to do, but they never seem to get around to it. Then there are the doers. Often the big difference between the two groups is that *serious writers have specific goals to reach through their writing.*

Initially you may not be able to articulate these goals for fear that you may never reach them or for fear that others might be critical; but few goals are ever reached before they become clear to their pursuers. And, for this reason, those who are serious about becoming writers must clarify at least to themselves their own reasons for writing.

Unlike students or those who work for a supervisor or boss, writers usually don't have people to spur them on. The world is full of people who dream about becoming something they aren't but who haven't the initiative to do the work that must be done to become whatever they wish to become. Most people who aspire to become writers are aware of some of the benefits of writing. They know that when you are a writer you are very much your own boss. You can decide *what* you want to write, *when* you want to write it, and even *where* you want to write. Authors can even choose their audiences.

Writing offers opportunity to earn recognition. Few professionals enjoy more admiration than successful writers. Most people also know that *writing offers authors an opportunity to apply their creative talents.* When you write, you invent; and then you share your creation with as many others as possible. *Our society places much value on creativity.*

On university campuses professors write to share their research findings, to promote their disciplines. For the most fortunate, dissertations and theses become lifetime pursuits. These professors use their publications to disseminate their findings, thereby contributing to the advancement of their professions.

Some people find that writing helps them clarify their own thinking. As strange as it may sound, they write to find out what they think and to remove inconsistencies in their own thinking. Some professional people, like college professors, are told that they must publish before they can earn tenure, promotions, or merit pay. Because grant writing and article writing are perhaps the best of all possible entrees into tenure track positions and to earning tenure, Chapter 16 is devoted to showing how you can design your own effective plan to garner a tenure-track position and to earn tenure. But writing is a proactive endeavor, and nobody can be forced to write. People write because they choose to.

Still others choose to write to earn money Our society has moved through a period when the main thrust of individuals was to compete with the Joneses, earning more money and buying more goods. Then our society experienced a period when the major thrust was to join and support group movements. Today, the greatest trend among our population is for individuals to improve their own talents and capabilities. Many people write to improve themselves. In their book *Megatrends 2000,* Naisbitt and Aburdene (1990) offer ten megatrends for the twenty-first century. Among these is the triumph of the individual. The authors say:

> *The great unifying theme at the conclusion of the 20th century is the triumph of the individual. . . . [I]t is the individual who creates a work of art, embraces a political philosophy, bets a life's savings on a new business, inspires a colleague or a family member to succeed, immigrates to a new country, has a transcendental spiritual experience. It is an individual who changes himself or herself before attempting to change society. (p. 298)*

Writing is an empowering activity. Many individuals enjoy the power they derive from writing and the power derived from subsequent publication. For example, professors enjoy the respect they get from colleagues and students when their articles and books are used in classes. Business people enjoy the power that writing gives them within their organizations. Perhaps the most meaningful empowerment is internal. Having a manuscript accepted for publication is evidence of your power; just knowing that your article has been approved by a national panel of experts in your field reassures you that you are on the cutting edge.

Often scholars view publication as a way to contribute to their professions. Some say that throughout their school years they took from the profession and that now, having completed their education, it is time to give knowledge back. Writing for publication provides a means for rendering this service. Professional people who hold this philosophy do not need the pressure of earning tenure, promotions, or merit pay to motivate them to write for publication. Perhaps this explains why many seasoned professionals, including retirees, continue writing and attending writing workshops. Incidentally, most participants in a recent week-long Phi Delta Kappa summer Writing for Publication workshop at Indiana University were retirees. Some entrepreneurs write to promote their businesses. For example, a realtor may write an article for a realtors' journal or the director of a medical clinic may write to publicize successful use of innovative approaches.

Some professionals see writing for publication as essential to their grant writing efforts. For example, one group of engineers whose entire profession is grant writing asked for a special workshop. They had two reasons. First, they wanted to improve their technical writing skills. Second, they wanted to increase their visibility through publication in professional journals because they knew that this would further enhance the acceptance of the group's future proposals.

Physicians, nurses, and nurse educators attend many of these workshops. They feel a need to share their expertise with their colleagues throughout the country. Clearly, many individuals write for publication because they anticipate benefits both to themselves and to others.

Regardless of their discipline, many professors enjoy the craft of writing. As they continue writing they gradually but consistently hone this craft until it becomes an art. I asked some contemporary writers why they write. Here are their responses.

Elliot Eisner cherishes the opportunity that writing provides him to improve his thinking and his expression.

I write for publication because it is through the process of writing that my own ideas get clarified and revised. When one is speaking, words have a very short life. In the process of writing, they are fixed on paper and they can be modified, expanded, and made more potent. In a sense, writing is an artistic activity in which matters of voice, precision, transition, and organization are critical. In fact, as a former painter, I see in writing a process analogous to painting: I am interested in creating an aesthetically coherent, insightful, and cogent statement. Painters too are interested in such an outcome.

Thus, for me writing is a way of learning to think more rigorously about ideas that I possess or want to develop. In fact, the act of writing is an invitation to discovery, to the location of new intellectual seas on which to sail. It is an act of exploration that provides the satisfactions that come from trying to make something beautiful.

> Elliot W. Eisner, Professor
> *Education and Art*
> *Stanford University*
> *Stanford, California*

Writing has a degree of permanency that many professors enjoy. Editor David Gilman appreciates this quality.

As a practitioner I had a lot of ideas, ideas that were important, and I wanted to share them. I thought you had to have a Ph.D. and teach at a university to get things published. Now that I am editor of a national magazine, I realize that articles written by practitioners can be extremely valuable.

Writing also helps me clarify my thinking. Often, after I've written a sentence or paragraph, I find myself reading it back and saying, "I didn't know that." I really did know it but the writing helped me realize it.

Articles that are written and published are then indexed and will influence students, practitioners, and administrators forever.

> David Gilman, former
> Professor and Editor
> *Contemporary Education*
> *Indiana State University*
> *Terre Haute, Indiana*

Researchers appreciate writing for the means it provides them to reflect on their own thoughts and mistakes. Thomas Good explains.

Writing for professional publication provides an opportunity to conceptualize, explore, and on occasion reformulate one's understanding of a topic. It presents an opportunity to consider what one understands and perhaps more importantly to confront one's misconceptions and one's limits. Writing is often frustrating, tedious, and forced. At other times it is spontaneous and rewarding. However, it is always the perfect medium for self-reflection and professional growth.

> Thomas L. Good, Professor
> *Educational Psychology*
> *University of Arizona*
> *Tucson, Arizona*

All of these goals are worthwhile and admirable. As some have confessed, writing is hard work. At times it is lonely. So, if you are going to spend
your time writing, do it right and make it pay off. *The main purpose of this book
is to help you prepare to write articles and books that will get published.* These are
immensely practical objectives and, as long as your writing is honest, they are
perfectly honorable reasons for learning to write. This book is written for
people who are committed to self-improvement and who want to enhance
their professional and personal lives.

But even people who write for such practical reasons as earning merit
pay and royalties must acknowledge that some people seek to learn to write
because they hold a deep respect for the beauty that lives in eloquent writing.
Pragmatists may question the wisdom of spending their time and energy
with only the goal of making something pretty; yet, even they can appreciate
knowing that others are willing to devote their writing to this end. To conclude that writers of prose seek only this end would be wrong. Many of the
most eloquent writers have deep-seated purposes, and they use their writing
skills to achieve these purposes. For example, we should appreciate the forceful nature of Eric Sevareid's writing. When he wrote the following lines, he
had been serving as news correspondent from the beginning of the United
States' involvement in World War II (Sevareid, 1976, pp. 497–498):

The last battle would be fought just across the river. . . . The Germans did
not know that this was the last day when the endless war would still be a
war. Tomorrow the great German raid against the human race would be
all over save for the meaningless odds and ends. . . . The whole situation
was selfishly satisfying, and I savored it. I, an ordinary man with a name
and origin of which Caesar (Hitler) was ignorant, was standing a couple
hundred yards from his camp knowing the secret of his fate and the fate
of his empire. And he didn't know. I, one of his intended slaves, was so
much mightier than he. I, who had never kicked a Jew, or looted a village,
or burned a bank, or stolen a country, or killed anything larger than a
hare, was standing with empty hands looking into his final citadel, pos-
sessed of the biggest, brightest fact in this moment in eternity—the fact
that the terror and tyranny of our times would come to an end this
night. . . . Now that I am here, I'll represent the whole human race, all the
millions of people who haven't done the things Caesar has done.

These few lines reveal the awesome power that rests in the hands of a
skilled writer. Few activities offer us power to represent the entire human
race. Writing does even more; the skilled writer can actually change the values and the behaviors of thousands or even millions of people.

If you value writing enough to pursue it, as you probably do if you are
reading this, you will appreciate the words that John Steinbeck set to paper

when he was asked to deliver a speech to the Kansas State Teachers Association (1959, p. 71).

> My eleven-year-old son came to me recently and, in a tone of patient suffering, asked, "How much longer do I have to go to school?"
> "About fifteen years," I said.
> "Oh! Lord," he said despondently "Do I have to?"
> "I'm afraid so. It's terrible and I'm not going to try to tell you it isn't. But I can tell you this—if you are very lucky, you may find a teacher and that is a wonderful thing."
> "Did you find one?"
> "I found three," I said.
> My three had these things in common—they all loved what they were doing. They did not tell—they catalyzed a burning desire to know....
> I shall speak only of my first teacher because, in addition to other things, she was very precious.
> She aroused us to shouting, bookwaving discussion. She had the noisiest class in school and didn't even seem to know it. We could never stick to the subject, geometry or the chanted recitation of the memorized phyla.
> Our speculation ranged the world. She breathed curiosity into us so that we brought in facts or truths shielded in our hands like captured fireflies.
> She left her signature on us, the signature of the teacher who writes on minds. I suppose that, to a large extent, I am the unsigned manuscript of that high school teacher. What deathless power lies in the hands of such a person.
> I can tell my son who looks forward with horror to fifteen years of drudgery that somewhere in the dusty dark a magic may happen that will light up the years, if he is very lucky....
> I have come to believe that a great teacher is a great artist, and there are as few as there are any other great artists. It might even be the greatest of the arts since the medium is the human mind and spirit.

Steinbeck knew how to hold on to the reader's attention. Equally important is the ability to grab the attention of today's busy readers. In his opening lines of *A Tale of Two Cities*, Dickens shows his ability to grab and hold readers' attention.

> It was the best of times, it was the worst of times, it was the age of wisdom, it was the age of foolishness, it was the epoch of belief, it was the epoch of incredulity, it was the season of light, it was the season of darkness, it was the spring of hope, it was the winter of despair, we had every-

thing before us, we had nothing before us, we were all going direct to Heaven, we were all going the other way.

Chapter 3 is included in this book to help you develop this skill.

At the beginning of *The Auctioneer,* Joan Samson (1975) used her words like an artist who carefully manipulates a brush to paint a picture. Her picture is full of motion and details.

> The fire rose in a perfect cone as if suspended by the wisp of smoke that ascended in a straight line to the high spring sky. Mim and John dragged whole dry saplings from the brush pile by the stone wall and heaved them into the flames, stepping back quickly as the dead leaves caught with a hiss.
>
> Four-year-old Hildie heard the truck coming even before the old sheep dog did. She scampered to the edge of the road and waited impatiently. It was Gore's truck, moving fast, rutting deeply in the mud and throwing up a spray on either side. John and Mim converged behind Hildie, each taking stock of what might be wrong to bring the police chief out to the last farm on the road.
>
> Bob Gore swung himself out and hooked his thumbs in the pocket of his jeans. He shifted from foot to foot for a moment as if his great belly were seeking a point of equilibrium. Gore had a taste for two things—trouble and gossip. By either route, he could talk away an afternoon without half trying. John glanced over his shoulder at the fire. (pp. 7–8)

Somewhere out there, someone may learn to write as eloquently as John Steinbeck, as forcefully as Charles Dickens, or as descriptively as Joan Samson. But most of us will never reach those superb levels of writing. Fortunately, though, you don't have to write eloquently or elegantly to become a successful writer and reach your goals. This book stresses simple, direct, and clear writing. The experts know that such skills give the author the ability to write assertively and forcefully. *This book provides the knowledge and opportunities needed to become a highly skilled author.* We should all take comfort in knowing that there are always good markets for important information that is clearly written.

Although the payoffs for writing are clear, the investment one makes to become a writer is far less frequently understood. Writing is hard work even to those who enjoy it. It requires self-discipline and self-denial. Becoming a successful, published writer requires becoming a good writer. Publishing is a buyer's market, and the writer is the seller. In publishing, the supply always far exceeds the demand. Publishers are always flooded with manuscripts, many of which are mediocre or worse, but there are always enough good ones to make writing for publication a competitive activity. To succeed, you must compete with and outperform many others who are just as bright and just as knowledgeable as you. The one saving grace is that few would-be writers are willing to invest the time and energy required to transform their mediocre skills into the sharp, refined skills required to compete in this buyer's market. For this reason all serious writers should rejoice. By taking time to develop sharp skills and by taking time to revise, improve, and polish your manuscripts, *you can dramatically increase your odds of succeeding.*

With today's hectic schedules, most writers find the answer to their need for more time in their ability to improve their self-discipline. Elaine Jarchow writes:

> *When I have a writing task—a grant proposal or an article—I know that I must engage in rigorous self-discipline to find the time to write. My obligations as associate dean, consultant, wife, and mother don't leave much writing time. I find my writing time from 4 to 6 A.M. I try to retire by 10 P.M. and arise promptly at 4 A.M. I proceed immediately to the dining room table where the writing space is organized (my books, supplementary materials, pens, pencils, scissors, paper clips, and paper) are all arranged symmetrically in neat piles the night before! I begin writing immediately. These early morning hours are great for me—no interruptions take place, and I produce text quickly and effortlessly. Although there are two computers in our den and although I am certainly computer literate, I produce my important writing pieces in longhand. I genuinely love seeing my pen move across the page, switching from print to cursive, crossing out, and drawing arrows to insertions. I also love delivering the text to my efficient secretary who quickly produces the computer printout.*
>
> *At 6 A.M. I take a 30-minute walk; then, I shower, awaken my daughter and proceed into the day. I also use all-day Saturday and Sunday marathons to complete a writing task. Of course, this "dining room" approach means we can't have dinner guests until I finish the task!*

Others find writing so stimulating that for them it seems to demand the necessary time. Rita Dunn has said,

> *It's what I like to do most. I can come home exhausted at 10 P.M. after a long, stressful day, feel as if I can't wait to get into a hot bath and bed, but sit down at the computer and, three hours later, realize the time . . . , but keep going until 4 A.M. At that point, common sense dictates that I have to get up in the morning and must get some sleep!*

A TIME AND PLACE FOR EVERYTHING

A well-known verse in the Old Testament says that there is a time for everything. Writing is no exception. Knowing where and when to apply your energy to this pursuit strongly affects your degree of success. My work with hundreds of aspiring writers in dozens of workshops and courses has produced many excellent questions. Of these many questions, the most frequently asked (and one of the most difficult to answer) is, How do you find time to write? In fact, this question was asked so frequently that it prompted me to write an article, "How to Find the Time You Need," for *The National Businesswoman.*

When we speak of "finding time," we are implying that time is a tangible object. When we travel, we speak of *making up* time that was *lost* because of mechanical failures or inclement weather. Actually, time—perhaps the most valuable commodity of all—is never created by humans, nor is it found. Usually, when we say that we should find time to do something, what we mean is that we should give that activity more of our attention. To do this we must learn to schedule our activities more carefully and assign more time to those activities that are most important.

The remark, I don't have time to write, actually means I have committed all of my time to other things or I have not yet learned how to effectively budget my writing time. Surely, in our busy world, this is no strange feeling to any of us. Yet, at this juncture you must make a decision. You must either choose to continue doing all the things that you are currently doing, in which case you should dismiss the idea of writing, or you must carefully examine your weekly calendar and *replace some of the less important activities with writing for publication.* (This may mean giving up an hour a day in the coffee room.) For most of us it requires giving up a few hours of television each week.

Once individuals do replace a few of these passive activities with writing, they often realize that the activities that were chosen to relax them are far less relaxing than writing. Paradoxically, *writing for publication is both exhilarating and relaxing.* Have you ever noticed that, after a hard day's work, an evening spent in front of the television leaves you exhausted? Why? Because you weren't so much physically tired as emotionally drained; and passive recovery is slow. Writing is different. It puts your brain in gear, enabling your frayed nerves to heal. Writers say that writing stimulates them mentally while relaxing them emotionally. Writing is good therapy; it lets you express yourself. Trading an evening of reruns for an evening of writing may be the best decision you've made in a long time.

WHEN IS THE BEST TIME TO WRITE?

Some writers do most of their work late at night, while others prefer to get up very early and write for a few hours before the day's obligations begin. Some writers carefully schedule a combination of mornings, afternoons, and evenings. Your own schedule should be determined by first considering your personal preferences. If you begin nodding and dozing off by 8 or 9 P.M., you should try to schedule your writing at other times. But, if you are the type who likes to stay up late and sleep late, an evening writing schedule will probably suit you best.

Next, check your daily obligations. Your present job may dictate that some times are unavailable for you to write. (Don't worry. Some of the most prolific writers are shut off from writing between 8 and 5 P.M. daily). You may have to block out time for carpooling children to and from school, helping with homework, preparing meals, cleaning the house, washing the clothes, or cutting the grass. Consider whether you need large blocks of time and whether you need to be free from noise or disruptions. Such concerns may restrict the *quality* times available to you for writing to late evenings or early mornings.

One final but important suggestion. *Be realistic about the amount of time you set aside for writing, and then, honor your commitment.* Save time for tennis, or golf, or exercise, or reading, or watching a special television show. If you are married, ask for the support of other family members. Let everyone know your writing schedule, and, when the phone rings during your assigned writing time, let someone else answer it. Instruct your family members to say that you are not free to come to the phone if the call is for you. Other disruptions—such as uninvited guests, door-to-door salespeople, or charity workers—can destroy your writing time. Taking time to solicit your family's cooperation can help ward off such interruptions from the outside and will impress on your own family members the importance of their respect for your writing time.

In the following passages, Robert Maddox tells about his strategies for getting time to write.

Finding time to write is one of the toughest parts of writing. I have found that it helps to set aside blocks of time that are devoted exclusively to writing. When I make up my schedule for the upcoming semester, I will block my calendar out for class times, office hours, and also blocks of time (minimum of one-half day in a block) just for writing. It is much easier, if I have committed myself to these time periods, to "stay on schedule."

If I am writing in my office, I close the door and put the phone on voice mail only. That way, it doesn't ring, but I know that I won't miss any important calls. I also use a beeper type pager which my family uses if they have an urgent reason to reach me.

I do, however, maintain a faculty study in the library just for writing, and try to do nearly all of my writing there. It has no telephone and no name on the door. I have it equipped with a computer and printer. I have a similar computer in my office and another at home so that I can move to the office if the library is closed (weekend, evenings, holidays, etc.), and also continue working at home, just by carrying a diskette with me. (I used to lug around a portable computer, which was a real chore.)

> Robert Maddox
> *Department of Management*
> *College of Business*
> *Administration*
> *University of Tennessee-*
> *Knoxville*
> *Knoxville, Tennessee*

Many writers do not have easy access to even one computer or to an answering machine. But, when available, this equipment and a hideaway office can make a major difference in an author's level of productivity. Perhaps you have found other ways to make your writing easier.

In addition to planning writing time into their weekly schedule, successful writers know how to capture additional valuable writing time. A writing friend who lives in New York and frequently travels to the West Coast has been accused of praying for delays. For her, the airport becomes a writing office. Such discipline has led this professor, housewife, and mother of six children to author some 20 books and 200 articles. Other writers take similar advantage of the time spent commuting to work on trains and planes.

TOOLING UP FOR THE JOB

Having a definite amount of time set aside each week is indispensable to most successful writers. Yet, the success of these writing sessions hinges on the writer's having the proper tools for the intended job. The importance of having the proper tools available is easy to understand if you have ever tried to repair a machine or cook a meal without the necessary equipment.

People often ask me what tools I consider essential for my office. I usually flinch a little and then remind them that the tools that one writer considers essential may offer no value to other writers. When pressed further, I give the following list of tools which, in addition to office supplies, proper lighting, and solitude, some writers consider staples for their offices:

1. Typewriter or word processor
2. Dictionary
3. Thesaurus
4. Book of quotations
5. Books in the writer's special field of study
6. Journals in the writer's special field of study

7. Style manuals (e.g., *The Chicago Manual of Style; American Psychological Association Manual*)
8. Grammar books (e.g., *The Elements of Style* by W. R. Strunk, Jr., and E. B. White)
9. Publishers' guides
10. Scissors
11. Tape and dispenser
12. Post-It tabs

A writer friend, Doug Brooks (a professor at Miami University of Ohio), explained the significance of having these tools on hand at the time he sits down to write. To him, "writing is like digging a well by hand." As you dig deeper and deeper, you must begin every day by climbing down into the well and then climbing back out of the well when you are done for the day. Much energy and time are spent entering and exiting the well; therefore, the efficient well digger will be sure to have all the necessary tools waiting at the bottom of the well. Likewise, *the writer must have all the necessary tools waiting.* As trite as this may appear, having to leave the office to sharpen a pencil or fetch paper or a dictionary often leads to diversions that delay and prevent the writer from getting on with the real task at hand—writing.

THE BEST PLACE TO WRITE

The more I think about my library, the more I realize that it is unique and critical to me in my writing. First, it contains those resources with which I am very familiar. For example, I have those textbooks that I used during my doctoral program. Because I had not done my undergraduate or master's work at the institution where I was pursuing my doctorate, I knew absolutely no one on the faculty. Recognizing that many of my classmates had already earned two degrees at this university and being aware that many of them knew our professors as friends and knew which researchers and authors would be stressed in classes and on exams, I needed a strategy to even the odds for my success. By inquiring, I learned which textbooks were most widely used in each of the four areas covered by my forthcoming qualifying exams. I chose the two most widely used texts in each area and spent ten hours a day for one full semester virtually memorizing these books. When exam time came, I was prepared to quote those authors and studies that were so familiar to the professors who would be constructing and scoring my qualifying exams.

The preparation process was so successful that I began tutoring the next class of doctoral students, preparing them for the educational psychology part of the qualifying exam. The adage "to teach is to learn twice" took on a new meaning. Needless to say, I became so well versed in this content area and so familiar with these textbooks that I will never forget much of this material. This is my best library of all; it is by far the most accessible because it's in my head. To make it even more valuable, I keep those source books in my library, and I still quote the classic studies found in them. What I am suggesting here is that you search out those books that are special to you and make them part of your library.

There is another unique aspect to my library. Each time I receive a professional journal or a research report, I scan it to identify areas of interest. Because I write on curriculum, educational psychology, teaching methods, and writing, I scan the table of contents for such topics. When I find one, I flag it with a Post-It tab and write the subject on the tab. Then, I shelve my journals with the open side outward. This means that I can sit at my desk and pull every resource that I own on any given topic—and this is exactly what I do when I begin writing an article or book chapter. In two minutes I am able to place all of my sources of information on any topic on my working table. I do this before writing a single word. So, when I do start writing, I can write for hours without even getting out of my chair.

Though you may not have shared my way of preparing for doctoral exams, chances are good that you became very familiar with a substantial body of knowledge in your field. This familiarity makes the content even more valuable, but only if you develop a system that permits you to use it. My system works for me. You may have already developed a system that works for you.

Whether you use a highlighter pen to accentuate the major points in everything you read, keep files of quotes to use over and over again, or develop a computerized database on your computer, your personal library will undoubtedly be your most powerful resource as a writer. Alter it in any way that will make it more "user friendly."

The exact location of your office may be dictated by physical realities. For example, your house or apartment may be too small to accommodate writing at home, or a young child may render your home environment unsuitable for serious writing. You may not own the reference books and journals that you need when you write, making a local library the best writing space for you. Some writers use more than one location to write. These writers have a portable office housed in their briefcase. The number of portable offices has increased by severalfold in the last decade. The next time you are on a plane or commuter train notice the number of workers who carry their office in their briefcases.

My grandmother, whom we all affectionately called Mama, was a woman of great determination. When Mama made up her mind to have something, she had it—*her* way. There were at least two problems, however. The first was that her grandchildren were responsible for delivering on whatever she had decided. The other problem was that, once Mama set her determined mind on a target, she had an unsurpassed capacity for changing her mind.

Mama's greatest single source of indecisiveness was hats; so, whenever she mentioned that word *hat*, her grandchildren disappeared for days. On one occasion my cousin and I were a little slow on the escape, and we ended up driving six miles to town for a hat Mama had seen in a display window. But by the time we drove to town and back, she had decided that the hat was just plain wrong for her. We dutifully returned it—only to have her regret sending it back. We made a third trip to town—and a fourth. Having traveled 48 miles, we arrived back on her front porch—with no hat!

Because most of us need more time than we currently have to write and we never know when we will be asked to make trips like the one I just described, many writers keep notepads and writing tablets in their vehicles. When asked to drive someone to the mall or elsewhere, the notepads are available to jot down ideas for topics or to make a quick and crude outline of a forthcoming article. Writing books and writing journals are also excellent topic sources and should be kept in the car or on the nightstand for idle reading.

For example, I had driven my son downtown to the music store to take a guitar lesson. While there, I was thumbing through a list of Reasons People Give for Not Writing. Noticing that the list contains some false beliefs or myths, I got the idea for an article. While waiting for my son to take his guitar lesson, I wrote an article titled "Six Myths That Haunt Writers." When I returned home, I wrote a query to *The Writer,* a favorite journal for professional writers. Sylvia Burack, editor of *The Writer,* liked the topic, so I sent her the manuscript "on inspection" (which means she was not obligated to accept it). Had she rejected it, I had identified two other journals for which this manuscript would have been appropriate.

Ms. Burack decided to use my article in a column called "The Rostrum" in the *The Writer.* That column usually includes short pieces that provide practical tips from authors. Although I would have preferred to have it appear as a feature article, I was happy to have it included in "The Rostrum"—especially when I learned later that it had been selected with articles by Dick Francis, Stephen King, Sidney Sheldon, and Mary Higgins Clark as one of the best 100 articles of the year. *The Writer's Handbook* also published this piece, placing it midway between articles by Stephen King and Sidney Sheldon. Not bad company for a writer who spent less than an hour drafting the piece, an hour that otherwise would have been spent waiting, daydreaming, and people-watching.

I confess that after my trip to the music store I spent additional time revising, rewriting, and polishing the manuscript, as I do for everything I write. Even if the topic is one in which I have some expertise and my mind remains clear, I find that about a half-dozen rewrites are needed before the work begins to shine. Seldom do I submit anything before completing at least five or six rewrites. "Six Myths That Haunt Writers" appears in Figure 1.1.

FIGURE 1.1   Sample article conceived and outlined while waiting for my son.

Six Myths That Haunt Writers
By Kenneth T. Henson

Among the many things I have learned in conducting writers workshops on campuses across the country is that there are several false ideas, myths, that haunt most writers and often impede and/or block beginners. The following are six of these myths—and some suggestions for dealing with them.

1. *I'm not sure I have what it takes.*
I have found that on each campus, coast to coast, there is a superstar writer who, I am assured, has only to put his fingers to the keyboard or pen to paper and, presto, words, sentences, and paragraphs—publishable ones—flow. And, it is thought, these creations are effortless.

These tales are as ridiculous as ghost stories, but more damaging, since most people *believe* them. And like ghost stories, their purpose is to frighten.

If I were a beginning writer and believed that writing comes so effortlessly to some, I would be totally discouraged.

You admit that you, too, have heard of such a superwriter? You may even know such a person by name. Well, don't believe it. It's probably the creation of a person who doesn't intend to write and therefore would prefer that you don't either. The next time someone mentions this super-person, think of Ernest Hemingway, who wrote the last chapter of *Farewell to Arms* 119 times. Or think of the following definitions of writing: "Writing is 10 percent inspiration and 90 percent perspiration" and "Successful writing is the ability to apply the seat of the pants to the seat of the chair." Contrary to the myth, all writers perspire; some even sweat!

2. *I don't have time to write.*
You have heard this many times, and if you're like most of us, you have even said it yourself: "If only I had time to write." Ironically, most would-be writers have more time to write than most successful writers do. Some writers even have 24 hours a day to do as they please. But they represent only a small fraction of all writers. The vast majority of writers are freelancers who have either part-time or full-time jobs and pick up a few extra dollars, a little prestige, and a lot of personal satisfaction through writing articles.

The reason behind the bold statement that you have more time than most successful writers have to write is that, probably like you, most of them must earn a living some other way. Yet, these individuals have allotted themselves some time for writing: they took it away from their other activities. Good writers don't *make* time, and they don't *find* time. Rather, they reassign part of their time to writing. And that part of their lives is usually some of their leisure time.

Continued

FIGURE 1.1 *Continued*

I don't suggest that you stop golfing or fishing or jogging or watching TV, but if you are to be a successful writer, you must give up part of the time you spend (or waste) in the coffee room or bar and you must also give up the idea that you are too tired to write or that watching a mediocre TV show relaxes you. Writing is far more relaxing to most of us who return from our work emotionally drained; it provides an outlet for frustrations, a far more effective release than our more passive attempts to escape from them. The next time you hear people say, "I don't have time to write" or "I would write for publications if I had time," observe how those persons are spending their time at that moment. If writing is really important to you, replace the activities that are less important with writing. Let your friends and family know that this is your writing time and that you're not to be disturbed. Then tell yourself the same thing. Disciplined people have much more time than do undisciplined people.

3. *I don't have anything worth writing about.*
We've all heard this for years. A significant percentage of aspiring writers really believe that they don't know anything that is worthy of publication. If you are one of them, you're not learning from your experiences: either you don't make mistakes or you don't adjust your behavior to avoid repeating them.

The truth is that you possess a lot of knowledge that would be valuable to others. And you have the abilities that successful writers have to research the topics you wish to write about. I don't know any successful writers who don't feel that they need to research their topics. Start with the subjects that are most familiar, then enrich your knowledge of these subjects by periodic trips to the library, or by interviewing people, or by conducting surveys on these topics.

4. *The editors will reject my manuscript because my name isn't familiar to them.*
Of all the excuses that would-be writers give for not writing, none is weaker than, "If my name were James Michener or Stephen King, editors would listen to me."

But these people don't consider the fact that the Micheners and Kings didn't always have famous names; they started as unknowns and made their names known through talent and hard work. And they would probably be first to say that they have to keep earning their recognition through hard work. Of course, these writers have unusual talent, but you can be equally sure that they work hard and continue to do so to sharpen their skills, research their topics meticulously, and to create and invent new, fresh ways to express their ideas. There's no guarantee that any of us can earn similar status and acclaim, but we can improve our expertise in our areas of interest and improve our communication skills.

5. *My vocabulary and writing skills are too limited.*
Many people equate jargon, unfamiliar words, complex sentence structure, and long paragraphs with good writing. Actually, though a good vocabulary is a great asset to writers, so are dictionaries and thesauruses, for those who

know how to use them and who are willing to take the time to do so. Jargon and long sentences and unnecessarily complex paragraphs harm writing more than they help it.

The sooner you replace words like *utilize* and *prioritize* with words like *use* and *rank*, the faster your writing will improve. Remember, your job is to communicate. Don't try to impress the editor. Editors know what their readers want, and readers seldom demand jargon and complexity.

6. *In my field there are few opportunities to publish.*

If your area of specialization has few professional journals (actually, some fields have only one or two), you may feel trapped, knowing that this uneven supply/demand ratio drives up the competition for these journals.

You might deal with this by searching for more general journals that cover your field, or journals whose editors often welcome articles written by experts in outside but related fields. For example, a biologist or botanist might turn to wildlife magazines, U.S. or state departments of conservation publications, forestry magazines, hunting and fishing publications, or magazines for campers and hikers.

Again, you could consider writing for other audiences, expanding your areas of expertise by taking courses in other disciplines, reading widely, and doing research in other fields to help you develop a broader range of subjects to write about.

Some fields have more journals than others, and some writers are luckier (and more talented) than others. But for those who are willing to work hard at their craft, writing offers a way to reach many professional and personal goals.

PERENNIAL EXCUSES

Professors who don't write often make excuses for not writing. Do any of these comments sound familiar?

- I don't have time.
- I don't have anything to say.
- I'm a good teacher.
- When I started teaching at this university, writing wasn't part of my job description.
- I'm too close to retirement to start something new.
- Most of my colleagues don't publish.
- My college is a teaching college, not a research institution.

At times, most of us are guilty of using some of these excuses. For most of us, the truth is that we know we lack the skills needed to do the job well and we are afraid we will be rejected. Our biggest error is failure to recognize that we can quickly develop the skills required to succeed at any level we choose. How can we expect others to respect us if we don't have the self-confidence needed to improve daily?

TAKING INVENTORY

So far, this book has been quite blunt. It says that *successful writing is hard work*. It requires self-discipline and sacrifice—and the rejection rates for many journals and book publishers are astronomical. I maintain that serious writers must give up some leisure activities, schedule time for writing, and discipline themselves to honor that schedule. To many people, such sacrifices appear foolish. Such individuals often criticize dedicated writers. For all this discipline and hard work the writer may get little more than criticism. Remember, it's a buyer's market, and the odds for success are indeed small.

I also maintain in this book that *successful writing is an activity that can be learned and mastered*—and that successful writing is not without rewards. Having mastered the craft of writing, you will have attained a variety of personal and professional goals, including earning money, advancing professionally, being creative, and being your own boss. Furthermore, such goals are within your reach if you are willing to demonstrate the self-discipline needed. The news even gets better; through practicing this advice *you can learn how to reverse the odds* of having your manuscript rejected.

In remaining chapters of this book, my aim is to help you master and use good writing skills. I hope you will use this book to gather the nuts-and-bolts knowledge of writing for publication. Decide what you really want to get out of writing, and use writing as a means to reach your personal and professional goals.

I have chosen to end this chapter with one writer's description of her personal process. Perhaps you will find ideas that have potential for helping you.

First of all, I must be in the mood to write. Before putting the proverbial pen to paper, I have a ritual or process I follow. To be ready to write, I must contemplate the issue or topic. I jot down my initial thoughts in outline form adding marginal notes such as "requires research," "quote reference from . . . ," "see so-and-so for more information," or the like. Once this research/organization aspect is completed, I set it aside and just "think about it for awhile." I allow myself two to three days for this step. My trusty calendar keeps track of due dates, and I always try to allow enough time to produce the final product. My calendar-planner pad is designed in such a way that I can jot down new ideas about an assignment.

A FINAL WORD

At a recent motivational seminar, the speaker worked hard to stretch our minds. His thesis was that through years of repeating routines, without realizing it, we become enslaved by our habits, even in how we think. The seminar reminded me of a philosophy course I took as part of my doctoral program. At the first class meeting, the professor expressed concern that students might become limited in their thinking by the need they feel to earn a good grade. So our first assignment was to give ourselves a grade that we thought would be fair, one that would motivate us to work hard—yes, a final grade for the entire course. I could tell that this was going to be my kind of course. To make certain that I would be highly motivated throughout the semester, I assigned myself an "A" for the course.

Next, the professor announced that he believed people achieve more when doing what they enjoy doing, so he let each of us choose our term project. We would spend the semester independently researching this topic. I remember making that error that most students make when selecting major thesis and dissertation topics: I took on more than I could possibly do justice to in one semester.

I had always wondered whether there were major identifiable differences in the way citizens think that affect their country's success. Do people in rising nations think differently than people in nations that are in decline?

My experiences as a department head, coordinator of doctoral studies, and dean have enabled me to observe the behavior of individuals and draw correlations between behavioral patterns and success levels. My work with teachers has convinced me that these differences not only exist, but can be categorized. Put simply, I believe that *the behavior of most highly successful teachers is highly proactive,* whereas *less successful teachers are mostly reactive.* My educational psychology text, *Educational Psychology for Effective Teaching* (Henson & Eller, 1999), carries the proactive theme throughout every chapter.

Writing for publication is a highly proactive activity. When we write, we create and make things happen. The combined activities of writing and publishing cause us to escape our routine ways of thinking. Thinking in new ways is energizing. If we are clever, we can direct this energy so that it helps us achieve many of our professional and personal goals. In my writing workshops I advise professors to escape the idea that their institution is forcing them to publish. Even if it can, it shouldn't. We should write and publish for our profession and for ourselves. Like my former professor, I believe we think better when we are pursuing activities that we choose to pursue than when we do it to please others.

If you are among the one in three people who read book prefaces, you may remember that I quoted Oscar Wilde as saying that all of us live in the gutter, but some of us look up and see the stars. I think Wilde was saying that most of us are comfortable just reacting to the pressures and ideas of others, but that a few of us refuse to have our behaviors and ideas dictated by others. Don't write because you think it will please your department chair or dean; do it for yourself.

Begin by setting a couple of long-term goals that you wish to reach. Don't be too modest—you can do it. Next, set a couple of short-term goals. Don't share these goals with anyone until you have begun having some success toward reaching them. Too often, we replace sincere effort with talk. Writing is proactive and it is fun. Just do it.

RECAPPING THE MAJOR POINTS

This chapter has introduced several important points. The following are well worth remembering:

- The competition among writers is keen. To succeed, writers must write excellently
- Good writers are self-made, not born. By learning a few hard facts, you can master the skills needed to succeed in writing.
- Successful writing for nonfiction magazines, journals, and books requires—above everything else—the ability to write clearly.
- Plain, simple writing is preferred over sophisticated, esoteric, pompous writing.
- Successful writers are well organized. They have designated times and places for writing.
- In our busy society, nobody *makes* or *finds* the time to write. Successful writers assign a higher priority to writing than to other activities.
- Clear goals give writers direction and incentive.
- Self-discipline and self-motivation characterize successful writers. You are the only one who can give yourself the kick in the pants that is needed to get started.

REFERENCES

Dickens, C. (1963). *A tale of two cities*. Intro. by D. G. Pitt. New York: Airmont. First published as a series of magazine articles and later as a book. The first book publisher for this work was Chapman and Hall, London, 1859.

Henson, K. T. (1991, May). Six myths that haunt writers. *The Writer, 104*, 24–25.

Henson, K. T. (2003, June). Writing for professional publication: Some myths and truths. *Phi Delta Kappan, 84*(10), 788–791.

Henson, K. T. (2005). *A brief guide to writing for professional publication.* 2nd ed. Fastback No. 538. Bloomington, IN: Phi Delta Kappa International.

Henson, K. T., & Eller, B. F. (1999). *Educational psychology for effective teaching.* Belmont, CA: Wadsworth.

Naisbitt, J., & Aburdene, P. (1990). *Megatrends 2000.* New York: William Morrow.

Samson, J. (1975). *The auctioneer.* New York: Avon Books.

Sevareid, E. (1976). *Not so wild a dream.* New York: Athenaeum.

Steinbeck, J. (1959). The education of teachers. In *Curriculum programs.* Washington, DC: National Education Association.

Strunk, W., Jr., & White, E. B. (1979). *The elements of style,* 3rd ed. New York: Macmillan.

2

FINDING TOPICS

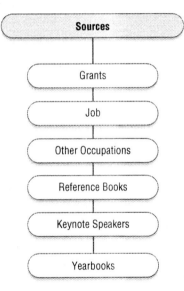

A former editor of a prominent journal tells the following story:

> *I was in Chicago making a speech on the topic "Writing for Publication." At the time, I was saying how easy it is for anyone to identify publishable topics, and I made the statement "All you need is one good topic. You don't need an unlimited number of ideas. All you need is one." It was precisely at this time when a small lady in the audience—very timid, yet serious and determined—raised her hand. What she said was the bravest thing I've ever*

heard. She struck straight to the heart of the fear that all writers, both new and experienced, feel at some time. In an almost inaudible whisper, she said, "But what if you don't have one good idea?" Then my hand went up and my mouth opened because that's what speaking is all about. You always say something *whether or not you have anything worth saying. Then I was stunned. For I realized that I didn't have an answer for that question. What if you don't have one good idea? So, I paused momentarily and with my hand raised high, I said, "Ahmmm. Let's take a break." And we did.*

Later, the speaker confessed that he worried throughout the break because he didn't have an answer for the woman who posed the question. Many professors can remember occasions when, as young instructors or assistant professors, they went into their office for one purpose and one alone: to write. Knowing that their pending tenure and their future promotion to assistant, associate, or full professor depended on their writing manuscripts and having them accepted for publication in recognizable journals, all they could do it seemed was to sit with pen in hand searching the boundaries of their minds for topics. This is the same desperate and lonely feeling expressed in the woman's question. Most writers will acknowledge that often they did not have even one good idea for a topic!

When people ask about the source of ideas for topics, seasoned writers understand the courage it takes simply to admit that lost condition. Yet, to succeed as a writer, people must acknowledge their inadequacies. Paradoxically, the reason writers must admit their inadequacies is the need to build their self-confidence. We cannot gain confidence until we face ourselves. Our weaknesses make us stronger, if we take steps to remove these weaknesses.

The goal of this chapter is to provide knowledge and perspective so that you will no longer feel that awful, lonesome fear of not knowing what to write or the fear of being rejected. I hope you will learn to perceive your own questions and your recognition of limitations as what they *can* and *should* be—indicators of personal growth. The remainder of this chapter provides some suggestions that will help you build a storehouse of good publishable writing topics.

THE DISSERTATION: A SOURCE OF TOPICS

There are many sources of ideas for writing topics. For those who have pursued graduate courses, dissertations and theses are excellent sources for article topics. One individual whose dissertation was titled "An Identification of Earth Science Principles Pertinent to Junior High School Programs and An Examination of Currently Adopted Textbooks in Terms of the Principles

Contained Therein" produced two or three good articles. An analysis of the title reveals that the study was divided into two major parts. Part One identified principles, and Part Two examined textbooks to determine whether or not they contained these principles.

Within a year following the completion of the study, an article by the author appeared in the journal *Science Education*. The title of that article was "Contributions of Science Principles to Teaching: The History and Status of the Science Principle," and it was actually a summary of the *literature review* contained in the dissertation. The *review of literature*—usually the second chapter in a thesis or dissertation—can easily be rewritten to form an article.

Concurrently, in the journal, *School Science and Mathematics,* another article appeared by the same author titled "Representation of Pertinent Earth Science Principles in Current Science Textbooks." This article was an abstract of Part Two of the dissertation. *Many dissertations have multiple parts; often each part can provide the substance for an article.*

Both of these articles appeared within a year following the author's dissertation. This means that they were written and submitted either while the dissertation was being written or almost immediately upon its completion. As you might guess, this was no accident. William Van Til, a leading expert on writing for publication, says that dissertations are like fish and company; they spoil quickly. Unlike cheese and wine, which improve with age, *as topics for articles, dissertations deteriorate rapidly.* If you have recently completed or are currently writing a paper, thesis, or dissertation, now is the time to draft articles.

If, however, you achieved this milestone earlier in life, and you fear that your thesis or dissertation has gone the way of old fish, don't worry. There is still hope. *To make your old dissertation a timely topic, you can always duplicate part of your original study.* The author of the science education dissertation did just that. Within a couple of years, an article titled "A Scientific Look at Science Textbooks in Indiana Junior High Schools" appeared in another journal, and still another article, "Applications of Science Principles to Teaching," appeared concurrently in the journal *The Clearing House.*

By now you may be asking, How long can this milking process go on? The answer is, indefinitely. As long as you update your study or parts of it, you can generate excellent substance for more good articles. For example, two years following the appearance of the article in *The Clearing House, School Science and Mathematics* published "Contributions of Science Principles to Teaching: How Science Principles Can Be Used." Later, when the author had an opportunity to repeat approximately one-tenth of the study, *School Science and Mathematics* printed still another article, "Principles of Conservation of Clean Air and Water Pertinent to the General Education Programs in Junior High School."

I have taken the time to relate this entire sequence because several lessons are contained in this series of publication. Even if you have not written a dissertation or thesis, you can still benefit from a few truths found in these examples. First, all good theses and dissertations offer the substance for more than one good article. Second, the sooner the articles are written, the better—but, more important, it's never too late to use your dissertation or thesis to generate good articles. A close look at the titles of these science articles shows that one may be on the general theme of the study while others focus on parts of the study, such as the *Literature Review* section. The author may choose to use part of the findings, such as the article on principles of conservation of clean air and water, and ignore the remaining 90 percent of the study.

One final note about using dissertations as the source of article topics: the material can—indeed, *must*—be rewritten to become more interesting and easier to read. If you write for applied journals or for magazines, your articles don't even have to follow the rigid steps of the scientific method upon which most theses and dissertations are designed. In fact, for most journals, the scientific method is inappropriate.

GRANTS AS A SOURCE OF TOPICS

Because times are financially tough for higher education institutions everywhere, professors continue to write grant proposals (the subject of Chapter 12). Beginning writers often miss an unusual opportunity to write articles describing their grants. This opportunity is unusual because writing an article on the topic of a recent grant allows you to share the grant with more people and also to use the forthcoming article to get additional grant proposals funded. This is tantamount to getting paid repeatedly for the same work—and it works. Think about it. If you were entrusted with the job of deciding who should receive support, wouldn't you want to put someone in charge of the funds who had been successful with an earlier grant and who had taken the effort to write an article telling others about your grant?

Each funded grant can be used to establish and reinforce your credibility. Writing an article about each grant further establishes you as a recognized expert on the topic. By using your grants as sources of article manuscript topics, you can enrich your grant-writing vita. It is a good investment of your time.

YOUR JOB AS A SOURCE OF TOPICS

Whether or not you are aware of your strengths, *all workers perform some parts of their jobs exceptionally well*. This means that you have information that is valuable to others who hold similar positions. But, month after month and year after year, aspiring writers attend writing workshops and openly acknowledge that they do not believe they have anything worthy of publication. This conclusion is unwise and it is wrong. You *do* have knowledge that is worth sharing, and until you acknowledge this truth you will remain unduly handicapped.

One beginning writer, a former teacher, had a job that required him to supervise student teachers in a public school setting. This new vantage point enabled him to see some of the barriers that prevent students from learning the content that teachers try to impart. This new job led to the publication of a series of articles including "Student Teachers Unlock Learning Barriers," "What the New Teacher Should Know About Learning Barriers," and "The Teacher as a Learning Barrier." All of these articles appeared in different issues of the same journal, *School and Community*. By shifting from teacher to observer, this person discovered a series of barriers that inhibit learning. What an excellent observation to share with other teachers! What an excellent topic! This observer even made a list of teacher behaviors that interfere with learning. To nonteachers this may be inane information, but to the right audience it is valuable knowledge.

OTHER OCCUPATIONS AS SOURCES OF WRITING TOPICS

Too often, we limit our writing to an unnecessarily narrow field; *professionals in many different fields could benefit from your expertise.* To avoid this myopic trap, try to think of as many audiences as possible who could benefit from your articles. For example, a nurse might wish to write an article titled "Strengths and Weaknesses of Today's Nurses." Who cares? Well, even if you and I don't care, there are others who care immensely about the strengths and weaknesses of today's nurses. Nurse educators must actively seek out feedback on the performance of graduates of their programs—feedback on what students learned that helps them in their work, feedback from employers on additional skills graduates need. This knowledge is essential for program evaluation, program improvement, and accreditation.

Practicing nurses need to know what they do well and what areas can be improved. Directors of hospitals and clinics need to know the strengths and weaknesses of today's nurses. Personnel directors must be aware of common weaknesses in the profession if they are to avoid hiring nurses who possess these weaknesses.

The author can now ask, *What do I know that is valuable to each of these audiences?* Practicing nurses? Nurse administrators? Nurse educators? Each question may lead to a similar, yet distinct, article. Whatever your ideas for topics might be, you can multiply these topics by asking these questions: "Who would be interested in this topic? Who else?" For a list of expectations of nursing journals and journals in other disciplines see Appendix A.

REFERENCE BOOKS AS A SOURCE OF TOPICS

One of the richest sources of ideas for writing topics is the reference section found in every library. For example, the *Readers' Guide*, the *Education Index*, the *Business Periodical Index*, *Psychological Abstracts*, *Index Medicus*, *Social Science Citation Index*, *Social Science Index*, *Humanities Index*, *MLA Bibliography*—these are but a few of the available reference books that can be used to identify topics.

Suppose you decide to write an article on a given topic. By checking the most current bound volumes of the appropriate index, you can see what topics are being published. Furthermore, you can readily identify those journals that are giving this topic attention. This is very important because most journal editors have topics they prefer to include and topics they prefer to exclude from their journals.

Book publishers are even more topic-limited. Each book publishing company has topics with which it excels because it has cultivated teams of experienced reviewers and marketers for those subjects. Although companies occasionally do break new ground, to do so is the exception. The acquisitions editor is far more likely to pursue tried and proven topics. Inexperienced writers are likely to purposefully avoid contacting publishers who already have a successful book on their chosen topic. This is a mistake. When the markets are large enough to support several books in a given area, publishers often actively pursue additional manuscripts in a subject area so as to increase their own share of the total market and to leverage their existing presence in that market.

Some topics will require the use of several key words. For example, say you have chosen to write on bicycle repair. There may be no entries under *bicycle repair*, but there are entries under *repair, small machines*, and other categories. A similar search on another topic may turn up no articles; now it is time to consider a computer search. For a nominal fee, most libraries offer this service. In addition to telling you what is being published and by whom, the computer search produces a review of the literature that you can use to expand your own knowledge of the topic and that can be used in your references and bibliography. Additional uses of the library to locate good topics are discussed in Chapter 6.

But suppose that neither you nor the computer can locate any articles on the topic you selected. Don't be discouraged. There's always a first time for everything. If you really want to write on this topic, do it anyway.

In the following passages, University of Nevada, Las Vegas professor Jesus Garcia talks about his topic-screening system:

> *When I write, I take an idea through what I call a "critical analysis process."*
> *I begin by placing an idea on pager/screen and "weigh its worth" to the educational community. Is what I want to tell the public novel, thought*

provoking, and practical? I discuss my idea with colleagues, particularly classroom teachers. I outline what I wish to do with the idea and again share the idea with colleagues. Third, where appropriate, I attempt to include suggestions that teachers would find useful for classroom use. Fourth, I do the research, begin writing, and continually sharpen the focus of the manuscript by returning to the original idea. The process is further heightened if I coauthor a manuscript, which I do regularly.

I find this process beneficial because I can look at an idea from multiple perspectives. More often than not, I am able to generate other ideas. As ideas are scrutinized, others surface. Moreover, I find that the process helps me to grow as I reinforce my commitment to an idea, modify my position, or reject an original idea.

FORECASTING THE FUTURE

By this time it should be obvious to you that with a little practice you will have no trouble identifying innumerable ideas for article topics or book topics. But this alone is not enough; *you must be able to identify topics that will be popular next year.* You see, the topics that you read about today are at least one or two years old. If you write about them and are lucky enough to get your work accepted, when your work is published it will be at least two years old! This figure is derived from taking a year-old topic; spending three months preparing, polishing, and submitting the manuscript; and waiting another nine months for it to be published. Does this place you in the seemingly impossible position of having to forecast the future? In a way, it does. But there are several strategies you can use—flawless strategies—to predict what topics will be popular in your field *one* or even *two* years from now. Here are three strategies that I use.

Using Speakers to Predict Future Topics

One effective way to identify topics of the future is to identify today's leaders in your chosen writing field(s). Take advantage of every opportunity you have to hear these leaders speak. The next time you visit a convention or hear a noted speaker, if at all possible, don't leave until you've spoken to this person. There is a sure-fire way to get most speakers' attention. Buy a copy of the speaker's latest book and, at the end of the speech, ask for an autograph.

As you stand in line waiting your turn, listen to the speaker's conversation with other members of the audience. Invariably, someone will ask about a recent article or book. Although the speaker did, indeed, write the article or book, the individual will be puzzled to learn how vaguely the author recalls the specifics of the work. Why is the author so vague?

Though far from obvious, the answer is simple. Before you suspect the author of plagiarism, consider the age of this work. Although the book or article carries a recent publication date, it has been at the publishing house for at least a year. Meanwhile, the author has moved forward to other topics. In fact, at this moment the admirer who has recently read the work has a better knowledge of the work than does its own creator.

Before taking time to talk to our speaker, we were looking for some ways to identify topics that will be popular one or two years from now. Actually, we haven't left our main path of pursuit because our side-track discussion introduced the best single way to identify next year's "hot" topics—*attend a conference or any assembly that affords you an opportunity to hear a speech by a recognized leader in your field of interest.*

The topic doesn't matter. You will know that it is on its way to becoming a popular item because the leaders in any field shape their field of study. While others are writing about the author's recently published, yet year-old works, the author is writing about something very different. Since the leading authorities in any field have a way of getting their manuscripts accepted (this technique is known as good writing skills) and since effective authors have a knack for getting mileage from their work (the subject of a forthcoming chapter), you can rest assured that this speaker's speech will be found alive and well dwelling in a book or an article (or both) in the next year or two. You can do far better than your competition if you take notes and prepare your own article, not on the author's book or article but on the much more current topic of the evening's speech.

Using Journal Editors to Predict Future Topics

A perhaps less exciting but equally effective way to discover the topics of the future is to contact the editors of the journals in your field of work. Ask these editors for a list of coming themes. Most nonfiction journals run a high percentage of theme issues. Editors always know the forthcoming themes for their journals at least a year or two in advance.

Using Professional Association Yearbook Editors to Predict Future Topics

Another excellent way to identify topics that will be popular one or two years from now is to contact your professional societies and ask for the topics of their forthcoming yearbooks and for the chapter titles in these books. Why is this method better? Because only the *best* of the *best* experts in the profession are invited to write a chapter in the yearbook. A trip to the reference desk of your local library can quickly identify the current members of the yearbook committee and the members of the journal publications committee.

Should you decide to write for popular magazines, examine your hobbies. A survey to determine sources of writers' first articles found the most common topic source to be personal hobbies.

Chapter 6 explains how writers can use their libraries to identify topics. With a little effort in the shape of purposeful planning, you can identify several excellent topics on which to focus your writing. With experience, you will be amazed to learn that locating topics is no problem. On the contrary, you will instinctively and unintentionally discover more topics—*good* topics—than you will ever have time to pursue.

For a look at the life of the development of an article from the time of its inception until it appeared in print, see Appendix H.

RECAPPING THE MAJOR POINTS

This chapter has pointed out that, although good, timely topics are essential for all writers, beginning writers often search desperately for suitable topics. You will always have a supply of topics if you remember these points:

- Dissertations, theses, and papers are excellent sources for journal articles.
- When possible, articles based on dissertations, theses, and papers should be written while those projects are still underway.
- Authors of dissertations can return to that document and duplicate part of the research to produce substance for a timely article.
- Your job (or any activity you do well) is an excellent source for article topics.
- You *do* have something to say that would make a good article topic.
- You can increase the mileage of each topic by considering the various audiences who would find it pertinent. This produces one or more articles for each audience.
- Topics that are popular today will lose their popularity in the year or two required for their publication; therefore, you must seek topics that will be popular a year from now.

REFERENCES

Henson, K. T. (1996, January). All the right reasons: Writing for publication. *Kappa Delta Pi Record, 33*(2), 57–59.

Henson, K. T. (2003, June). Writing for professional publication: Some myths and truths. *Phi Delta Kappan, 84*(10), 788–791.

3

GETTING STARTED

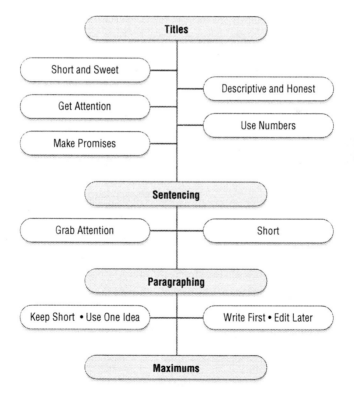

THE RIGHT TITLE

The skeptic asks, "What's in a title?" The answer is, "Only the most important key for the writer." *A good title captures the reader's attention.* Without this, the book stays on the shelf, and the article is instantly and painlessly flipped out of the reader's life.

When I was a small child, taking vacations was something special, something to really get excited over. My brother and I were barely tall enough to look out ahead above the tall seats in Dad's big Buick. But occasionally we saw something that was well worth the strain. The company that made Burma Shave, a popular shaving cream, had created a new way of advertising its product—a clever saying would be broken into phrases, and each phrase was painted on a simple sign, which was then positioned strategically beside the highway. For example, on one stretch of road, the first sign read "Why is it." Then, around the next curve we saw another sign, "when you try to pass." And over the next hill, a third sign appeared, "the guy in front." Quickly, we would try to guess the ending. Around another curve we saw it, "steps on the gas?" And always the last sign read simply "Burma Shave."

Maybe today's high-tech, "flash and trash" world of advertising finds that earlier lifestyle boring; more likely, today's advertisers recognize that adults read only a small percentage of road signs and only a slightly higher percentage of books and magazines. Instead, today's readers are very selective. They know they haven't time to read even a small percentage of the books and articles with which they come into contact. Today's readers have two reasons for reading. They read for *information* (nonfiction) or they read for *fun* (fiction), hoping to get lucky and find material that delivers both information and fun.

An astute author can capitalize on this knowledge. As you search for the right title, select one that hooks the reader's interest and/or promises to deliver information the reader deems important. Consider, for example, Tipper Gore's book *Raising PG Kids in an X-Rated Society.* To catch the reader's attention, Gore uses a little levity, playing on motion picture ratings. Her title also makes a definite promise to the reader. Experienced writers know that to protect their integrity their writings must deliver whatever the title promises. Whether a book title or an article title, the reader will feel disappointed if the work fails to deliver.

The writer must also remember to *keep the audience in mind at all times.* With a title like *Raising PG Kids in an X-Rated Society,* it is clear that Gore's intended readers are parents and guardians, so each paragraph and each sentence must be written to provide information that parents and guardians need. This title contains an implied promise to help these people meet the challenge of raising good kids in a less-than-wholesome society.

Once such a promise is made, it must be kept. It might help to remember that as a writer you are creating a product that you want to sell. Therefore, your product must provide something of value in return for the reader's time, attention, and money. In a society as busy as ours, a person's time and energy are precious. As a writer, you are competing with many other vendors for people's time. In every sentence, you must be sure that the reader won't feel shortchanged. Give something valuable to the reader, and you will have gained a loyal customer; but break your promise, and you will lose the reader's support.

Consider the following titles. Do they hook *your* attention? Does each make a promise?

How to Turn $15 into a Money-Making Business
Megamergers
Breaking Up Is Hard to Do
The One-Minute Manager
Finding the Freedom of Self-Control
Existentially Speaking
39 Forever
Help for the Battered Woman
Thoroughbred Handicapping as an Investment
The Facts on FAX
How to Save Your Child from Drugs
Eating on the Run

A quick glance at this list tells the reader that these are nonfiction books. They promise to provide useful information and help the reader.

Titles of fiction books and articles may be far less descriptive because the purpose of fiction is to entertain. Consider the following list of current fiction titles:

Letter from Home
The Arraignment
By the Light of the Moon
Crossroads
Forever
Life of Pi
Light in Shadow
Whispers at Midnight
Foxcatcher

Although fiction book titles may or may not be descriptive, they usually stir the imagination. For example, the reader doesn't have to know that *Foxcatcher* is about espionage to find the title captivating. Good fiction writers know that their readers are imaginative, and good writers use this knowledge when choosing titles.

Choosing Titles for Nonfiction Journal Articles

Writers of nonfiction journal articles have a special opportunity to use titles to engage their readers. Knowing that their readers have even less time to dedicate to their reading than fiction readers who read for fun, successful authors of nonfiction articles make even more definite promises to their readers. For example, consider the following article titles and their respective audiences.

Article Title	*Audience*
Ten Ways to Avoid Litigation	Physicians
Six Ways to Resolve Discipline Problems	Middle school principals
Knowing Your Clients' Needs	Realtors
Interviewing: Accentuating Your Assets	Job applicants
How to Make Your Car Last 150,000 Miles	Car owners

All of these titles promise to help the reader, but what is more important is that finding solutions to the problems addressed is perceived by the intended audience as being very important. With litigation on the rise, in number of cases and in the number of dollars and number of awards to patients, what physician could ignore an article titled "Ten Ways to Avoid Litigation"? What middle school principal, who must deal daily with children of the most awkward and rebellious age, could fail to be intrigued by an article that promises to make his or her own life easier?

The two titles just mentioned also contain another element to attract the reader. The first title specifies that *ten* concrete suggestions will be provided to the reader, and the second offers *six* substantive solutions. When asked what he looked for most in an article, the editor of a research journal responded: "I suppose that what I want more than anything else is that each article makes some contributions." Readers of research journals and readers of applied journals want—even demand—substance from the articles they read.

The last title on the preceding list, "How to Make Your Car Last 150,000 Miles," is an article that appeared in *Consumer's Digest*. Interestingly, the first page of this article carries a chart that lists the 10 least expensive cars to maintain to 50,000 miles and a corresponding list of the 10 most expensive cars to maintain to 50,000 miles. With just a glance at this first page, this chart immediately tells the reader that this article offers substance. The author did his homework and researched his topic, which means that he reviewed the literature to discover new and helpful information to enrich his article. Incidentally, he reprinted the charts, with the permission of *The Car Book,* and gave that source credit. Good writers use lists, charts, and graphs so that readers won't have to "sniff out" or look for the main ideas in their articles.

Another important aspect of selecting a title is that a good title gives direction to the author. The importance of having each sentence throughout your document advance your theme cannot be overstressed. A specific descriptive title can put you on track and keep you there. The right title can help you select words and construct sentences to make this direct, straight-line advancement happen. *Use your title to guide the writing of each page and each paragraph.*

Often during the writing process an author will discover ways to improve the work by shifting the direction of the manuscript. Such a short interruption to explain or offer an example is fine as long as the end result does not alter the theme to the extent that the document no longer delivers on the title. This need not be a problem—the title can always be revised to correct the mismatch. Even the best writers make such adjustments. To neglect to do so would either result in a title that doesn't live up to its promise or an article written in one limited direction, with limited creativity.

WRITING THE FIRST SENTENCE

The author of nonfiction must immediately tell the reader exactly what this article or chapter will do. This is the function of the lead (or leading) sentence. For example, the first sentence may introduce a problem; the rest of the lead paragraph will explain how and to what degree the author will solve this problem. Or the article might begin with a question, and the rest of the lead paragraph tells exactly what this article is going to do about answering the question. The remainder of the manuscript must then step-by-step, sentence-by-sentence, paragraph-by-paragraph begin resolving the issue, solving the problem, or answering the question.

Fiction writers may have no question to answer or problem to solve, but they must use the first sentence and paragraph to begin establishing the climate, introduce and develop characters, and introduce conflict. Early attention to these tasks enables the writer to capture and hold the readers' attention.

A wide variety of types of lead sentences is available to writers. Factual statements are among the most common, although they are not necessarily the most captivating. You be the judge of what constitutes an interesting lead sentence. Examine the following three examples to see which type you prefer.

- Early Sunday evening, unaware of the plot against his life, Tom Simms walked into the dimly lighted parking lot.
- Americans are killing themselves, and they don't even know it.
- What is your consumer IQ?

These three examples are all good lead sentences, but they differ greatly. One is fictitious, one is factual, and one asks a question. Like all good lead sentences, they *hook the reader to want to know more*. What is it about these sentences that compels the reader to read the next sentence? Each one focuses on a topic that contemporary Americans find important. Crime continues to rise. Concern and commitment to better health are evidenced in the sale of exercise videos and books. Consumer awareness is a deep concern because of the increase in all types of fraud—credit card, mail-order, and investment, not to mention the customer-service fraud such as medical malpractice or interstate auto mechanics fraud.

A nonfiction article should begin with a lead sentence that addresses the topic revealed in the title, and it must extend this topic in a logical way. For example, an article titled "Our Foods Are Poisoning Us" may begin with the following sentence: *Americans are killing themselves, and they don't even know it.* The next sentence is very important, for it must reveal the purpose of this article. If the author plans to write about cholesterol, this sentence might read, "Each day Americans consume more cholesterol than . . . " Or, if the writer wishes the article to focus on salt consumption, the next sentence might read, "Each day we eat ten times as much salt as our bodies need."

While still in the first paragraph, the author must articulate the purpose of this article. Here the author must tell readers what the article offers that will enable them to cope with this problem or situation. For example, the next sentence may read, "Fortunately, through planning, we can control our consumption of . . .". This sentence implies that the rest of the article will tell the reader how to do this planning, and the rest of the article—each paragraph, each sentence, and each word—should be used to deliver this promise.

Examine again the first sample lead sentence. "Early Sunday evening, unaware of the plot against his life, Tom Simms walked into the dimly lighted parking lot." Although this sentence could be used to start a nonfiction article, it seems more likely to be the beginning of a fiction piece. Assume that Tom Simms is a leading character and that he will survive the parking-lot scene. The author must now let the reader know who Tom is by describing his appearance and his personality. The reader can appreciate this story only by knowing and perhaps identifying with Tom Simms. To ensure that the reader will read on, the author must continue to build Tom's character, explaining why he behaves as he does.

As you have seen, authors often use more than a single lead sentence just to grab the reader. Consider the following article opening: "It's happening on college campuses everywhere. It's exciting, and it isn't even illegal. But it should be." These three short sentences are written to stir your curiosity and make you wonder, what's happening everywhere? What's exciting? What isn't illegal but should be?

This was the lead I used for an article in the *The Chronicle of Higher Education* warning writers about publisher rip-offs. The title of the article is "When

Signing Book Contracts, Scholars Should Be Sure to Read the Fine Print." Once past this hook, I immediately begin describing the traps, using lists and subheadings to highlight each one. This shows that the article has substance and makes the content easily visible to even the most casual reader.

PARAGRAPHING

Two mistakes account for a large percentage of the poorly written materials. Both of these mistakes concern paragraphing. Inexperienced writers seldom know when to end a paragraph. Some writers use the surveyor's approach. They step back and look to see how much of the page has been used, then hit the return key. Other writers just keep on writing and writing until their pens and ribbons run dry. You can do better.

The paragraph is an important tool available for all writers who know how to use it. As readers read, they make associations between the sentences. The author can help shape these associations so that the reader thinks as the writer thinks. This is important if the reader is to draw the author's intended conclusions. By lumping the related sentences together, the author tells the reader which sentences to associate. By correctly assembling the sentences, the author helps the reader comprehend the overall meaning of the paragraph. However, many authors fail by packing too much information into one paragraph. There is a simple rule: *one major theme per paragraph.*

A second useful way to determine the best length of a paragraph is to purposefully keep each paragraph short enough so that you (and the reader) can remember all of the ideas contained in the paragraph. Usually half of a double-spaced typewritten page is as much as a reader can retain. Remember the reader, and *keep your paragraphs short.*

Paragraphs can be simplified by using a process which psychologists call "chunking." Consider the following numbers: 386914. Try to remember them. If you succeeded, you may have put the numbers in groups such as 38–69–14 or 386–914. This is chunking. Now try to remember the following paragraph.

A good way to add power to your writing is by keeping your subject and verb in close proximity. Good, strong paragraphs have only one major idea and good, strong sentences start with concrete nouns and use action verbs. Writing can be weakened by hiding the subject in the middle or at the end of the paragraph.

Now consider how much easier it is to remember this same information when it is organized into chunks:

There are three ways to make paragraphs powerful: (1) use concrete nouns, (2) put the subject up front, and (3) follow it quickly with an action verb.

Once you complete your manuscript, read through it to see if each paragraph advances the ideas in previous paragraphs. If not, the paragraphs must be reordered. There is a good way to do this. Those who use the pencil or pen can write each paragraph on an index card and then sequence and rearrange the order until you are satisfied. Those who write on computers also have unlimited flexibility to experiment until they find the best sequence.

GO AHEAD AND WRITE

The first and foremost job of a writer is to write. Tom Buttery (1996, p. 112) reminds us that the one uncompromising prerequisite to become a successful author is to write. "The more you write, the more you are forced to think through the process, dissect the components, and then synthesize new entities; however, the prerequisite behavior is simply to write."

Recognize that you do have something that is worth saying. Identify your target audience and ask yourself: If I were in their shoes, what would I want to know? What would I find interesting? Helpful?

Some people find it helpful to make an outline. They say that making an outline forces them to rethink and sequence their ideas. It helps them identify the most important issues. But other people find that making an outline stifles their creativity, and they prefer not to be restricted by an outline. But what about *you?* Should you use an outline? The decision is simple. If you like to work with outlines, use one. If not, don't.

The main thing to remember about getting started is to forge forward without worrying about errors in spelling or punctuation and without trying to avoid superfluous words and sentences. All of these errors can be corrected later. Don't make the mistake of perfectionists who ponder over word choice even during the first draft. Don't worry that you may be straying from the title. Writing is a creative process, even nonfiction writing. So just write. Whenever you think that you might have something to say, just write it down. The first draft doesn't have to be good. *Getting something on paper is half of the challenge. You can do it. Just write.*

PROFILE

Arnold B. Cheyney received bachelor's and master's degrees from Kent State University and a Ph.D. from Ohio State University. He began his career as an elementary school teacher, principal, and supervisor in Canton, Ohio. Now University of Miami Professor Emeritus, he lives in Wooster, Ohio. Jeanne Cheyney, his wife, attended the Cleveland School of Art, graduated from Kent State, and taught in Ohio and Florida at elementary schools. She is a professional writer, illustrator, and novelist.

They have done 12 GoodYearBooks, a series of curriculum books for primary teachers. In addition, the Cheyney's curriculum materials for primary grade Sunday Schools are used throughout Canada and the United States.

Arnold Cheyney's book *The Ripe Harvest: Educating Migrant Children* (U M Press, 1972), was selected by the American Library Association as an outstanding academic book for 1972–1973. He has published over 500 articles in newspapers such as *The Miami Herald, Detroit Free Press,* and the late *Chicago Daily News.*

Jeanne Cheyney's novels include *Captive's Promise* (1988) and *The Conviction of Charlotte Gray* (Zondervan, 1988) which have since been republished in condensed versions by a book club; *A Patch of Black Satin* (Silhouette, 1985); and *The Secret of Giltham Hall* (Cook, 1980). She has several other novels completed and ready to make the rounds of publishers.

The Thirteen Cheyney Maxims for Would-Be-Published Writers

1. Know for whom you want to write, send for writer's guidelines, and follow them explicitly.
2. Read widely and much, especially in the area in which you intend to write.
3. For practice, copy exceptional paragraphs when you find them in your reading, and analyze them. Do the words flow? Why are the words the writer used good choices? Do the sentences describe a scene in as few words as possible?
4. Be sure the first paragraph in your book or article captures your reader's interest.
5. Become familiar with the latest issue of *Writer's Market.* It gives you editor's needs and how to prepare manuscripts and queries. Your public library has a copy.
6. Send only your very best work.
7. Keep to deadlines.
8. Proofread and proofread again.
9. Do not take rejection of your manuscripts as a personal affront.
10. Do not talk about what you are writing—if it's publishable, others will find out in due time.
11. Let your manuscript rest in a drawer for seasoning, and read it again before sending it to an editor.
12. Be kind but honest when evaluating your collaborator's writing.
13. Read all lists, tips, and maxims on writing with suspicion.

RECAPPING THE MAJOR POINTS

Getting started is the most difficult challenge that writers face. The goal of this chapter has been to help you begin getting words on paper. Getting started will be easier if you remember these points:

- Choose topics that are interesting to the reader.
- Begin by writing a title that describes your forthcoming article.
- Feel free to stray from your title; you can always change the title at a later time.

- For nonfiction articles, choose a title that makes a promise to the reader, then use the article to deliver that promise.
- For fiction articles, write a title that hooks the reader's attention.
- Use the first sentence to tell the readers exactly what the article will do for them.
- Make every sentence extend the message found in the preceding sentence.
- For nonfiction articles, use the first paragraph to tell what the article is going to do to help the reader.
- For fiction articles, begin developing the characters in the first paragraph.
- Keep your paragraphs reasonably short, limiting each to one major idea and a reasonable number of supporting ideas.
- If you like outlines, use them; if not, don't.
- During the first draft, ignore any need that you might feel to make your article grammatically correct.

REFERENCES

Buttery, T. (1996). Writing for publication in professional journals. *North Carolina Journal of Teacher Education, 8*(1), 112–119.

Henson, K. T. (1990, October 24). When signing book contracts, scholars should be sure to read the fine print. *Chronicle of Higher Education,* p. B2.

Henson, K. T. (1996, January). All the right reasons: Writing for publication. *Kappa Delta Pi Record, 33*(2), 57–59.

4

ABOUT STYLE

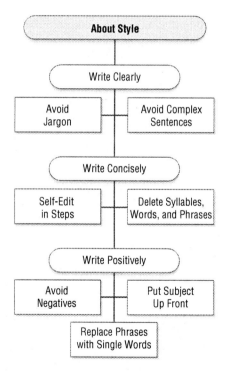

About Style

Write Clearly

Avoid Jargon

Avoid Complex Sentences

Write Concisely

Self-Edit in Steps

Delete Syllables, Words, and Phrases

Write Positively

Avoid Negatives

Put Subject Up Front

Replace Phrases with Single Words

In your quest for facts and tips on becoming a better writer, nothing is more important than style. What is the meaning of style? It might help if you think of someone familiar, say Fred Astaire, whom most people recognize as having style. Ginger Rogers had style, too—she did everything Fred did except, as Ginger herself said, she did it backwards and in high heels. People with style are poised and confident. They are eager to display their talents, yet they never "toot their own horns"—their performance and behavior speak for them.

Style is not just the particular combination of dance steps; it's *how* the dancer takes those steps. Style is not just the words a writer chooses; it's also *how the writer uses them.* Here's where many beginning writers trip on their own thoughts. Their failure to see their own potential and purpose for writing limits their ability to master an effective writing style. Style requires a few basic understandings. These understandings shape how writers think; and, in turn, how they think shapes how they write.

To appreciate the role that style plays in writing, refer to the passage from *The Auctioneer* by Joan Samson (p. 8). Suppose, instead, she had written:

> *The man and woman were burning brush. Their daughter was with them. She saw a truck coming toward them and went over to get a better look. It was Bob Gore, the police chief.*

Instead, Joan Samson chose to have the dead leaves hiss, the truck tires rut, the mud spray, and Gore's belly seek a point of equilibrium. This writing style is entertaining, and it puts the reader on the scene. Obviously, Joan wanted the readers to share this experience and enjoy it. But, suppose most of your writing is for professional or academic journals. There, you will not choose to entertain but to inform. Consider your other reasons for writing, and develop a style that will serve your purposes. For example, if you write to earn promotions, tenure, or merit pay, consider the qualities that your evaluators will be looking for, and work those qualities into your manuscript. A good way to develop this sensitivity and flexibility is to write a manuscript for a specific audience, and then rewrite it for a different audience.

Now, it's time to dispel some common myths that impede the development of writers. Among these is the common belief that *it's who you know* that determines your success as a writer. It's visible and audible. Skepticism is in the eyes of aspiring writers, and some beginners are bold enough to announce it openly. Some just bare their souls and say, "I don't know if I have what it takes to become a successful writer." At this point let me share a little good news. Although it may sound deceptively simple, to become a successful writer, you must set aside your modesty and believe in yourself. My promise to you is that *anyone of average or above intelligence can become a successful writer.*

Occasionally skeptics will openly challenge this assertion. They say, "Sure, it's easy for people like you. You have published so much that the editors recognize your name. But what about me? Nobody knows me!" Although mine isn't a household name to most editors, I will admit that having editors recognize your name probably causes them to consider your manuscript a little more carefully, resulting in a slight edge. But I emphatically insist that having an editor recognize your name is far overrated. Any advantage is good to have, but you don't need this edge to get published. All you need to do is to turn out a good product, and you can do this by learning a few simple but essential nuts and bolts about writing. Then you carefully apply this knowledge to developing your own writing style.

Let's examine a little logic. Suppose you were the editor working for an important magazine, journal, or book publisher. It's fair to assume that most people would consider important any journal that happened to be their source of income. Your own success as an editor hinges on your ability to give your journal subscribers or book buyers what they want and need. If you succeed and your readership increases, your board of directors will be happy, making the company president happy, your boss happy, and you happy. Why would any editor who values success let friendships and familiar names seriously influence the decision to accept or reject a manuscript? Only a very shortsighted (and probably short-tenured) editor would run such a risk.

For several summers I have enjoyed traveling to college campuses to give writing workshops. Part of the enjoyment comes from visiting journal offices. For example, I have been shocked at the smallness of the staffs of some premier journals and at the physical smallness of other offices. Most readers would be surprised to learn that the amount of released time from teaching given to some editors is only one course per term; some get none.

Sometimes the editors of these journals share some interesting stories. For example, on one visit I learned that one of the most respected leaders in his field, both nationally and internationally, received a rejection letter for an article he submitted to a journal for which he had previously served as senior editor. In fact, it was generally acknowledged that this journal had been elevated to a rank unsurpassed by similar journals during this author's editorship. His manuscript was rejected because he had failed to give his own manuscript the attention and hard work that it needed to meet the standards of that journal.

If not a recognizable name, then what does one need to become a successful writer? Some say luck. It's hard to deny that luck does play a part in the success of writers. But many insist that real winners make their own luck. Rather than waiting for luck to come to us, each of us can *develop* an effective writing style that will increase our odds of success. What is the best style? One that works for you.

Now let's get specific about writing style. Basic to success for both nonfiction and fiction writers is the ability to write clearly, succinctly, and positively—to communicate. And whether writing fiction or nonfiction, all successful writers are able to communicate ideas, thoughts, and feelings with clarity and accuracy.

WRITING CLEARLY

In writing, clarity is best achieved through the use of a simple, concise, straightforward approach. Writing simply and clearly sounds easy, but for most people it is not. Why? There are two reasons. First, most beginning writers believe that the task before them is to impress the editor. Second, they think the best way to impress the editor is to use big words, complex sentences (well seasoned with jargon), and long paragraphs. Both of these ideas are dead wrong. The way to impress an editor is to communicate clearly. This is not easy for most academicians who are steeped in jargon. Experienced writers and editors know that *anyone can take an easy topic and make it appear difficult, but only a skilled writer can take a complicated topic and make it appear simple.* Furthermore, the author's job is not to please the editor: it's to please the readers—the people who subscribe to the journal or buy the books or magazines. Editors have a common expression that sounds strange to the novice but has precise meaning to other editors. Editors are often heard saying: "It's *right* for our journal" or "It's *not right* for our journal." Good editors develop a keen and accurate sense for what their readers want and expect in terms of both content and style.

By now, perhaps you are asking, "How do I know what content and style are right for a publisher?" There are two easy, sure-fire ways to learn what editors expect from their writers. First, get a recent copy of the journal and study its style and content. Second, you can contact the editor to request a list of needs, future themes of the journal, and guidelines for contributors.

Write Concisely

In their classic reference book *The Elements of Style,* William Strunk, Jr., and E. B. White (1979) say:

> Vigorous writing is concise. A sentence should contain no unnecessary words, a paragraph no unnecessary sentences, for the same reason that a drawing should have no unnecessary lines and a machine no unnecessary parts. (p. 23)

Good writing is achieved by deleting unnecessary words and arranging the remaining words in active order. By this standard, parts of some translations of the Bible exemplify some of the best writing we know. For example, John 11:35 reads *Jesus wept.* Although our educational background may tell us that such simple writing should be avoided, this is powerful writing. Ironically, it is difficult to shed the pedagogical jargon that we have learned to use so effectively to cloud our meanings. For most of us, developing a good, simple writing style requires *unlearning* years of poor word selection and complicated sentence structure. But, with determination and practice, you can master the art of straightforward, simple writing.

It is now time to learn how to write clearly and simply. Figure 4.1 contains an editing exercise designed to help you recognize stylistic problems. Try to simplify each of the following statements by deleting unnecessary parts of each sentence. Be careful not to change the meaning of the sentence. Then refer to Figure 4.2 for an edited version of the exercise.

Although your results may vary from the revisions in Figure 4.2, you probably will agree that most of these statements are improved over those in Figure 4.1. If you look carefully, you will discover even more ways to shorten some of these sentences without changing their meanings. For example, sentence 7 still contains the superfluous words *There is no doubt that.* These words are excess baggage. Delete them. Sentence 8 has the useless words *The reason is that.* Sentence 9 could be shortened further by deleting *no doubt* and by changing *was right in finding* to *correctly found.* It is important to note that this editing takes place in steps, and each step improves the quality of the product. This is precisely how good writers work. The popular belief that good writing is the product of geniuses is quite mistaken. Polished manuscripts result from a series of editing sessions, each bringing gradual improvement to the work.

FIGURE 4.1 Editing exercise.

Delete the unnecessary words.

1. The truth of the matter is that the company was not successful.
2. The judge, who was a distant cousin, set him free.
3. She is a woman who does not usually stumble forward without giving considerable thought to the possible consequences.
4. His cousin, who is somewhat older than he, himself is, will stand a good chance to inherit the entire estate.
5. The fact is, he's finished.
6. His job is a highly demanding one.
7. There is no doubt but that he responded in a highly hasty manner.
8. The reason why is that the Hawthorne control group was shocked out of its complacency by the supervisor's presence.
9. There is no doubt that the jury was right in finding him guilty.
10. Were you aware of the fact that excessive salt produces hypertension?

FIGURE 4.2   Effect of close editing.

1. The company was not successful.
2. The judge, a distant cousin, set him free.
3. She does not usually proceed without considering the consequences.
4. His older cousin will stand a good chance to inherit the entire estate.
5. He's finished.
6. His job is highly demanding.
7. There is no doubt that he responded hastily.
8. The reason is that the Hawthorne control group was shocked out of its complacency by the supervisor's presence.
9. No doubt the jury was right in finding him guilty.
10. Were you aware that excessive salt produces hypertension?

Write Positively

Classes in public speaking teach us to speak assertively. When writing, we should write forcefully. Forceful writing results from writing concisely, actively, and positively. The present tense is usually more active and therefore more forceful than the past tense. Refer to the "close editing" examples in Figure 4.3. Sentence 1 can be made more positive and forceful by changing *not successful* to *unsuccessful*. The words *does not* in sentence 3 can be replaced by the word *seldom* and, of course, the word *proceed* must be changed to *proceeds*. Eliminating negative words such as *not* is often a key to making writing more positive and forceful.

Figure 4.3 shows the results of step-by-step editing of the statements from the earlier exercise. First, read a sentence in the left column and then follow that statement to the right to see how each editing step contributed to the improvement of the existing statement. Next, compare the statement in the left column with the final edited statement in the right column. Most of these examples show dramatic improvement. Finally, notice that the objective of the first two steps was to shorten the statements. In the last step, the objective is to make the statement more active. From these examples, can you make a statement about how writers can make their writings more active? *To add power to their writing, good writers put the subject at the beginning of the sentence.*

Throughout most of the century, Americans have used the term *jump-start* to refer to the process of starting a stalled car engine. When former President George Bush applied the term to the country's lagging economy, suddenly it seemed as if we were jump-starting everything. Inexperienced writers often try to jump-start sentences with words such as "it" and "there" at the beginning—but these lifeless words are no more effective than using a dead battery to jump-start a car.

FIGURE 4.3   Writing positively.

Original Sentence	First Revision	Second Revision	Third Revision
The truth of the matter is that the company was not successful.	The company was not successful.	The company was unsuccessful.	The company failed.
The judge, who was a distant cousin, set him free.	The judge, a distant cousin, set him free.	The judge set him free. (Wrong— valuable meaning is lost.)	
She is a woman who does not usually stumble forward without giving considerable thought to the consequences.	She seldom proceeds without giving considerable thought to the possible consequences.	She seldom proceeds without considering the consequences.	She thinks before she acts.
His cousin, who is somewhat older than he himself is, will stand a good chance to inherit the entire estate.	His older cousin will stand a good chance to inherit the entire estate.	His older cousin will probably inherit the entire estate.	
The fact is he's finished.	He's finished.		
His job is a highly demanding one.	His job is demanding.		
There is no doubt but that he responded in a hasty manner.	He responded in a hasty manner.	He responded hastily.	
There is no doubt that the jury was right in finding him guilty.	No doubt the jury was right in finding him guilty.	The jury was right in finding him guilty.	

For example, consider the sentence *It is a good practice to always lock your car.* The first part of this sentence drags. You can read *four* words and still know nothing. Why not put a concrete subject up front? *Locking your car is a good practice.* You might even make it a command: *Always lock your car.*

The most common of these jump-start words is *there.* This word should be used to give directions, yet it is often used to get sentences going—for example, *There is a good chance that the person who buys the most tickets will win.* Instead of this slow start, how about *The person with the most tickets will probably win.* Or *Buying more tickets increases your chance of winning.*

Because the sentences we have been examining are exaggerated, they may seem contrived and ridiculously obvious. But many serious writings are full of superfluous words assembled awkwardly, and with passive verbs. Figure 4.4 contains sample sentences from the first draft of a book manuscript. This exercise will be more challenging.

After you have edited all of the sentences, examine Figure 4.5. The same editing process used in the previous exercise has been applied to these more advanced statements. Because the original statements are more complex, the improvements are more pronounced.

Sentence 1 in Figure 4.4 has two major problems. First, it has a very weak beginning; and second, it is too wordy. *To give the sentence more force, put the subject up front: Teachers should* or *teachers must* identify routines . . . give the sentence thrust. Shortening the sentence clarifies the meaning while making the sentence more powerful. The words *that need to be established* can be replaced with the single word *necessary.* A reversal in the sequence of the last two words is needed.

Sentence 2 suffers from too many words and colloquialisms. By removing the colloquial expressions, you can reduce the number of words while removing the distractions. For example, use *much* instead of *a great deal of.* Replace *how to teach* with *teaching methods* or *teaching strategies.* Simply delete the word *information.*

In sentence 3 replace *will be a result of* with *result from,* giving the sentence more force. Change the remainder of the sentence to *a lack of awareness of ways to prevent and resolve problems.* The expression *once they do occur* is superfluous since this is the only time one could respond to problems.

Sentence 4 begins with a conjunction. This is not as strict a taboo today as it once was, but don't do it casually. For example, sometimes starting a

FIGURE 4.4   Advanced editing exercise.

1. It will help if teachers will identify routines that need to be established.
2. Teacher preparation programs typically spend a great deal of time acquainting prospective teachers with how to teach information.
3. Such fear may well be a result of a lack of understanding of some ways of preventing problems and of responding to them once they do occur.
4. However, repetition should not be overdone. If it is, boredom can set in.
5. In general, people who are acknowledged to have a great deal of expertise in a given area exercise considerable influence over others.
6. Efforts are being taken in schools of nearly every industrialized nation to improve the quality of their schools.

FIGURE 4.5 Good editing is a step-by-step process.

Original Sentence	First Revision (to shorten)	Second Revision (to shorten more)	Third Revision (to make active)
It will help if teachers will identify routines that need to be established.	It will help if teachers will identify necessary routines.		Teachers should identify necessary routines.
Teacher preparation programs typically spend a great deal of time acquainting prospective teachers with how to teach information.	Teacher preparation programs typically spend considerable time acquainting prospective teachers with how to teach.	Teacher preparation programs typically spend considerable time on teaching about methodology.	Most teacher preparation programs emphasize methodology.
Such fear may well be a result of a lack of understanding of some ways of preventing problems and responding to them once they do occur.	Such fear may result from a lack of understanding of ways to prevent problems and respond to them.	Such fear may result from a lack of understanding of ways to prevent and respond to problems.	Not knowing how to prevent and respond to problems can frighten teachers.
However, repetition should not be overdone. If it is boredom can set in.	Repetition should not be overdone. If it is boredom can set in.	Excessive repetition can result in boredom.	Excessive repetition can cause boredom.
In general, people who are acknowledged to have a great deal of expertise in a given area exercise considerable influence over others.	In general, experts in a given area exercise considerable influence over others.	Experts in a given area exercise considerable influence over others.	Experts often influence their peers.
Efforts are being taken in nearly every industrialized nation to improve the quality of their schools.	Efforts are being made by most industrialized nations to improve their schools.		Most industrialized nations are working to improve their schools.

sentence with *however* or *but* can make a stark contrast to the previous sentence. Sentence 4 should read, *Excessive repetition causes boredom.* Did you think of another way to eliminate the colloquialism *set in?*

Sentence 5 is far too wordy. You might begin by replacing "people who are acknowledged to have a great deal of expertise" with *experts,* thereby reducing the number of letters and spaces from 61 to 7. This is economical writing through good editing. Good writers are good editors. The ending of the sentence, "exercise considerable influence over others," can be reduced to "influence others."

The sentences in this second exercise are representative of those found in actual manuscripts. Writing an article or book requires several editings. Indeed, *good writing is the result of good editing, and good editing occurs in gradual steps.*

Treat Genders Fairly

The 1970s was the decade that brought concern for equal treatment of the sexes into the public consciousness, and that change was accomplished largely through our literature. As great efforts are made to portray the sexes equally and fairly, too often the results are awkward writing. Our society has moved from using the single pronoun *he* and *him* to the double pronouns *he or she* and *him or her*—we even take care to reverse the order much of the time. Then we learned to combine *she* and *he* by using a slash (s/he). All of these attempts to treat the genders fairly result in awkward reading. Some textbook authors have attempted to handle the problem by using masculine pronouns throughout and by prefacing the book with a disclaimer directing the reader to think masculine half of the time and feminine the other half of the time. None of these strategies is acceptable.

Two easy strategies will skillfully handle the gender issue in almost all circumstances. Either you can simply choose to pluralize the subject or the antecedent, or you can reconstruct the sentence so that the need for identifying the gender of the subject or antecedent is eliminated. Figure 4.6 provides

FIGURE 4.6   Treating genders equally.

1. There is no relationship between a learner's self-concept and the likelihood that he or she will develop acceptable patterns of self-control.
2. The teacher can continue to monitor the entire class at the same time that he or she is working with the small group.
3. If someone is liked and respected as an individual, people are more willing to accept his or her advice than if he or she is not liked.

an opportunity for you to develop skill in treating the genders fairly without disrupting the flow of each sentence. First, see if you can resolve the problem by using the pluralizing strategy. Then see if you can resolve the problem by reconstructing the sentences. For this exercise, ignore the superfluity of these statements, and do not edit for any purposes other than dealing with the gender problem.

Now that you have had an opportunity to apply these two strategies, examine Figure 4.7 and compare the changes with those you made. Should you find discrepancies, don't worry. Usually you will find several ways to improve statements. Some improvements may be better than others, but *all* improvements are good!

Study Figure 4.7. Notice that for each statement, both pluralizing and restructuring methods are applied. Do you prefer the results of the revisions by pluralizing over those by reconstructing? Is your preference consistent for all three statements? This may give you some insight into how you want to handle this concern in your writing.

The net result of developing and using an effective writing style is capturing and holding the reader's attention—a goal that all successful writers keep in front of them at all times. Developing conciseness requires concerted

FIGURE 4.7   Eliminating sexism through pluralizing and restructuring.

Original Statement	Pluralizing	Restructuring
There is no relationship between a learner's self-concept and the likelihood that he or she will develop acceptable patterns of self-control.	There is no relationship between learners' self-concepts and the likelihood that they will develop patterns of self-control.	Self-concept has no effect on self-control.
The teacher can continue to monitor the entire class at the same time that he or she is working with the small group.	Teachers can continue to monitor the entire class at the same time that they are working with the small group.	The teacher can continue monitoring the entire class while working with the small group.
If someone is liked and respected as an individual, people are more willing to accept his or her advice than if he or she is not liked.	If people are liked and respected as individuals, others are more likely to accept their advice than if they are not liked.	Friends have more influence than enemies.

effort. Figure 4.8 lists some of the most common examples of expressions that can clutter writing.

The expressions in Figure 4.9 are some of many that make writing unnecessarily wordy. Long words have already been identified as contributing to needlessly complex writing. A list of such words and their simpler substitutes appears in Figure 4.9.

This list is intended to stimulate you to think of more two-dollar words that can easily be replaced with 25-cent words. Understandably, politicians hear a lot of fancy words that lack meaning. Texas congressman Maury Maverick coined the word *gobbledygook* to represent those words that sound fancy but have little meaning. For him, such words conjured up the image of a turkey gobbler which spreads its wings, struts around, and gobbles. Like the gobble-gobble sounds made by Old Tom, such words make their users look like turkeys.

You might be surprised to know just how often you use unnecessarily long words and expressions. John Locke said "We are what we do. Therefore,

FIGURE 4.8   Replacing long expressions with fewer words.

Bulky	*Concise*	*Bulky*	*Concise*
until such time as	until	on a daily basis	daily
a high rate of speed	fast	in a hasty manner	hastily
on account of	because	in close proximity	near
in the event that	if	there is no doubt that	undoubtedly
provides information	tells	administrate	administer/run
in the majority of cases	usually	a large percentage of	most
each and every one	each	once upon a time	once
has to do with	concerns	during the past year	last year
has the capability of	can	can't help but think	think
in spite of the fact that	although	almost everyone	most
cancel out	cancel	need to be established	needed
mandatory requirement	requirement	filled to capacity	full
at that point in time	then	give consideration to	consider
at this point in time	now	as to the question as	why
in attendance	there	to why	
improve the quality of	improve	rank order	rank
a new innovation	an innovation	as to whether or not	whether
in short supply	scarce	put in an appearance	attend
in the final analysis	finally	revert back to	revert to
continues to occur	reoccurs	a great deal of	much
in the forseeable future	soon	with the exception of	except
she is a woman who	she	in the amount of	of
in the majority	usually	to have to tell you	to say
of instances		have no other choice	must
in view of the fact that	since		

use
FIGURE 4.9 Writers should ~~utilize~~ small words.

utilize	use
prioritize	rank
medication	medicine
origination	origin
established	set
irregardless	regardless
administer	run/give

excellence is a habit." Obtuse writing is also a habit, and like all habits, it is difficult to break. Figure 4.10 provides further opportunity to practice using shorter sentences and shorter words.

When you have completed the exercise in Figure 4.10, examine the following edited version:

If you attended the meeting last year, you know why the room was full and why that meeting usually improves our sales. She can give each innovation a boost.

Consider the difference this type of editing can make when applied to an entire manuscript.

For several years, I have taught a course on writing for publication. Most students in this class have published. To earn an A, students must produce two completed, edited, polished, and mailed manuscripts. Half as much is required for a B. No student has failed to earn a B, and half have earned As. But, notice that the course does not require manuscript *acceptances,* only that the manuscript is mailed to a national journal. Acceptance is not required

FIGURE 4.10 Additional editing practice.

In the event that you were in attendance at the most recent meeting this past year, you have a pretty good understanding of why that presentation improves the quality of our sales, at least in the majority of instances. You also have a good understanding as to why the room was filled to capacity.

I have to tell you that she has the ability to give each new innovation a boost.

because the turnaround time for some of the journals is longer than the entire semester.

One student shocked herself, her classmates, and me by breaking the world's speed record for acceptances *and* by a leading journal whose acceptance rate is about 5 percent. As a class we edited her manuscript on Friday. The following Friday this student announced to us the acceptance of her manuscript. Her article appears in Figure 4.11. It seems an appropriate ending for this chapter.

FIGURE 4.11   Sample student article.

> **One-Pulse Words: Short, Sweet, and to the Point**
> by Anne Davis Toppins
>
> Once a day I try to state in short words what I think. The words I use are words of one pulse. The rest of the day I use words that are two-, three-, or six-pulse words—just the way school folks ought to talk. But each day for a short time I work at plain speech. My aim is to clear my head.
>
>   I learned this mode of speech a few years back. Dave Blum wrote of the Club for One-Pulse Words, a group of friends who write and speak this way as much as three hours a day. The group lives by these rules:
>
> 1. Use no words of more than one pulse.
> 2. Words that make use of a small mark (such as "don't") are fine but should be used with care.
> 3. Folks' names that have more than one pulse should be changed to code words.
> 4. Don't be a pest.
>
> Their point is that "words don't have to be long to be good."
>
>   To help you get a grip on this kind of speech, look at how I have changed what most school kids say each day:
>
> > *I pledge my troth to the flag of the states that are joined in this land and to the form of rule for which it stands; one large state with trust in God, not to be split, in which all can be free and for whom the law is just.*
>
> See what I mean? Some of this may seem forced, and it is. I'm new at the task, and it's hard to speak in one-pulse words. The art is to use them so well that they sound smooth. Those skilled in the craft have done this for years. The Bard, whose first name is William and whose last name is a blend of shake and spear, left us a store of one-pulse quotes. "To thine own self be true." "Out, damned spot! out, I say!" "What's in a name?" "To be or not to be." And what school child was not stirred by:

> *Give a man a horse he can ride,*
> *Give a man a boat he can sail;*
> *And his rank and wealth, his strength and health,*
> *On sea nor shore shall fail.*

That 12-line verse, by a scribe named James whose last name tells us he was Tom's son, has just two words of more than one pulse in the whole work.

The fair sex, too, have used this form to say what they feel. The maid whose first name is the same as the queen of the Brits and whose last name is Brown with an -ing on the end wrote:

> *How do I love thee? Let me count the ways.*
> *I love thee to the depth and breadth and*
> *height my soul can reach. . . .*

Much of our lore—the truth passed on from one group to the next—is found in words of one pulse: "Where there's a will, there's a way." "Where there's smoke, there's fire." "A bird in the hand is worth two in the bush." "All things come to him who waits." "Three's a crowd." And the well-known Book of God has a large stock of one-pulse lines. "And God said, 'Let there be light.' " "You shall know the truth and the truth shall make you free." No doubt you can think of more.

Since I have learned this game, I find strings of one-pulse words in use each day by all sorts of folks. When I read a book, talk with a friend, or watch the tube, I hear such things as, "Let me give it to you straight." "What shall I do with my life?" "You can't mean that!" "Keep your chin up." "This is a piece of cake." "Are you out of your mind?" "Where's the beef?"

I once asked a class to write a thought in one-pulse words. Some could not. Some would not. Some slipped in a few two-pulse words and were shocked when I found them. Most thought the task was weird. Three or four vowed not to choose my course the next term.

At times I try to get my peers to talk with me this way. A few laugh and join in the fun, but some look at me as if I were on the wrong train. Most who teach in my field want to stretch their words, not cut them short. They have heard that they must write or die. And they think that what they write needs to sound big if it is to be seen in print. So they add -ize, -tion, or -ing to plain words and hope that they sound wise.

You may think I write these lines with tongue in cheek, so to speak. In a way I do, but my point is that great truths can be said in one-pulse words. Who knows? My own thoughts may last if I can do the same. And, as the words carved on the tomb of the wit John Gay make clear:

> *Life is a jest, and all things show it,*
> *I thought so once, and now I know it.*

Reprinted with permission of Anne Davis Toppins, Associate Professor Emeritus, College of Education, The University of Alabama.

RECAPPING THE MAJOR POINTS

While learning how to write concisely, actively, and positively, you are well into the process of developing an effective writing style. Take every opportunity to edit your own writing and the writings of others. Only with practice will your skills continue to improve. As you continue your writing, remember these points:

- Most editors base their decisions to accept or reject manuscripts on the quality of the manuscript and its relevance to the readers.
- Nobody has time to write. Successful writers must reassign time for their writing, time which they need for other activities.
- Everyone with average intelligence has much information that would make an excellent article, if correctly written and aimed at the right market.
- All good writers must write, edit, and rewrite each manuscript several times.
- Writers should place clarity above all else.
- Rejections don't always imply low quality.
- Good writing is more plain than fancy, more simple than complex.
- Editors and writers are partners who share the same goal: to produce the best possible product for their readers.
- Authors don't need pomposity and arrogance, but they do need self-confidence.
- The best way to impress editors is to write clearly and accurately.

REFERENCES

Blum, D. (1982, July 15). Some guys I know march to the beat of one weird drum. *Wall Street Journal*, p. 1.

Daugherty, G. (1996, January). Get motivated . . . and stay motivated. *Writer's Digest*, pp. 28–29.

Samson, J. (1975). *The auctioneer*. New York: Avon Books.

Strunk, W., Jr., & White, E. B. (1979). *The elements of style*. New York: Macmillan.

Toppins, A. D. (1986). One-pulse words: Short, sweet, and to the point. *Phi Delta Kappan, 66*(4), 286–287.

5

ORGANIZING ARTICLES

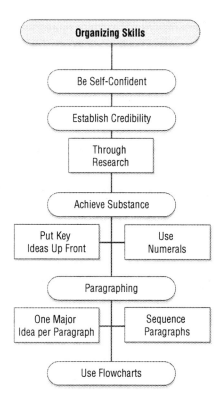

Conducting workshops for writers is a gratifying experience because of the many different people who attend them. Over two hundred such workshops, some with hundreds of participants, have had no known disinterested participants or, indeed, no participant who was only mildly interested. Unlike the members of many audiences who arrive early to get a seat in the back of the room, these people arrive early to get a front seat! Nor does the speaker have to strive to get their attention. They arrive motivated and, for the duration of the workshop, they remain motivated.

Educators tell us that learning requires only two factors: motivation and ability. The students must want to learn, and they must be capable of learning at the same level that the teacher is teaching. Aspiring writers are seldom short on either motivation or ability. When writing workshops fail, it's usually the presenter's fault. Too many participants blame themselves. *Never doubt your ability to succeed as a writer. Just set your goals and go for them. You can astound yourself.* This chapter will help you develop your organizing skills, and the ability to organize will help you produce a more successful manuscript.

The facts and tips on writing are easy to teach. Given highly capable and motivated audiences, most of the *how-tos*, the *what-tos*, and *what-not-tos* of writing are easily taught. This is not always true for helping people become better organizers. One aspiring writer was completely baffled over writers' abilities to assemble hundreds of pages of ideas. This confused but brave beginner asked a very simple, yet poignant question: How do you know how to organize a manuscript? The fact is, most people who are good organizers would be hard pressed to explain how they do it. They just do it. But they do it well. An answer such as this is of little help to individuals who have not yet mastered the skill of organizing writing. Fortunately for some of us who struggled with outlining assignments in our high school English classes, organizing writing content for the purpose of publishing is easier than other types of organizing.

Have you ever watched while someone prepared a meal? If so, and if your acquaintance with the kitchen is limited to the refrigerator and microwave oven, you may have been amazed at the complexity of the task. (Some items are baking while others are skewering; and the cook is mixing others.) To a novice, just the timing alone is a miracle. But the experienced cook usually manages to have all the dishes and the bread and drink completed at the same time. This is organizing!

If you are an accomplished cook (which by my definition means that in two tries out of three you can prepare a simple meal without burning down the kitchen), then you are an organizer, even though you may find it difficult to explain how you do it. The same is true for writers. *Successful writers are good organizers* although they may not be able to help others learn how to organize. But there is good news. Organizing manuscripts for publication can be learned if you are willing to heed some advice that may sound elementary and trite. Maybe the following is just that, elementary and trite, but it is also a sure-fire way to improve your organizing skills.

ORGANIZING NONFICTION ARTICLES

Organization can be thought of as a separate tool that you can use to hold your readers' attention, make your writing clearer, and give your writing more force. There are skills that you can easily master and use to achieve better organization. These skills include establishing credibility, achieving substance, paragraphing, and using flowcharts.

Organizing Skill No. 1: Establishing Credibility

Nonfiction readers are critical of the authors whose works they read. When receiving a professional journal, the typical professional scans the index to examine the article titles *and* to see who wrote each article. They have a common thought in mind. "Who is the author? Who is he or she to be telling me about this topic? Does this person have expertise that I don't have?" In other words, "Why should I read this person's writings?"

Some authors may find such critical questions annoying, but many experienced authors recognize this as an opportunity to score a point with the reader while also scoring a point with the editor. But to accomplish this, you must be familiar with some of the sources of evidence that the reader finds credible. In almost every workshop, I ask participants to tell me what they consider good evidence that an author has necessary expertise to write on a given topic. Almost without exception the first response is the author's title. Running a close second is the author's degree(s). You can do better.

Far more convincing than degrees and titles is evidence that the author has researched the topic. Nonfiction authors can and should immediately show the readers that they have researched the subject. The article in Figure 5.1 shows how this can be done quickly and easily.

In the very first paragraph of their article, the authors leave no doubt that they have researched this topic. In this short, two-sentence lead paragraph, they cite eight references—an excellent model for establishing credibility early in the article.

Organizing Skill No. 2: Achieving Substance

Nonfiction readers go to the libraries and bookstores in search of substance just as grocery shoppers go to the supermarket. Just like the grocery shoppers, readers look over the products. They don't want just anything to fill their baskets. They want substances that have specific uses. The producers of every product in the stores know that their economic survival depends on their ability to help the customers find what they need. Through cleverly designed, eye-catching advertising, they make the advantages of their products known to everyone who comes down the aisle. Book and magazine buyers shop just as selectively. They browse through the bookshelves and the card files until they find something

FIGURE 5.1   Establishing credibility.

FROM TEACHER-CENTERED TO LEARNER-CENTERED
CURRICULUM: IMPROVING LEARNING IN DIVERSE CLASSROOMS

KATHY LABOARD BROWN

Assistant Professor
The Citadel

The premise "one teaching style fits all," which is attributed to a teacher-centered instructional approach, is not working for a growing number of diverse, student populations. New challenges facing classroom teachers: legislative mandates for school renewal, diverse student needs, technological advances, and school violence prompted this researcher to look for an alternative. Examination of the literature detailed the assets of teacher- and learner-centered approaches for meeting the challenges of 21st century teachers. Findings indicated that for diverse populations who are not experiencing success with a teacher-centered approach, an instructional paradigm shift is needed to implement a learner-centered approach.

Introduction
Twenty-first century classrooms challenge traditional, teacher-centered curriculum to meet the increasingly diverse needs of students and make the required increases in achievement gains. School violence, diverse student needs and populations, educational renewal, and technological advances place demands on teachers in areas for which they were formally held accountable. With teacher educators, problems occur when teaching styles conflict with students' learning styles, often resulting in limited learning or no learning. Altan and Trombly (2001) offer learner-centeredness as a model for countering classroom challenges because of its viability for meeting diverse needs. Learner-centered classrooms place students at the center of classroom organization and respect their learning needs, strategies, and styles. In learner-centered classrooms, students can be observed working individually or in pairs and small groups on distinct tasks and

projects. The transition from teaching the entire group to meeting individual learner needs involves extensive planning and task specific classroom management.

Purpose
The premise—one teaching and learning approach fits all—is not working for a growing number of student populations and has prompted this researcher to examine what is required to move from a teacher-centered to a learner-centered approach. McCombs & Whisler (1997) identified two essential factors for a learner-centered approach to education: (a) characteristics of the learner and (b) teaching practices. By contrasting the use of reflective inquiry, thinking-centered learning, and assessment of program quality to satisfy McCombs & Whisler's essential factors, this article examines whether moving from a teacher-centered to a learner-centered approach requires a transition or a paradigm shift.

Learner Characteristics

Learner-Centered Approach

An essential factor for a learner-centered approach is placing the learning characteristics of all learners under the microscope with specific emphasis on low-performing learners. McCombs (1997) explained that the focus in a learner-centered approach is on individual learners' heredity, experiences, perspectives, backgrounds, talents, interests, capacities, and needs. She defined learner-centered, from a research-based perspective, as a foundation for clarifying what is needed to create positive learning contexts to increase the likelihood that more students will experience success (Defining "Learner-Centered", ¶ 2). Cultural factors impact the connection teachers must make to scaffold students' learning (Singham, 1998; McCombs & Whisler, 1997). The focus is on *metacognition,* how individual students learn. Milambiling (2001) extended the learner-centered definition by characterizing learner-centered education as context-sensitive. She said that the culture of the learning context is as important to learning as the content and the methods used. Milambiling recommended curricula which address the culture of the learner within specific learning contexts.

Teacher-Centered Approach

The teacher-centered approach is associated chiefly with the transmission of knowledge. McDonald (2002) clarified

---

Source: From *Education,* Vol. 124, No. 10, pp. 49–54, Fall 2003. Reprinted by permission.

promising. Then they track it down and, opening to the table of contents, they resume their shopping. They check the article or chapter titles. Everyone knows that people today are selective, but few realize just how selective people really are. Newspaper publishers know. They know that only one reader in 10 completes reading a front page article that continues on another page. This is why papers such as *USA Today* don't extend many articles beyond one page.

Knowing that the readers are looking for specific content and knowing that the average reader will give only a few seconds to survey the table of contents of a journal or book gives you an advantage over your less-aware competitors. You have already learned how to select captivating titles. Now consider the reader's next move. After finding a title that promises content, the reader will either begin reading or will thumb through the article to see how long it is and what it looks like. Either way the author wins, so far.

This is where the experienced writer takes care to see that the reader doesn't take a quick glance and reject the article. This can be done by openly displaying the major parts of the manuscript. By clearly identifying the distinct parts and by structuring the article appropriately to display these parts, you can achieve the same effect that the washing powder producers hope to achieve by labeling their products with "Effective in hot or cold water" and "Gets out ugly stains." *Arrange your manuscript so that its major messages are visible to even the casual reader.*

The article in Figure 5.2 uses similar structuring techniques to communicate clearly that it, too, has something definite to say. This article, titled "Middle Schools: Paradoxes and Promises," identifies several major nuggets of material. Some of these nuggets are labeled "paradoxes" and some are called "promises." The paradoxes are listed sequentially and all of them are presented before the promises are addressed. Numerals are used to give emphasis to the fact that this article has a definite number of separate and distinct pieces of substance.

FIGURE 5.2   Communicating visually through structure.

Middle Schools: Paradoxes and Promises
Kenneth T. Henson

Anyone who has read Charles Dickens' *A Tale of Two Cities* will recall the opening lines:

> *It was the best of times, it was the worst of times, it was the age of wisdom, it was the age of foolishness, it was the epoch of belief, it was the epoch of incredulity, it was the season of light, it was the season of darkness, it was the spring of hope, it was the winter of despair, we had everything before us, we had nothing before us, we were all going direct to Heaven, we were all going the other way.*

To the uneducated person, these lines may appear foolish, but the alert mind finds them stimulating. With these few lines, Dickens was able to tell his readers that they were about to set out on a journey full of suspense and action. Such is often the case with paradoxes; they challenge us to investigate, and yet they are difficult to understand.

The American middle school is one of the most misunderstood institutions in our society. It is also one of the most interesting and challenging concepts, with unlimited possibilities. Like Dickens' novel, the American middle school is full of paradoxes that not only make it a worthy challenge to study, but that also fill it with promises for becoming a better educational institution than any of its predecessors. The following presents some of these paradoxes and discusses some of the promises for hope and success of the American middle school.

Paradox Number 1
Teaching in the middle school is both frustrating and rewarding.
Interestingly, few students plan to teach the middle grades; yet, attrition alone assures that the number of middle school and junior high school teachers is greater than the number of high school teachers. Therefore, most middle school teachers begin their experiences somewhat reluctantly and without confidence. They find their students at a very awkward age. This brings an inordinate number of problems to the middle school teacher.

But after teaching this level of students for a year, many teachers find themselves hooked on this age group for life. The reason for this paradox is found in the rewarding feeling teachers experience when they help youths who have either no direction or too many directions in their lives. The middle school teacher is often identified as the one individual in a youth's life who is most influential and whom the students would most like to emulate.

> *I continued with two additional paradoxes and then introduced three promises as follows:*

Promises of the Middle School
Although the middle school offers contradictions and challenges, these should not be interpreted as indicators of a dismal future for the middle school. In recent years, research on classroom teaching offers much to counterbalance the limitations imposed by these paradoxes. Following is a generalized representation of the research that can make the future of the middle school increasingly bright and successful.

Promise Number 1
Many popular myths that limited progress in academic achievement have been disproved. According to Hunter,

> *Current findings are in direct contrast to the former fatalistic stance that regarded I.Q. and socioeconomic status as unalterable determinants of academic achievement. Gone also should be the notions that different ages, ethnic deviations, or content to be learned require a completely different set of professional skills, or that effective teachers must be born and can't be made.* (1983, p. 169)

Although no one denies that genetic inheritance sets limits on learning, recent research shows that many students' learning has been curtailed by their acceptance of limits imposed by intelligence-test scores, limits that have often been far below their real levels of ability. In fact, studies have shown that contrary to popular belief, a full 90 to 95 percent of all secondary-level students are capable of mastering all of the content and objectives found in modern schools (Bloom, Hastings, & Madaus, 1981, p. 51).

> *I continued with Promises Numbers 2 and 3, and then wrote the following conclusions:*

Conclusions
The middle school has not failed in the many ways that the junior high school failed, and it will not likely achieve the poor image of its predecessor

Continued

FIGURE 5.2   *Continued*

because, unlike the junior high school, the middle school has a clear set of purposes. Among these purposes is that of nurturing the emotional, social, and cognitive growth of students. Despite the many paradoxes that make these goals difficult to reach, recent progress in educational research gives reason to hope that all teachers at all levels will become more effective in their power to enhance cognitive growth in their classrooms.

Since its origin, the middle school has been dedicated to nurturing the growth of its students, and middle school teachers have always viewed change positively. As research on classroom teaching continues to enhance cognitive attainment at all levels (K–12), these characteristics of the middle school and of middle school teachers should accelerate this progress among students in the middle schools.

> *I always count the number of references in articles in my intended journal and I purposely include a few more than average. Can you guess why? You'll find the answer in a later chapter.*

References

Alexander, W. M., et al. (1968). *The emergent middle school* (2nd ed.). New York: Holt, Rinehart and Winston.

Bloom, B. S., Hastings, G, & Madaus, J. T. (1981). *Evaluating to improve learning.* New York: McGraw-Hill.

Dickens, C. (1963). *A tale of two cities.* New York: Airmont.

Epstein, H. T. (1976, April). A biologically based framework of intervention projects. *Mental Retardation, 14:* 26–27.

Good, T. L., & Brophy, J. (in press). *Third handbook of research on teaching.* New York: Macmillan.

Henson, K. T. (1981). *Secondary teaching methods.* Lexington, MA: D.C. Heath.

Henson, K. T., & Saterfiel, T. (1985, January). Are recent state-wide accountability programs educationally sound? *NASSP Bulletin,* 23–27.

Hudson, L. (1968). *Contrary imaginations: A psychological study of the English school boy.* Middlesex, England: Pegasus Books.

Hunter, M. (1983). Knowing, teaching, and supervising. In P. L. Hosford (Ed.), *Using what we know about teaching.* Alexandria, VA: Association for Supervision and Curriculum Development.

Konopka, G. (1973, Fall). Requirements for healthy development of adolescent youth. *Adolescence, 8,* 10–11.

Offer, D. (1969). *The psychological world of the teenager.* New York: Basic Books.

Saylor, J. G. (1982). *Who planned the curriculum? A curriculum reservoir model with historical examples.* West Lafayette, IN: Kappa Delta Pi.

Source: The Clearing House, Vol. 59, issue 8, pp. 345–347, April 1986. Reprinted with permission of The Helen Dwight Reid Educational Foundation. Published by Heldref Publications, 1319 18th Street, N.W., Washington, DC 20036–1802. Copyright 1986.

Organizing Skill No. 3: Paragraphing

English texts frequently discuss several types of paragraphs, such as introductory, emphatic, transitional, and concluding. As mentioned earlier, writers need to know how to write each of these types, but the major problem that writers experience with paragraphs is their inability to identify one. That's right. Many struggling writers don't know a paragraph when they see one! Furthermore, they often fail to recognize one when they themselves have written it. A review of a few journal articles will show that some published writers fall into this category. As simple as it sounds, without the spacing and indenting, could you tell where another writer's paragraphs should begin and end? Would you see paragraphs exactly the same as another writer sees them? Probably not.

Your elementary or junior high science class probably first introduced you to concepts. There, you learned that concepts are categories made up by people. What a friend considers a long pencil with a soft lead, you may consider a short pencil with hard lead. So it is with paragraphs; yet, some general guidelines are available. As was discussed in Chapter 3, each paragraph should focus around one major idea. When the author progresses to a new idea, a new paragraph should be used. Sounds simple, but is it? For example, examine this paragraph that you are now reading. Does it focus on one idea? Two? More? Should it be divided to form more than one paragraph? If so, where? Figure 5.3 consists of the first two pages of an article—but all of the author's paragraphs have been removed. Take some time to decide where *you* would begin each new paragraph.

Ideally, new paragraphs begin every time the author moves from one clear idea to another. Learning to paragraph takes practice. Don't be too harsh on yourself if your paragraphs and the author's are not identical. Paragraphing remains an art; some variation is to be tolerated. In fact, variation is expected, since the author's personal preferences affect the length of each paragraph.

Paragraph Sequencing

Writers are often confused over the search for the "correct" sequence for their paragraphs. Sometimes the sequence of paragraphs is of little significance. It usually doesn't matter which set of pros and cons follows another set or which axiom follows another—but it is always good to *check to see if a logical paragraph sequence exists*. For example, in an article titled "Ten Ways to Increase Your Safety at the Ice Rink," an author might put *follow the direction of the crowd* before giving advice about exiting the rink. Perhaps you noticed in the article about the myths of corporal punishment that Myth Number One is introduced first because the other myths explain the basis for Myth Number One.

The word processor makes paragraph sequencing easy. If you do not use a word processor, an alternative is to write each paragraph on an index card. When all paragraphs are written, you can simply organize and reorganize the

FIGURE 5.3   Paragraphing exercise.

Grant writing is all about power. We write grants because they bring us prestige, programs, equipment, travel, and time. Grants free us to do the kind of research, teaching, and service that we enjoy most. So why is such an essential skill so difficult and mysterious for so many academics? You can be as successful as you want to be with grant writing, but you have to realize that it's a craft, and like any other craft, being successful at it requires developing and polishing a few skills. It starts with attitude. You must believe in your own ability to master this craft and to succeed as the level you choose. Then you must have some clear reasons for writing grants. As the Cheshire cat told Alice, if you don't know where you are going then it doesn't matter which direction you take. So, begin by taking a step backward and asking yourself, Where do I want to go in my career? Five years from now? Ten years from now? Grant writing can be a powerful force to get you there. In the past two decades, I've written millions of dollars worth of successful grant proposals and traveled the country giving workshops on grant writing. I've encountered a lot of myths about this subject, and believing them can, and often does, derail even the brightest professor's grant-writing program. I'd like to tackle a few of the myths and then offer some tips. Myth 1: There is no money available; the grant-writing well has dried up. Wrong! Money is tighter these days but there is still hundreds of millions of dollars waiting to be taken. Furthermore, those who are entrusted with dispersing this money are just as eager to give it away as we are to receive it. Myth 2: The money that is available goes to big, prestigious institutions, not to individual or to small institutions. That statement is half true. Enormous amounts of money are given to the same institutions, year after year. But it is not simply because grant agencies are impressed with the institutions' prestigious names. It is because certain individuals at those institutions have proved themselves good stewards of the money. Furthermore, small institutions and people who are "unknown" to the general public are getting hundreds of millions of dollars. But these people are not so unknown to the grant agencies. They have established reputations for delivering quality service and managing their budgets wisely—two skills that you can easily master. Myth 3: Successful grant writing requires connections, and I don't have any. This excuse begs for rebuttal. Connections can help but they aren't required. What's required is the ability to craft a quality proposal that will convince grant givers that you will give the most and best in return for . . .

Source: From "Debunking Some Myths About Grant Writing," by K. T. Henson, *The Chronicle of Higher Education,* Vol. 60, No. 3, June 26, 2003. Reprinted with permission.

cards until they are in the sequence that makes the most sense to you. Remember that each paragraph, from the first sentence to the last sentence in the article, should advance the discussion.

Organizing Skill No. 4: Using Flowcharts to Organize

Another way to organize your article or book chapter is to develop a visual diagram of a flowchart. The illustration in Figure 5.4 is an example of how authors can use a picture to explain a concept described in their article.

If you share my frustration with authors such as William Faulkner who with all ease slip into and out of trains of thought, you can appreciate the power of flowcharts such as the one shown in Figure 5.4 to simplify the writing job as well as the job of the reader.

This figure describes the physics teachers institute described in Chapter 13. Notice that it begins with the signing of the contract and describes the steps taken to implement the proposed program. It is labeled "Sample Timetable" because it presents the steps in chronological order and includes the anticipated date for each step to occur. Notice that Roman numerals and arrows are used to add clarity.

Actually, when developing such a flow chart, the grant proposal writer begins setting the date for each step in the project at the opposite end and works backward. For example, in this project, the developer would choose an autumn date to visit the participants after the summer institute was over.

FIGURE 5.4   Using flowcharts to show organization.

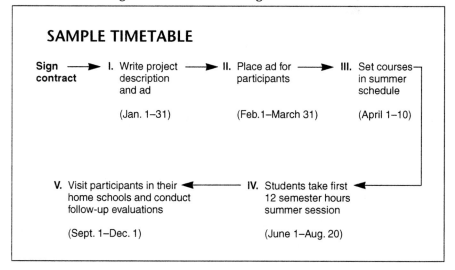

Source: From "Debunking Some Myths About Grant Writing," by K. T. Henson, *The Chronicle of Higher Education*, Vol. 60, No. 3, June 26, 2003. Reprinted with permission.

PUTTING IT TOGETHER

Occasionally, a desperate beginner tells me that what would really help would be to have a history of the life of an article, showing each step of action that occurred from the time of the idea for the particular topic until the article appeared in a journal. Such a profile is available in Appendix H.

RECAPPING THE MAJOR POINTS

Learning the how-tos, the what-tos, and the what-not-tos of writing is easy, but learning how to organize an article is not so simple. In this chapter you learned the following:

- Trust yourself. You have the ability to develop essential writing skills.
- Successful writing requires good organizing skills.
- Immediately establish your credibility.
- You must show your readers that your article contains substance that they consider valuable.

REFERENCES

Henson, K. T. (1986). Middle schools: Paradoxes and promises. *The Clearing House, 59*(8), 345–347.

Henson, K. T. (2004). *Grant writing in higher education.* Boston: Allyn & Bacon.

Johnson, M. K., Hashtroudi, S., & Lindsay, D. S. (1993). Source monitoring. *Psychological Bulletin, 114*(1), 3–28.

Tallman, I., Leik, R. K., Gray, L. N., & Stafford, M. C. (1993). A theory of problem-solving behavior. *Social Psychology Quarterly, 56*(3), 157–177.

6

USING JOURNALS, LIBRARIES, SURVEYS, AND ACTION RESEARCH

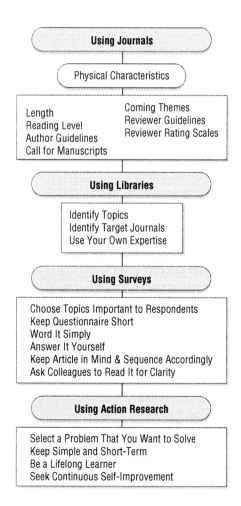

Using Journals

Physical Characteristics

Length
Reading Level
Author Guidelines
Call for Manuscripts

Coming Themes
Reviewer Guidelines
Reviewer Rating Scales

Using Libraries

Identify Topics
Identify Target Journals
Use Your Own Expertise

Using Surveys

Choose Topics Important to Respondents
Keep Questionnaire Short
Word It Simply
Answer It Yourself
Keep Article in Mind & Sequence Accordingly
Ask Colleagues to Read It for Clarity

Using Action Research

Select a Problem That You Want to Solve
Keep Simple and Short-Term
Be a Lifelong Learner
Seek Continuous Self-Improvement

USING JOURNALS

For years higher education institutions have encouraged their members to write and submit their works to journals for publishing. Major research universities have held the strongest expectations for their academic employees, often requiring them to publish in research journals. Recently, however, many regional, private, and parochial colleges and universities also have begun requiring their ranks to write and submit their manuscripts to professional journals.

Whether writing for a research-type journal or other professional journals, writers can begin improving their skills in this craft by using the journals as models. Few novice writers and perhaps only a few experienced writers make maximum use of the journals to perfect their writing and publishing skills. Editors will tell you that you should begin writing each article by reading a few recent issues of the journal to which you plan to submit your manuscript. This chapter will present other ways that you can use the journals to increase the likelihood of acceptance of your manuscripts.

Physical Characteristics

Interestingly, readers can read every issue of a journal for years and still know very little about the physical makeup of the journal. Think about a journal that you often read. If asked, could you accurately describe this journal's average article length, average reading level, the average number of references per article, frequency of themed issues, whether manuscripts are sent out for review and if so to what degree? Each of these questions is very important to the aspiring writer; each one can increase the chances of manuscript acceptance—and the answers are in the journals. The secret to understanding what the editor thinks is right for a journal can be unlocked by studying that journal's physical characteristics.

Article Length

One of the most obvious physical properties of any journal is the length of its articles. You want to know the minimum, maximum, and average lengths. Determining these lengths requires examining only one or two recent issues. Simply count the pages of each article and note the longest article and the shortest article. Use the lengths of all articles in the issue(s) to compute the average. Then your answers must be translated from journal pages to manuscript pages. The conversion is simple. Each typed manuscript page has about 250 words. So, to change from journal pages to manuscript pages simply count the number of words on an average journal page, multiply by the number of journal pages, and divide by 250.

$$\frac{\text{words/journal page} \times \text{no. of journal pages}}{250} = \text{no. of manuscript pages}$$

Now you have the average number of manuscript pages per article. Try to keep your article length between the length of the shortest article and the average article length for that journal. The reason for aiming at the shortest length is that editors often need a short manuscript to finish out an issue. Because your manuscript is short, it may be chosen over others that are equally well written.

Reading Level

A somewhat less obvious quality of manuscripts that makes them "right" in the editor's eyes is the manuscript's reading level. Some journals have high reading levels; others have low reading levels. You can easily determine the reading level for your journal by following these steps:

1. Randomly select a page from each of three articles, and count out 100 words for each, starting with the beginning of a sentence in each article. Count each proper noun, acronym, and numeral group as a word.
2. For each 100 words, count the number of sentences, estimating the length of the last sentence in tenths.
3. Count the number of syllables in the passage.
4. Compute the average sentence length and average number of syllables. Then use the graph in Figure 6.1 to plot the point where the two lines intersect. Most reading charts use grade levels to calibrate reading levels. This answer is the approximate grade level of the journal.

The readability level of your manuscript should approximate the level of readability of the target journal. If your manuscript's reading level varies substantially from that of the journal, examine the sentence lengths and the lengths of the words in the two, and edit your manuscript accordingly.

Guidelines for Authors

Most professional journals have a page or two of instructions or guidelines for authors to follow when writing and preparing a manuscript for the particular journal. Check your target journal. Guidelines may be labeled "Suggestions for Contributors," "Information for Authors," or "Manuscript Guidelines." Study these guidelines carefully. They are the quickest route to understanding those qualities that can make your manuscript fit the particular journal. Notice the style and be sure to put your manuscript in this style. If the guidelines call for a 50-word summary, prepare a 50-word summary. If the guidelines forbid tables, charts, or figures, don't include these in your

FIGURE 6.1   **Graph for estimating readability—extended.**

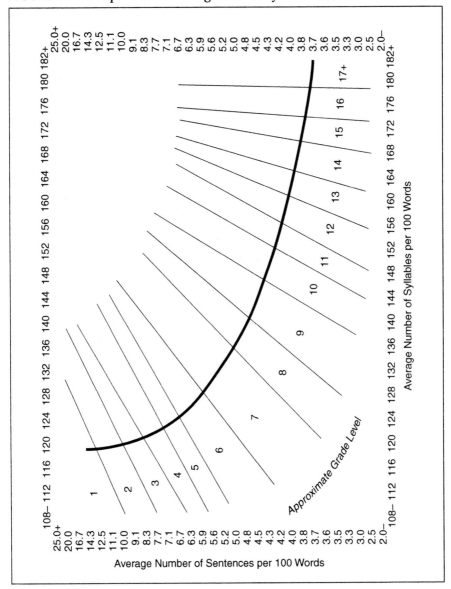

Source: Reprinted from "Fry's Readability Graph: Clarifications, Validity, and Extension to Level 17," *Journal of Reading,* Vol. 21, No. 3, 1977, p. 249.

manuscript. Most guidelines ask for a self-addressed, stamped envelope (SASE). Whether or not your journal asks for this item, *it is always appropriate to include a self-addressed, stamped envelope with your manuscript.* If the journal you have targeted has no guidelines for authors printed in it, simply request a copy. But a precaution is necessary. Editors are proud of their journals. They like to think that most members of the profession are familiar with their journal, and asking for a copy of guidelines may be interpreted as a lack of familiarity with the journal, which surely is not in your best interest when you are about to submit a manuscript. There is a way out of this dilemma.

Instead of writing or calling the editor, phone or write your request to the managing editor, the editorial assistant, or the secretary. These individuals can fill your request, freeing the editor to edit and without calling the editor's attention to your lack of familiarity with the journal.

Another way to learn the expectations of journals is through directories and journal articles. For example, the expectations of several types of journals are given in Appendix A.

Call for Manuscripts

Occasionally professional journals issue a "Call for Manuscripts," "Call for Papers," or "Request for Manuscripts." See Appendix B for a sample. These items usually appear when a journal is new, has new management, or is altering its goals or operating procedures. Whatever the specific reason, when you see a Call for Manuscripts you know that the journal is searching for material to publish. The common supply/demand ratio that makes writing a buyers' market puts you at a major disadvantage as you try to get editors to accept your manuscript. The Call for Manuscripts tells you that if you act quickly, you can submit your manuscript at a time when the editors need more manuscripts. *Don't miss the opportunity to act when the odds are in your favor!*

Coming Themes

A recent survey showed that editors receive about three or four times as many manuscripts for general issues as for themed issues. Thus, solicitation of manuscripts on upcoming themes is not unusual. (Appendix C shows an announcement of coming themes.) Notice that each theme is accompanied by a corresponding deadline for submission. Clearly, your chances of having your article accepted are enhanced by preparing your manuscript well and ensuring its arrival at the editor's office prior to the deadline.

Reviewers' Guidelines and Rating Scales

Many journals rely on a cadre of content specialists to judge the appropriateness of manuscripts for publication. These reviewers are given a set of guidelines and a rating instrument, which helps to maintain objectivity.

Rating scales help editors attain consistent information from all reviewers of the same manuscripts. The reviewer's job is also simplified in that the rating scale tells the reviewer what qualities to look for in the manuscript. (By sending a self-addressed, stamped envelope and a note to the secretary at the journal address, you can obtain a copy of the rating scale used by reviewers.) *But more important to you, rating scales can tell you, the writer, what qualities to put into manuscripts.* Figure 6.2 shows a rating scale with seven criteria against which manuscripts submitted to this journal are measured. Notice that the first item on this scale is "significance to teacher education." How important is it that authors choose topics that are considered pertinent by the audience who subscribes to the journal? Actually, for this particular journal and many others, this is the most important quality of its articles. According to the journal's editor, failure to write on topics pertinent to the journal's audience is the most frequent reason that manuscripts sent to this journal are rejected. These seven criteria are typical of those included in many journal rating scales.

Writers often ask, "Which, if any, of these criteria are indispensable?" Although the answer may vary slightly from journal to journal, it is safe to say that most editors consider criteria 2 and 6 indispensable. As for the quality of writing, writers often ask, "If the content in an article is accurate and important, won't editors just rewrite manuscripts that meet the other six criteria?" The answer is almost always a resounding no because editors usually have an abundance of good, accurate, well-written articles from which to build each issue. Why should they be willing to use their time to do work that the writer should do?

Only on the rare occasion when editors receive an *unusually* important and timely manuscript will they be willing to rewrite the manuscript. One editor said that in a *decade* of editing a journal, only once had he bothered to rewrite a poorly written manuscript. The message, here, is that authors should study these physical characteristics and consider each one essential to getting their manuscripts accepted.

Most rating scales contain a place for the reviewer to recommend action on the manuscript, or the editor asks for the recommendation in his initial letter to the reviewer. Usually, reviewers must recommend one of three actions:

1. Acceptance as is.
2. Conditional acceptance (provided that the author makes specific, requested changes).
3. Rejection.

Authors often ask what they should do if an editor asks them to alter their manuscripts. Unless you think the changes misrepresent your manuscript or distort your intended meaning, you should be eager to make those changes. The additional time and energy put into fulfilling an editor's request are usually much less than you would spend sending the manuscript to

FIGURE 6.2 Rating scales raise the quality of manuscript evaluations and simplify the evaluators' work.

JOURNAL OF TEACHER EDUCATION
Reviewer Response Form: Manuscripts

Assessment of Manuscript Quality

CRITERIA	ASSESSMENT				
	Weak	Marginal	Acceptable	Strong	Excellent
1. Significance to teacher education	1	2	3	4	5
2. Suitability for JTE audience	1	2	3	4	5
3. Stimulating quality of material	1	2	3	4	5
4. Originality	1	2	3	4	5
5. Accuracy of content	1	2	3	4	5
6. Quality of writing	1	2	3	4	5
7. Overall manuscript evaluation	1	2	3	4	5

CRITIQUE (Please type):

Source: American Association of Colleges for Teacher Education.

another journal. The greatest benefit of making the requested changes is the time you will save on the life of the manuscript. In most cases editors' requests for changes significantly improve the quality of the article. We will discuss this topic further in Chapter 9.

USING LIBRARIES

Most experienced authors spend endless hours in libraries. They spend most of this time researching their topics. Even those writers who are leading experts in their field of study realize that their writings should reflect the current literature, and the only way to do this is by reading the most current books, journals, magazines, and monographs on the topics they have selected.

Unfortunately, many novice writers only use the library for research. Some experienced writers get far more writing help out of libraries. You, too, can get many valuable writing benefits if you learn how to make maximum writing use of the library. The following profile suggests a method for using the library to perform several writing functions.

Identifying Topics

Experienced authors learn to identify good topics much as news editors learn to "smell" a good story. As they go about their daily work, experienced writers carry a big question in their subconscious memory: What would be a good topic for my next article or book? Then they filter all of their observations through this perceptual screen. Consequently, at any one time, experienced writers can tell you several topics they plan to write about.

Unfortunately, beginning writers often do not have on hand this supply of good topics. Consequently, they spend a lot of valuable time trying to "think up" good topics. This process is too slow, and it seldom results in quality topics. You can do better.

Chapter 2 provided detailed information that you can use to perfect your topic selection skills. But, you may feel that you do not have time to become a master at this task. You may want a quick way to identify a topic so that you can get on with the author's business at hand—writing. Here's where the library can help.

The library is the best, richest source for identifying good topics, topics that editors and readers will find captivating. Here's how the process works. First, locate your library's reference periodicals. They may be in the reference room, but in some libraries they are kept in the periodicals room or in yet another room. Find the *Business Index, Medical Index, Education Index,* or whatever annual reference index your discipline offers. Begin by examining the annual topics list if your index has such; if not, examine the most recent issue.

Scan through the categories of topics until you find a topic that relates to one of your own professional roles. Now, see how many articles are being published on this topic. You want a topic that has some degree of popularity in the literature. Repeat this process until you have found a topic that you find interesting. *Don't worry if you don't currently possess enough knowledge to write on this topic. One benefit of writing is to enlighten the writer on new topics.*

By now, hopefully you have thought of some topics and are ready to begin; however, if you still feel a little uncomfortable, see Appendix H. This appendix profiles the life of an article from its inception until it was published.

Identifying Target Journals

Suppose you have an idea for a topic. Let's say that you decide to write about the case study as a teaching method. As you think about this topic, you realize that there are several audiences who would benefit from learning more about the case study method. Elementary, middle, and high school teachers could surely profit from learning more about this method. In fact, many junior college and university professors make extensive use of case studies, so another audience would be higher education faculty. Since teacher education colleges prepare teachers, teacher educators should know about the case study method. Today, K–12 school administrators are perceived as instructional leaders and are held accountable for the achievement level of all learners in their schools; thus, many administrators would be interested in learning about the case study method.

You could continue identifying target audiences but to do so wouldn't be a good use of your time. It is now time to tentatively identify a target audience and direction for this topic. Suppose you decide to write for teacher educators. What journals are written for this audience? Which of these journals would be interested in your topic? Some of them include *Educational Forum, The Journal of Teacher Education, Action in Teacher Education, The Professional Educator, Theory into Practice,* and *Phi Delta Kappan.* This is an opportunity to really use the library to improve your writing for publication. Most contemporary libraries have computer facilities. Most have programs that you can use to do quick searches on topics.

If your library does not offer this facility, don't worry; a simple reference index such as *Business Guide* or *Education Index* will do well. Looking under "Case Study Method," you will see several articles on this topic. Now, see what journals published these articles. This tells you that the editors of these journals consider this topic relevant for their readers. If the list is short, a few alternative topics such as methods of teaching, lecture, simulation games, questioning, discovery, and inquiry can extend the list. Any editor who has published articles on any of these topics would probably welcome a manuscript on the case study method.

So far, you have used the library to collect data on publishers. Now you can use these data in two ways. First, you know which journals are interested in your topic. You will remember and use this information when you begin selecting a journal to consider this manuscript. You also have more immediate use for this information. You can use it to shorten your search for data to use in writing this article.

Take a full-size writing tablet and follow these steps. First, draw two horizontal lines one-third and two-thirds down the page, dividing the sheet into three equal parts (see Figure 6.3).

Second, at the top of each one-third section on your note tablet, write complete bibliographical information for an article that sounds promising. *Caution: Do not abbreviate or omit any of the bibliographical information.* Should you have to return to look up this information, you may spend several times as long searching for the information as is required to copy it down at this time. A similar search should be made of books, using the card catalog or computer. This task is easy and fun. You just look over the lists as though you were shopping and you have the money to buy anything you want. You will need several pages completed with three articles and/or books listed on each page.

Third, scan each article or book. Copy verbatim one or two quotes. Look for quotable quotes—those that say something meaningful and say it clearly.

Suppose the search revealed that the journal *Educational Forum* has recently published several articles aimed at improving teaching methods through improving practices in colleges of teacher education. Then, perhaps you should tentatively choose this journal and audience as targets for your article. Figure 6.3 also shows some quotable quotes from books, one of which dates back to 1931. Were this the only reference used in your article, it would be too old; yet, this is a valuable source of data. Because the other journal article quotes are more recent, the age of the references will be balanced. The most sensible approach is to begin your journal searches with the current issues and work backward.

Read the second quote by Dewing in Figure 6.3. This is a powerful testimony supporting the topic on which you may wish to write. Having quoted verbatim from the books, you can now choose between paraphrasing and quoting.

Using Your Own Expertise

As you plan and research your article topics, remember that prolific writers don't start at square one or point zero with each article. On the contrary, you must draw upon your own previously accumulated material. Suppose you have previously written a research paper or conducted research for a professional convention presentation where the paper or speech topic was "The Role Concepts Play in Learning." Suppose you also read in John Goodlad's school reform report, *A Place Called School,* that teachers must help students identify major concepts in their discipline. Go back to that study and find a quote that says concept identification is important to teaching, and one that explains *why* concepts are important to teaching. Your goal is to use your ex-

FIGURE 6.3   Systematic research method.

W. B. Donham, "Business Teaching by the Case System," in C. E. Prager, ed., *The Case Method of Instruction,* (New York: McGraw-Hill, 1931).

"The distinguishing characteristics which make the case system of teaching law, in the hands of a competent instructor, an instrument of great power is the fact that it arouses the interest of the student through its realistic flavor and then makes him, under the guidance of the instructor, an active rather than passive participant in the instruction."

A. S. Dewing, "An Introduction to the Use of Cases," in M. P. McNair, ed., *The Case Method at the Harvard Business School,* (New York: McGraw-Hill, 1954).

"Of the many theories of education, there are actually only two. Education is the gathering of important information accumulated by humankind through the ages, followed by its refining, categorizing, and systematizing before presentation to students (p. 3)."

"Human thinking and the new human experience are indissolubly bound together. If we teach people to deal with the new experience, we teach them to think. In fact, power to deal with the new and power to think are pragmatically the same" (p. 4).

B. J. Biddle and D. S. Anderson, "Theory, Methods, Knowledge, and Research on Teaching," in M. C. Wittrock, ed., *Handbook of Research on Teaching,* 3rd ed. (New York: Macmillan, 1986), pp. 230–252.

"Case studies provide an open invitation to generalize."

"Correctly used, the case study method will allow students to draw many conclusions, some of which the instructor may not even be aware."

isting repertoire of quotations to enrich and embellish this article. You might also look up *concept teaching* on the library computer or in the *Education Index* to gather another current reference. Continue your search until you have as many good references as you need to write your article.

USING SURVEYS

A recent survey of the requirements of over 50 journals found that 90 percent report some research, and two-thirds of all the articles published in them cite some research—either the author's or that of others. This means that all serious writers should report research, and whenever feasible some portion of that research should be original.

Correctly designed and implemented, a survey can easily produce a large amount of important information. Furthermore, the survey can facilitate the writing of articles. The questionnaire in Figure 6.4 has produced a series of articles for several premiere journals. By comparing this questionnaire with the list of articles it produced, you can readily see a correlation. (See Figure 6.5 for the list of articles.)

Carefully examine the survey questionnaire in Figure 6.4. This questionnaire was designed by simply asking those questions the author would ask should he meet with the editors. The questions were sequenced with a number of article ideas in mind. For over a decade now, this questionnaire has been revised and readministered biennially. The results have provided the substance for eleven articles in the *Phi Delta Kappan;* one article each in *Writer's Digest, The Writer, Kappa Delta Pi Record, Thresholds in Education, NASSP Bulletin,* and *Writer's Journal;* and a chapter in *The Writer's Handbook.*

When first used, this questionnaire had a 75 percent return rate. By its fourth use, the return rate had increased to 98 percent. This unusually high return rate can be attributed in part to the covering letter (see Figure 6.6). The letter explains that there will be an advantage to the editors for completing the questionnaire. Two followup letters were sent, and one followup phone call was made to each editor who failed to respond to the second mailing. Notice that the cover letter for the 1990 survey (Figure 6.7) was revised to save the editor time, which also helped to increase the return rate. When designing questionnaires, remember to:

1. Select a topic of importance to the respondents.
2. Keep the questionnaire short—no longer than one page whenever possible.
3. Word each question so that it can be answered easily and quickly.
4. Answer the questions yourself. When you find a question ambiguous, rewrite it.
5. Keep your article in mind, and sequence the questions accordingly.
6. Ask a couple of colleagues to complete the questionnaire and, if clarification is needed on any question, rewrite it.

When sending questionnaires, you can ensure a high return rate by doing the following:

1. Alert each recipient of the forthcoming questionnaire.
2. Promise to send the results to those subjects who wish to see them.
3. Thank respondents for their cooperation.
4. Enclose a self-addressed, stamped envelope.
5. Send a followup letter to recipients who fail to respond within a certain time period.
6. Follow the letter with phone calls to those who still have not responded.

FIGURE 6.4   Sample survey questionnaire.

EDITOR'S INFORMATION FORM

Name of Editor _____

Name of Journal _____

Address _____

1. a. _____ Approximate number of subscribers.
   b. Your primary audience is _____

2. _____ % of the contributors are university personnel.
   _____ % are graduate students, and _____ % are K–12 classroom teachers;
   _____ % are K–12 administrators; _____ % specialists; _____ % other.

3. Refereed 10 yrs ago? _____ Refereed now? _____ If yes, nationally?
   _____ , or in the office? (by the editor and/or the editorial staff) _____
   If refereed, is it anonymous? _____ Other? _____
   Please explain _____ .
   Do you provide the referees with a rating instrument? _____ .

4. _____ % of the articles in your journal report research data, i.e., what percent of the articles report the results of a study conducted by the author(s)?
   _____ .

5. _____ % of the total number of articles published in one year relate to a particular theme issue.

6. _____ % of all manuscripts received are accepted for publication.

7. _____ days lapse before we answer query letters. (please estimate)

8. _____ days lapse before we acknowledge receipt of a manuscript.

9. _____ weeks lapse before we make the publishing decision.

10. _____ months lapse between acceptance and actual publication.

11. _____ manuscript pages is our preferred article length. Our max. length is
    _____ pp. Our min. length is _____ pp.

12. In addition to the original, how many photocopies do you require? _____

13. Required style: APA _____ , MLA _____ , Chicago _____ , Other _____ .

14. Accept dot matrix? _____ Letter quality? _____ Photocopies? _____ .

15. Good black & white photos would enhance acceptance in this journal?
    none _____ , possibly _____ , likely _____ .

16. To inquires about possibly submitting a manuscript, do you welcome query letters? _____ , phone calls? _____ Which do you prefer? _____ .

17. Some common mistakes made by contributors.

18. Recommendations to contributors:

FIGURE 6.5   Articles produced by periodically readministering the survey to editors.

Henson, K. T. Writing for professional publication. *Phi Delta Kappan,* December 1984, *65,* 635–637.
Henson, K. T. Writing for publication: Playing to win. *Phi Delta Kappan.* April 1986, *67,* 602–604.
Henson, K. T. Writing for education journals. *Phi Delta Kappan.* June 1988, *69,* 752–754.
Henson, K. T. Writing for education journals: Some facts to consider. *Phi Delta Kappan.* June 1990, *71,* 800–803
Henson, K. T. How to shake the six myths that haunt all writers. *The Writer.* May 1991, 24–25.
Reprinted in the 1991 *Writer's Handbook,* Chapter 13, pp. 53–56.
Henson, K. T. How to write for education journals—and get published. *NASSP Bulletin.* September 1991, *75*(536), 101–105.
Henson, K. T. Six ways to capture and hold the attention of nonfiction readers. *Writers' Journal.* January–February 1993, 19–20.
Henson, K. T. Writing for successful publication: Advice from editors. *Phi Delta Kappan.* June 1993, *74*(10), 799–802.
Henson, K. T. Writing for education journals: Some mistakes and suggestions. In *NASSP Bulletin.*
Henson, K. T. All the right reasons: Writing for publication. *Kappa Delta Pi Record,* January 1996, *33,* 57–59.
Henson, K. T. Writing for publication: Some perennial mistakes. *Phi Delta Kappan,* June 1997, *78,* 781–784.
Henson, K. T. So you want to be published? *Kappa Delta Pi Record,* 1999, *35,* 79–81.
Henson, K. T. Writing for professional journals. *Phi Delta Kappan,* 1999, *99,* 780–783.
Henson, K. T. Writing for professional journals: Paradoxes and promises. *Phi Delta Kappan,* 2001, *82,* 765–788.
Henson, K. T. Writing for professional publication: Some myths and some truths. *Phi Delta Kappan,* 2003, *84,* 788–791.
Toppins, A. D., Henson, K. T., & Solezio, E. What editors want: How to get published in HRD Journals. *Training and Development Journal,* March 1988, 26–29.

Consideration in undertaking large research studies is the possibility of collaboration. Novice authors often ask if they should work with other colleagues. The answer depends on whether you have colleagues who are congenial, whose areas of expertise complement your own, and whose work habits are efficient. For example, the middle school survey just discussed

FIGURE 6.6   Sample questionnaire cover letter.

_____ , Editor
Journal of _____
Street Address
City, State 00000

Dear _____ :

During the autumn of each odd year, I collect information to help prospective contributors improve the quality of manuscripts that they submit to education editors. I then attempt to report the results in a journal article.

If you would like to have your journal included in this report, please complete the enclosed questionnaire. For your convenience, I am enclosing a self-addressed, stamped envelope. I realize that your schedule is very demanding and thus will be most grateful of your time. Hopefully, the information you provide will save you time by reminding your future contributors of your requirements. Thank you for your consideration.

FIGURE 6.7   Revised questionnaire cover letter.

_____ , Editor
Journal of _____
Street Address
City, State 00000

Dear _____ :

Enclosed please find a questionnaire that you completed for a survey several months ago.

The last time this questionnaire was mailed, one editor suggested that, to save all the editors some time, I might return the last questionnaire and ask everyone just to note any changes, an excellent suggestion. So, will you please examine your questionnaire carefully and note any changes at your journal. I have erased the last two items to provide room for your suggestions. Thanks very much for your participation.

Gratefully,

proved to be highly productive because each collaborator had a unique area of expertise. The team included a researcher, an editor, and an author—all of whom were task oriented. In addition, each member had harmonious working relationships with the other two.

USING ACTION RESEARCH

Some participants in my workshops on writing for publication and on grant proposal writing cringe when I mention research. Perhaps because their dissertation experience was less than pleasant, they have promised themselves never to engage in another research study.

I understand this reaction. Although my study, itself, was rewarding, trying to please a committee of individuals with different—sometimes even mutually exclusive—expectations was highly frustrating.

I assure these research skeptics that there is an alternative to the type of research they engaged in when writing their dissertation. Then I introduce them to action research. I especially like action research because it is less threatening, more expedient, and often far more practical than many empirical dissertation studies. I also like it because it is an easy and convenient way for university faculty to become involved with public school teachers and administrators.

RECAPPING THE MAJOR POINTS

- By modeling your article after the characteristics of the articles in a journal, you can significantly improve your chances of acceptance in that journal.
- You can determine the average manuscript length of a journal's articles by counting the words in an average line, multiplying by the number of lines in the article, and dividing by 250.
- You can increase your manuscript's chances of acceptance in a journal by keeping it near the length of the shortest article in the journal.
- The reading level of your article should approximate that of articles already published in the journal.
- The surest and easiest way to make your manuscript fit a particular journal is to read a couple of recent issues of that journal and design your article accordingly.
- Most journals have a set of author guidelines. If these are not printed in the journal, you can get a copy by writing to or phoning a secretary, assistant editor, or managing editor.
- Journals are inflexible; therefore authors must follow the guidelines closely.

- Most manuscripts are rejected because they are not appropriate for that publication's audience.
- Only *rarely* will editors rewrite a poorly written manuscript.
- The *Education Index* and similar reference guides can be used to identify appropriate article topics and to identify appropriate journals for given topics.
- Prolific writers relate their writing topics to their previously acquired knowledge, enabling them to use references with which they are already familiar.
- References should always include a few current entries.
- Whenever possible, surveys should be kept to one page. Long surveys have lower return rates.
- The return rate for surveys can be increased by choosing a topic of concern to the respondents and by designing the questions so they can be answered quickly and easily.

REFERENCES

Biddle, B. J., & Anderson, D. S. (1986). Theory, methods, knowledge, and research on teaching. In M. C. Wittrock (Ed.), *Handbook of research on teaching,* 3rd ed. (pp. 230–256). New York: Macmillan.

Copeland, M. T. (1931). The development of principles by the use of cases. In C. E. Fraser (Ed.), *The case method of instruction.* New York: McGraw-Hill.

Henson, K. T. (1996). Teachers as researchers. In J. Sikula, T. Buttery, and E. Guyton (Eds.), *Association of Teacher Educators' handbook of research on teacher education,* 2nd ed. (Chapter 4, pp. 53–66). New York: Macmillan.

Tallman, I., Leik, R. K., Gray, L. N., & Stafford, M. C. (1993). A theory of problem-solving behavior. *Social Psychology Quarterly, 56*(3), 157–177.

7

COMMON ERRORS IN WRITING FOR JOURNALS

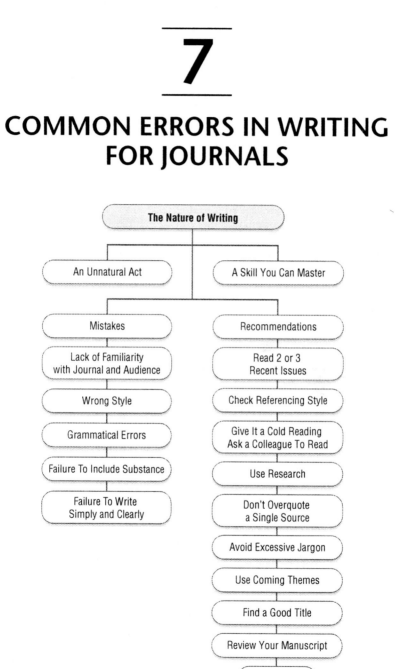

The Nature of Writing

An Unnatural Act

A Skill You Can Master

Mistakes

Lack of Familiarity with Journal and Audience

Wrong Style

Grammatical Errors

Failure To Include Substance

Failure To Write Simply and Clearly

Recommendations

Read 2 or 3 Recent Issues

Check Referencing Style

Give It a Cold Reading Ask a Colleague To Read

Use Research

Don't Overquote a Single Source

Avoid Excessive Jargon

Use Coming Themes

Find a Good Title

Review Your Manuscript

Think!

THE NATURE OF WRITING

Almost every college campus has its own story of a resident genius super-writer who has only to pick up a pen or put the fingers on the keyboard, and—presto—words, paragraphs, and pages begin to flow. Even more astounding, this superwriter doesn't have to edit or rewrite: the first draft comes out perfect. The story must be true because it is told often by the superwriter's own colleagues, and it is told with conviction.

Why would anyone purposefully distort the truth to such a degree, knowing the harm that it does to aspiring authors? Could the purpose of such a fib be to demolish the would-be authors who are merely human? Indeed, many novices who are already insecure about their ability to write publishable articles must be devastated by the thought that for some of their peers, perfect writing is an effortless process, a gift granted at birth.

James Raymond (1986) used the title of his book to remind would-be writers that *good writing doesn't come naturally or easily.* Raymond's book is titled *Writing (Is an Unnatural Act).* William Zinsser, author of *On Writing Well* (1988), cautions would-be writers that successful writing requires clear thinking, which must be learned. Says Zinsser,

> *Thinking clearly is a conscious act that the writer must force upon himself.*
> *Just as if he were embarking on any other project that requires logic. (p. 12)*

James Kilpatrick, author of *The Writer's Art* (1984), says, "The construction of a good, solid sentence is no more a matter of instinct than the putting together of a dovetailed drawer" (p. 11). Although to many aspiring writers these comments may appear trite and unnecessary, they obviously are quite necessary because contributors to journals and magazines continue to make the same mistakes over and over. But you can do better. By knowing these mistakes before you write, you can avoid them.

The rest of this chapter reports, in order of their importance, the mistakes that editors say their contributors make most frequently. This information is based on 172 editor responses to two open-ended questions: What are the most common mistakes made by contributors? What recommendations would you give to contributors? The answers are reported verbatim as they appeared on the questionnaires returned.

MISTAKES AND RECOMMENDATIONS

Mistake: Lack of Familiarity with the Journal and Its Readers

Ignorance about the target journals causes the most common error that contributors to these journals make—failure to design their articles so they fit the intended journals. Of all the comments that these editors made, the advice they offer most frequently is for authors to read some recent issues of the journal. A former editor of the *Journal of Teacher Education* says that one of the most frequent mistakes made by contributors to that journal is "not addressing a topic of concern to their readers." For example, such journals as *The Journal of Teacher Education, Action in Teacher Education, The Teacher Educator,* and *The Professional Educator* are published for a specific audience: teacher educators. Yet, many, if not most, of the manuscripts sent to these journals are written for classroom teachers—clearly the wrong audience. The following comments are taken from the questionnaires returned by editors of many well-known journals.

"(The authors) do not understand the journal's purpose."

"Read articles in the journal to which you are submitting."

"Most mistakes . . . could be avoided if authors studied our journal . . . beforehand."

"Read the journal before submitting!!"

[A common error of contributors is] "not reading past issues to become familiar with the types of articles we publish."

"[Authors] need to read the editorial [in the journal to which they plan to submit] to find out what's appropriate."

Another editor advised, "Read a few copies." This will help acquaint you with both the audience and the journal. In Chapter 6 it was noted that editors often use the expression, "It is not right for our journal." This can mean that the manuscript is directed to another audience or it may mean that the way the article is written is unsuited to the audience. For example, the article may be either too research oriented or too pragmatic, too long or too short, too pedantic or too elementary; or it may mean that the article uses the wrong style for footnoting and referencing.

The two article excerpts in Figure 7.1 show the wide range in style among journals in the same field. Part One shows a complete article; Part Two is but a short paragraph taken from a very long article. Suppose you have prepared a manuscript for submission to one of these journals. In what ways would it be inappropriate to submit this article to the other journal? In addition to submitting their manuscripts to journals within their fields, most prolific writers also have a group of journals outside their subject specialty to which they occasionally submit manuscripts, which further increases the diversity of journal styles. It is essential to make certain that your manuscripts are adapted to fit each journal to which you submit.

"It's not right for our journal" might also mean that the topic is not a topic of interest to the journal's readers. It could also mean that the language is inappropriate. Once again, examine the two articles in Figure 7.1. One

FIGURE 7.1   PART ONE   Sample article style A.

SCHOOL AND COMMUNITY

Student Teachers Unlock Learning Barriers
Kenneth T. Henson

The degree of learning which develops in any classroom is affected by the atmosphere in that classroom. The experienced teacher knows this varies so much that each class has its own personality. This atmosphere of "personality" is somewhat determined by a number of factors present in the class which prevent or disrupt the learning process. These factors may be labeled "learning barriers." The method which the teacher uses successfully today to remove learning barriers may not work so well tomorrow. A method successful with one class may be a failure with another. A method successful for one teacher may never be successful for another. Such variations have prevented the discovery of methods which can be prescribed to overcome learning barriers in all situations; however, this is no indication that research cannot contribute to the removal of learning barriers.

Each teacher should be aware of the existence of learning barriers and of several methods for overcoming them. A number of methods afford selection of alternatives when the first attempt is unsuccessful. Analysis can identify these barriers and provide the teacher with a selection of methods and the knowledge of the degrees of success achieved through their use in situations similar to his own.

Following is a record of responses of ten student teachers of high school mathematics to some learning barriers which developed during a semester of student teaching. A conference was held with each student teacher immediately following each teaching period. During this meeting, the student teacher was reminded of his attempts to overcome barriers which threatened to disrupt the learning process during the preceding period. He then explained why he selected the particular method to deal with each situation.

Introducing a Concept:
Mister Wells observed that in his classes certain behavioral problems which disrupt the learning process are most abundant immediately following an introduction of new subject material and decrease after the students began to grasp an understanding of the new material.

This suggested to him that failure to understand is often the cause of inattentiveness and a special effort should be taken to make sure that the boisterous students understand new lessons. Since more misunderstanding is present during this period, the teacher should avoid traveling at a pace which students cannot follow. He should be careful to explain newly introduced material thoroughly, not assuming that students have information which is basic to the new concepts, but assuring that each student has this necessary background, before proceeding into the new area.

Source: Henson, K. T. Student teachers unlock learning barriers. *School and Community, 56* (February 1970): 43–44. Reprinted by permission.

FIGURE 7.1   PART TWO   Sample article style B.

THE ELEMENTARY SCHOOL JOURNAL

**Long-Term Academic Effects of the Direct
Instruction Project Follow Through**
Linda A. Meyer

There are generally high correlations between MAT and WRAT end-of-third-grade reading scores and ninth-grade reading. Third-grade MAT total reading scores and ninth-grade total reading scores correlate .78 for cohort 2 and .81 for cohort 3. The end-of-third-grade WRAT reading scores and ninth-grade reading scores correlate .47 for cohort 1, .71 for cohort 2, and .73 for cohort 3. End-of-third-grade WRAT math scores correlate with ninth-grade math scores .49 for cohort 1, and .39 for cohort 2. Ninth-grade math scores and Slosson IQ scores correlated .20 for cohort 1, and .49 for cohort 2.

Source: Meyer, L. A. Long-term academic effects of the direct instruction project follow through. *The Elementary School Journal, 84*(4), 1984, pp. 380–394. Reprinted by permission of the University of Chicago Press.

journal is read by professors and doctoral students; the other is read by practicing teachers. As you compare these, listen to the tone of the language. Is one more pedantic? Scholarly? Chatty? One of the articles has no references; the other has 26. Can you tell which audience is professors and doctoral students? How?

Now consider how much better the editors of these journals know their readers. The next time you hear an editor say "It's not right for our journal," realize that the editor has discovered a polite way to say that you haven't done your homework. It's your responsibility to study the journals and make your articles fit the audiences' expectations. You must write about topics that have special appeal to those who read the targeted journals, and you must learn to be flexible, adapting your writing style to conform to the style of each journal. By examining the table of contents of a few copies of each journal, you can easily develop a sense of what these readers consider important. By studying the style of each journal—the topics, the reading level, tense, amount of research reported, and the amount of statistical description—you can prepare manuscripts that will appear familiar to the readers. You *can* do it, and you must.

Mistake: Wrong Style

Rita Dunn (1986), who has authored and collaborated to produce hundreds of articles and monographs, says that she has learned that the journals won't change, nor will they make exceptions to accommodate the style of manuscripts. Journals that use *The Chicago Manual of Style* by The University of Chicago Press will not accept manuscripts that use the style of the American Psychological Association and vice versa. Journals that accept 10- to 12-page manuscripts are unlikely to accept 20- to 30-page manuscripts and vice versa.

Just inside the front cover, most journals tell prospective contributors which style to use. If the style is not mentioned, authors can write or phone for a copy of the guidelines.

Many manuscripts are rejected because authors fail to follow the journal's designated style. Following are some style-related reasons for rejection particular editors give.

- "Not (failure to use) APA style."
- "Need to use the APA format."
- "Not (failure to follow) Chicago style."
- "Failure to follow style guidelines."
- "Wrong style, level, and focus."

Many other editors in this same survey cautioned their contributors to follow the author guidelines, which always address style.

When your manuscript is completed, always make a final check to see that the citations (or footnotes) in the manuscript match those at the end of the article.

Mistake: Failure to Check for Grammatical Errors

How serious is this error? One editor says that he counts grammatical errors the way an umpire counts strikes. Incidentally, he allows some errors, but just one mistake over the number allowed earns the manuscript a place in the rejection file.

Nobody can avoid mistakes; yet, you can and should refuse to share your errors with editors. Never let the editor be your first reader. Several of these editors recommend that you let at least two or three colleagues read your manuscript before sending it to anyone. Preferably those readers should read critically and react honestly. You need someone who offers specific feedback and suggestions, not a doting spouse, not an envious colleague, but an objective critic who will offer specific suggestions and who will tell you if the manuscript is confusing or shallow.

Another suggestion is to give your manuscript a cold reading. This means put it aside for a few days before your final reading. This allows errors to crystallize and become visible to the author. A good practice is to begin writing another manuscript immediately upon completing the current one. Some authors work on several manuscripts simultaneously, putting each aside for a day or two and returning later with a fresh perspective.

Mistake: Failure to Include Substance

When researching the art of writing for research journals, Halpin and Halpin (1986) asked the editors, "What is the most important quality that you look for in a manuscript?" An editor responded, "I suppose that the most important quality is that the article makes some unique contribution, however small." Yet, the comments of the editors in my more recent survey reveal that many manuscripts fail to offer anything new. Responding to the question about the most common mistakes that contributors make, the editor of *Contemporary Education* said, "Old Hat; Old Stuff." The editor of *Vocational Education* said, "Rehash of well-known information." The editor of another journal said, "Much ado about nothing."

An examination of some of the other responses gives a definite clue as to how writers can avoid this criticism. The editor of *The High School Journal* lists as a common mistake, "No data base." The editor of *Journal of Research in Science Teaching* says, "Not making a new contribution."

These comments imply that not all writers should write for research-type journals. Unless your employer requires such, your time and energy can be much more economically invested in writing for journals that do not follow the research format. Nonresearch formatted journals, such as journals written for practitioners, usually have higher acceptance rates; they are far less demanding on authors; and they have a much shorter turnaround (response) period, which permits authors to move their publishing program at a much faster pace.

If, however, you do intend to write for research-type journals, remember that you are not limited to reporting your own research; relevant data and the opinions of other experts in the field can be used to buttress your article (see Figure 7.2).

But beware of including lines and lines of quotes. Like William Faulkner's and James Joyce's stream-of-consciousness style, very long quotes take the readers off course. If and when the reader realizes what has happened, the point you were attempting to make has been lost.

To avoid this confusion, break up long quotes and just talk to the reader. Offer examples. These will serve two purposes; they will clarify the meanings hidden in the long quotes, and they will remind the reader that they are still in the quote.

A similar common error among research articles is quoting the same source too often. Pretty soon the readers begin to wonder why they are reading your article when they could be reading the original source.

Some other errors that you will recognize include:

- Referring to *data* in the singular (*data* are always plural).
- Personifying the document (e.g., this paper will . . .)

FIGURE 7.2   Referencing the work of others.

[T]eachers must first learn proper methods of using inquiry learning. When using inquiry, the main role of the instructor is that of a catalyst to encourage students to make and test their own hypotheses,[22] since "case studies provide an open instruction to generalize."[23]

Finally, the instructor can use the case study method to cross-examine the students. Although we typically recognize the word "cross-examine" as a legal term, this approach is also widely used in business education programs and has been cited by some as the most desirable way to use the case method in business.[24]

These four approaches are the most common for using case studies.[25] Instructors should mix and sequence these approaches so that their students will be exposed to the benefits of all of them, while simultaneously learning to enjoy a variety of activities in their daily classes.

A recent variation for using the case method is the development of case study computer simulations. According to Zappia, "Many computer simulation games are designed so that they provide all the positive elements of the case method, but games have an added dimension . . . they permit the students to see the actual consequences of their decisions."[26]

When using the case study, all decisions should be based on involving the students in positive ways. As Ahmadian explains, "The key to capturing potential (that has got to be tapped) is to cause students to become deeply involved, both emotionally and intellectually, in the analysis and resolution of cases. It has been found that case analysis and resolution must be supported by textual material and instruction guidance."[27] Used in such a way, the case study method becomes a tool that can help instructors bring meaning to the increased field experience components of their programs.

Source: Henson, K. T. (1988, September). Case study in teacher education, *The Educational Forum,* 52(3), 240.

- Using abbreviations.
- Using an acronym without first spelling it out.
- Referring to yourself in the third person (e.g., the author, the investigator, or the researcher).
- Pairing a singular subject with plural antecedent or vice versa. Perhaps the most common cause of this problem is the word *each,* as in "*Each* of the researchers shared *their* findings."
- Claiming "research shows" but failing to immediately cite a study. If you say that research studies have found, you should immediately cite *two* or more studies.
- Using colloquialisms, including:

  Used to (*did*)
  Come up with (*discovered* or *introduced*)

Has to do with (*concerns*)
On the other hand (*in contrast* or *conversely*)
Brings to mind (*recalls* or *reminds*)

Mistake: Failure to Write Simply and Clearly

Having something to say is one thing; saying it simply and clearly is another. Time after time these editors made emphatic statements addressing this need. Tying the two needs together, the editor of *American Middle School Education* said, "Articles [in our journal] are evaluated for substantive content and quality readability or thought flow." The editor of *Contemporary Education* said that his journal often rejects manuscripts because they "lack coherence."

First, the article must have a distinct message, and this message must be clearly stated in the title. Then, the message must be clarified in the first paragraph. The comments of the editor of *Middle School Journal* captured both of these ideas: "Entice your reader with a title and (with your) opening paragraph." Communicating the purpose of the article immediately is absolutely essential. The *NASSP Bulletin* editor said, "Contributors do not write interesting opening paragraphs. If editors aren't excited with openings, how will readers react?" The editor of *Journal of Reading Behavior* mentioned as a problem: "Including identifying information in the body of the manuscript which the editor must sniff out."

The editor of the *Journal of Allied Health* advised contributors to, "Avoid too much professional jargon. Be concise, be consistent, be thorough, be direct, and avoid administrative language." The editor of *Theory and Research in Social Education* advised, "Be thorough, clear, factual, and scholarly." *The Social Studies* editor added a valuable suggestion, "Avoid passive voice." The common thread in all of these comments is the message to authors that their number one objective should be to attain clarity.

Just how important is getting your idea across clearly in the beginning of your article? Think of yourself as a salesperson. If your income came from the sales you made, you would find a way to clearly and quickly communicate the strengths of your product. *Writers, too, are salespeople who must compete with all other writers who submit to the same journal.* Like potential customers who purchase goods, readers of professional journals will turn to other sources rather than labor to understand your meaning.

One editor emphasized his desire for simple language when he cited "overuse of jargon" and "pedantic style" as common problems with manuscripts. The editor of *The Reading Teacher* and *Journal of Reading* echoed this concern by deploring "writing in pompous, academic style." She advised, "Write in a straightforward manner as if speaking to practitioners." *Educational Record's* editor says, "We look for nonacademic [writing style]." The editor of *Theory into Practice* makes an excellent suggestion to improve clarity: "Examples should be used to explain difficult concepts."

Following are some additional suggestions to improve clarity:

- If the journal permits, use headings. A brief survey of a current or recent issue can provide this information.
- Use short, familiar words. For example, the word *use* is preferable to *utilize, change* instead of *effectuate.*
- Use short sentences and short paragraphs.
- Avoid clichés.
- Edit your work. As you reread your drafts, remove unnecessary paragraphs, sentences, and words.
- Read and follow the advice in such works as *The Elements of Style* by William Strunk, Jr., and E. B. White.

Never settle for a level of quality in your writing that causes the reader to have to reread a single sentence for understanding.

In summary, the most common mistakes that contributors to professional journals make are:

Common Mistakes	*Recommendations*
• Lack of familiarity with the journal	Read a few recent issues.
• Wrong style	Check inside the front cover for directions. If there are none, write for a copy of the journal's guidelines for contributors.
• Grammatical errors	Proof and correct. Wait a few days and give it a cold reading. Ask associates to read and critique your articles.
• Failure to include substance	Consider using a survey to gather data. Review current articles and important books and reference these works in the body of your manuscript.
• Pedantic writing	Avoid using unnecessary jargon. State your message in the title. Use familiar words, short sentences, and short paragraphs.

Although the preceding errors are the most common mistakes contributors make, they are by no means the only mistakes. The editors responding to the questionnaire offered the following recommendations.

Recommendation: Select Your Target Journals in Advance

Even before you begin writing, you should take time to select some target journals. Only then can you design your manuscript to make it fit these journals. The assistant editor of the *Peabody Journal of Education* says, "Scholars should do their homework when selecting a journal." This task is just as much a part of becoming a successful writer as writing the manuscript itself. This is why the editor of *Educational Record* wrote, "Read our magazine before you submit (or ideally, [before you] write) an article." Failure to select your target journals and tailor your articles to them could lead to the problem referred to by a former editor of the *Journal of Teacher Education*—"Not addressing a topic of concern [to our readers]."

Recommendation: Identify Coming Themes

Most professional journals publish some themed issues each year. Alexander L. Pickins, editor of *Educational Perspectives,* was referring to these themes when he suggested, "Inquire regarding forthcoming themes—write toward a theme for which your expertise exists." Some journals have no themed issues; others have *only* themed issues. But most journals have both themed and general issues, and considerably fewer manuscripts are received for the themed issues than for the general issues. Often three or four times as many manuscripts are received for general issues as are received for themed issues. This means that *you have an opportunity to increase your chances for acceptance by 300 to 400 percent*. To achieve this goal, you must write your article and submit it before the deadline date. You can learn about forthcoming themes and deadline dates for submitting to the themed issues by examining several recent issues of each journal. At least one issue will carry this information for the coming year.

Recommendation: Find a Good Title

Responding to the question about common mistakes contributors make, the editor of *Middle School Journal* wrote, "Terrible titles." Entice your readers with a title that is inviting and that describes the content of your manuscript. Whenever possible, use your title to make a commitment to your readers. (See Chapter 6.)

Recommendation: Focus on the Opening Paragraph

Like the title, the opening paragraph should hook and hold the reader's attention. Like those boring speakers who use the first few minutes to get to the subject of their presentation, many would-be writers use the first paragraph or two to begin focusing their writing. By the second or third page, they attain clarity in their own thinking about the article, and the reading picks up. Unfortunately, many readers will become bored and give up before reaching the "good stuff."

The editor of the *NASSP Bulletin* listed as a common mistake, "Contributors do not write interesting opening paragraphs. If editors aren't excited with [the] opening, how will the readers be?" To make your opening paragraphs more stimulating, immediately tell the reader what the article is about and what you intend to do about it. Too often, writers fail to achieve this goal.

Recommendation: Avoid Provincialism

The preceding recommendations were taken directly from responses to a recent survey. Now permit me to make a couple of additional recommendations which my workshop participants have led me to consider essential.

Beginning writers have a tendency to write about their own experiences. Perhaps the best advice that can be given to fiction writers is to write about the people and places they know best. This usually translates to mean that you should write about your own community. Maxwell Perkins, editor for such writers as F. Scott Fitzgerald and Ernest Hemingway, advised Marjorie Rawlings to stop trying to write Gothic novels of which she knew very little and instead to write about her own community and the people she knew. She did, and her book, *The Yearling,* won a Pulitzer Prize, and her autobiography, *Cross Creek,* was a best seller.

Without much effort you can think of great writers in your own locale— Zane Grey, Eudora Welty, Samuel Clemens, or James Street—who were successful because they captured the lifestyles of the people they knew best. Yet, for the nonfiction writer, provincialism can become a deadly trap. So, you are an entrepreneur who wants to write about the business that you personally nurtured to health against overwhelming odds. Fine. This is a story that should be told. The dilemma is that few people will want to read a nonfiction business book unless they can identify closely with the circumstances—so closely that they can transfer your story to their own situation. Here's where you must help. *By offering examples, you can make your story pertinent to other types of businesses and to other geographic areas.* A novice writer in Eastern Kentucky is currently writing about a partnership program between a local school system and a coal mining industry. Initially the author wrote specifically about her home town, providing names of the town, industry, local school superintendent, and company officials. Unlike the characters in well-written fiction, her characters were not developed so that the reader could identify very strongly with them. Therefore, to talk extensively about them is inappropriate. Her intent was not to have the reader feel compassion, anger, or other emotions about the characters. Introducing the name of the town, the industry, and the people was not inappropriate, but talking extensively about them would run the risk of shutting out entrepreneurs in other areas and in other types of business.

A second approach to overcome provincialism is to offer examples to explain how people in other businesses in other locations can benefit from your article. The writer could tell how other partnerships could be developed. Figure 7.3 is an example of such an article.

This sample article has encouraged other school systems in other college towns to develop similar partnerships. Notice that much of the article focuses on the how-to process rather than on the characters involved.

In your own department you may have discovered a way to overcome a major problem that confronts you and your colleagues. Figure 7.4 illustrates such a discovery. Notice that this article also focuses on the process involved. *The Physics Teacher* printed this article because it addresses a critical problem that every state in the country faces, and it offers the readers a step-by-step way to resolve similar problems. Notice that the authors of this article tell the readers precisely how they can use this process to provide more qualified physics teachers in their respective states.

Recommendation: Review Your Manuscript

Before sending your manuscript, take time to check it thoroughly. One editor advises, "Prior to submitting any manuscript, anywhere, have at least two or three colleagues read (the) text for critical commentary." This is good advice because we often make the same mistakes repeatedly, and we are prone to overlook some mistakes again and again. *The Social Studies* editor advises, "Have a naive reader read and comment on the article before sending it for review."

The coeditors of *Psychological Reports* and *Perceptual Motor Skills* take a different perspective but a very good one. They say "Be of good cheer. Take time to do the job correctly, and check everything yourself. Consult with an expert when you need to." Remember that time spent clearing out errors is a very economical investment. Once the manuscript is in the mail, it is impossible to make corrections.

All of these citicisms and suggestions are both sound and necessary. Their credibility is ensured by the fact that they come from experienced, professional editors. Their absolute necessity is reflected in the fact that these editors reject four out of every five manuscripts they receive.

I am going to end this chapter with the recommendation (which captures my own advice to writers) offered by one of the responding editors. "Think!"

FIGURE 7.3   Expanding application beyond one geographical region.

The Teacher in Residence Partnership Program

Introduction

The central theme of the commission reports and task force studies has been that we must improve the quality of education. These reports have not prescribed standardized answers, but they have encouraged entrepreneurship at the state and local levels. Collaborative efforts and programs have been initiated to lubricate the wheels of progress. These include programs between state and federal levels, schools and communities, businesses and schools, and colleges and schools. The focus of this "Promising Practice" is on a partnership program among the Tuscaloosa City School System, the Tuscaloosa County School System, and The University of Alabama's College of Education.

The program, titled "Teacher in Residence (TIR) Partnership Program," involves two outstanding classroom teachers selected to serve as regular full-time faculty members in the College of Education's Early Childhood and Elementary Education undergraduate teacher preparation programs.

Planning sessions were held between the two superintendents of the local city and county school districts, the dean, the Head of Curriculum and Instruction, and the Chairperson of Early Childhood and Elementary Education. After approval from the appropriate boards, the following guidelines were instituted.

Fellows

An outstanding primary (1–3) grade teacher would be cooperatively selected from the County school system and an outstanding intermediate (4–6) level teacher would be selected from the City school system. The TIR Fellows would serve as faculty members with the University in a fashion similar to an adjunct or visiting professor.

Qualifications

The following objective requirements were set: current classroom teaching experience at the designated grade levels; tenure in the respective school systems; and a Master's Degree. Additionally, affective qualifications included the ability to work with university students and faculty, and a positive and enthusiastic manner.

Selection

In June of 1985, teachers in the two participating school systems were sent letters of notification regarding the program. Interested candidates were asked to submit to their Superintendent's Office an application, a one-page statement of educational philosophy, and any additional facts which might favorably influence their selection. The Assistant Superintendents for Personnel (Dr. Nora Price for the City system and Dr. Sydney Poellnitz for the County system) and the Chairperson of Elementary Education reviewed the applications and selected finalists. The Area Head of Curriculum and Instruction and the Chairperson conducted the final interviews during July. In future cycles of the program the selection process will be conducted during the spring to allow greater transition time.

Continued

FIGURE 7.3 *Continued*

Duration
The TIR positions are for one academic year and are renewable for a second year upon mutual agreement. Teachers serving two years as a Fellow are guaranteed a return to the same school and grade level from which they left. The two-year time frame was selected as the optimal time length because of the breadth of learning that would be required of the Fellows. A period of time less than two years would reflect more of a novelty approach rather than a sustaining program. The school systems agreed to reverse the primary and intermediate levels of the teachers for the next cycle of the program in 1987.

Salary
The University contracts with the respective school systems for the services of the teachers. The Fellows' salary and benefits will continue in accordance with their permanent positions. Salary checks are issued by the participating school systems. This program was not designed to save money by hiring non-doctoral personnel for the University. The teachers' regular salary exceeds the salaries that would be paid to starting assistant professors on nine-month contracts. If the Fellows choose to teach during summer school, their salaries will be paid directly by the University on a visiting professor basis.

Schedule and Assignments
During the Teacher in Residence Program, the Fellows follow the annual and daily University schedule as do regular University faculty members.
   Their assignments revolve around a 12 semester-hour core of teaching undergraduate courses. Regular faculty teach 9 semester hours, generally including at least one graduate course, and are assigned 3 semester hours of research and publication time. The Fellows also serve on program committees, advise students, have voting power on departmental issues (excluding promotion and tenure), and generally function in the same manner as regular faculty members. They enjoy having equal status with other full-time faculty members as is reflected in one of the TIRS, Mrs. Jo-Ann Schweer's, comments: "The opportunity to be chosen as a participant in this program has been a highlight of my teaching career."

Evaluation
Fellows serve as members of the Early Childhood and Elementary Education Program and report directly to the program Chairperson. An annual evaluation of the Fellows will be completed by the Chairperson and shared with the participants, the Area Head of Curriculum and Instruction and the LEA Superintendents. The school systems will meet annually with the Fellows to go over the reports and to assess the quality of the program.

Advantages
The advantages of this program are numerous. The Fellows have the opportunity to experience new, invigorating roles. Mrs. Schweer has observed, "I anticipated the University staff being cautious about my participating; but

in reality, I experienced complete cooperation and acceptance." Both Mrs. Schweer and Mrs. Nancy Rogers have expressed their interest in gaining a first-hand understanding of the program philosophy, objectives, and sequencing. Additionally, they have the satisfaction of directly influencing future teachers. Mrs. Rogers observed, "I believe that because of my everyday classroom teaching experiences, I can personalize and bring to life methods and procedures that might otherwise seem only theory."

Upon completion of the program, the school systems gain teachers who have had experiences which will be invaluable in helping them to plan and institutionalize inservice programs. Both school systems employ many University of Alabama graduates. Having their own teachers directly participating in the preparation program significantly increases the sense of joint ownership in the task of preparing new teachers for the profession.

Source: Buttery, T. J., & Henson, K. T. (1987). Partnership in teacher education: The teacher in residence model. *The Professional Educator, 10,* 21–23.

FIGURE 7.4   Expanding the relevance of information.

The University of Alabama Summer Institute for Physics Teachers: A Response to a Critical Shortage
Kenneth T. Henson, College of Education, University of Alabama
Philip W. Coulter, Department of Physics and Astronomy
J. W. Harrell, College of Arts and Sciences

For several years, the state of Alabama, like most other states, has had a severe shortage of qualified physics teachers.[1,2] Responding to this need, three years ago the Head of Curriculum and Instruction in the College of Education joined with an Assistant Dean in the College of Arts and Sciences to write a cooperative grant. The result was a rigorous, 10-week summer institute for uncertified physics teachers, funded by the State Department of Education. The proposal has since been revised twice by the Head of Curriculum and Instruction and by faculty in the Department of Physics and Astronomy. Both revisions have been funded, providing a second and third summer institute.

All three institutes have received excellent evaluations from the participants and from representatives from the State Department of Education. Several features have enabled this institute to compete successfully with other universities for funding for three consecutive years.

First, all teachers selected for participation in the institute are inadequately prepared to teach physics and do not hold teacher certificates in physics. Though unqualified, all participants are selected to teach physics next year. Therefore, they arrive motivated, wanting to learn everything they possibly can about physics. This sense of purpose and the inquiring attitude that it promotes are essential to the endurance and the success of the participants in the institute.

Second, the University of Alabama Physics Teachers Institute is very rigorous. It runs for 10 full weeks, all participants take 12 credit hours of physics

Continued

FIGURE 7.4 *Continued*

courses, and all courses must be taken for credit. The intensity of this program draws serious teachers who come determined to succeed.

> *This article was easy to write. I just described the program step by step. The first draft took about two hours to write.*

Third, the University of Alabama Physics Teachers Institute is practical. Most of the laboratory experiments chosen complement the high school textbook and require inexpensive equipment. (A special course uses the state's most frequently used high school textbook, examines applicable software, and emphasizes classroom demonstrations).

Fourth, a weekly seminar utilizes the resources of a major research university. Faculty from throughout the University campus give lectures and demonstrations on such topics as lasers, quasars, robotics, and biophysics.

The University of Alabama Physics Teachers Institute has one goal—to enable every participant to be more effective next fall, and it has ways to assure that this happens. Following the institute, co-directors will make a follow-up visit to all teachers' schools. The purposes are: (1) to determine which aspects of the institute the teacher has found most useful and (2) to determine further ways to improve the quality of the institute for another year (in hopes that the institute will be funded the coming year).

Each summer, adjustments have been made to improve the institute. First, a special section of introductory physics was created for these teachers alone, providing them freedom to ask questions that concern teachers and eliminating the initial anxiety that comes from competing with regular University students. Second, a first-year attempt to use a high school physics teacher to teach the high school text was not successful. Although the teacher was truly a master teacher, the participants did not give her the respect that is automatically afforded a university professor. Therefore, a high school teacher was replaced by a university physics professor. Finally, the third summer, teachers were provided opportunities to have their demonstrations and experiments videotaped to take back with them and use in their classes.

Because of the high degree of success of these institutes, and because of the help that they are giving to small, rural schools throughout the state, the Alabama Coalition of Citizens for Excellence in Small Schools has funded an Advanced Physics Institute at the University. The first advanced institute was held during the early 1986 summer term. Six teachers who had attended either the 1984 or the 1985 institute attended the advanced institute.

References
1. R. L. Stanford and W. S. Zoellner, "Alabama Teacher Supply and Demand for 1984–85," *The Professional Educator,* 7(2), 1984, pp. 31–36.
2. R. L. Stanford and W. S. Zoellner, "Alabama Teacher Supply and Demand for 1986–87," Unpublished study, University of Alabama, 1986.

RECAPPING THE MAJOR POINTS

Many errors never seem to go out of style. Through the years, they continue to trip authors. You can escape the damage these errors do if you remember to:

- Identify a few journals that you wish to publish your manuscripts. Consider journals in your specific content field, general journals, and journals in related fields.
- Familiarize yourself with those journals to which you submit your manuscripts. Very carefully read a few recent copies of each journal, paying close attention to its level of complexity, article length, types of topics, and documentation style.
- Check your manuscript for errors. Then ask an impartial colleague to critique it. If your typewriter or computer provides a spell check, use it. Finally, put the manuscript aside for a few days and proofread it again.
- Be sure that each of your manuscripts offers substance. Put simply, be sure you have something worthwhile to say. You can begin by selecting topics that you really know about; then use the library to add more substance. You may also wish to consider using a questionnaire to collect data to report in your articles. Finally, check the title and the lead sentence to see that both reflect the article's main message.
- Write simply and clearly. Begin by knowing your main message, then structure your articles to make sure that this substance stands out to even the most casual reader. Avoid jargon, clichés, and unnecessarily complex and lengthy words, sentences, and paragraphs.
- Having selected your target journals in advance and having read a few recent issues of each, adapt your manuscripts to fit each journal.
- Give each manuscript a captivating title that reflects the main message in the manuscript; then give it a lead sentence and lead paragraph explaining what the article is going to communicate about this topic.
- Because your chances of acceptance by a journal are three or four times as great in themed issues as in general issues, know when theme issues are coming in your target journal, and time your manuscripts to coincide with the deadlines set for these themes.
- Explain how your manuscript content can be applied to programs throughout the country.

REFERENCES

Cole, R. (1986). *Professional journal writing.* Videotape. Raleigh: University of North Carolina at Raleigh.

Dunn, R. (1986). *Writing for professional journals.* Videotape. New York: St. John's University.

Henson, K. T. (1988, June). Writing for education journals. *Phi Delta Kappan, 69,* 752–754.

Henson, K. T. (1997, June). Writing for publication: Some perennial mistakes. *Phi Delta Kappan, 78*(10), 781–784

Henson, K. T. (2003, June). Writing for professional publication: Some myths and some truths. *Phi Delta Kappan, 84*(10), 788–791.

Henson, K. T. (2005). *A brief guide to writing for professional publication.* 2nd ed. Fastback No. 538. Bloomington, IN: Phi Beta Kappan.

Kilpatrick, J. J. (1984). *The writer's art.* New York: Andrews, McNeel, & Parker.

Raymond, J. C. (1986). *Writing (is an unnatural act).* New York: Harper & Row.

Strunk, W., Jr., & White, E. B. (1979). *The elements of style,* 3rd ed. New York: Macmillan.

Zinsser, W. (1988). *On writing well,* 3rd ed. New York: Harper & Row.

8

COMMUNICATING WITH JOURNAL EDITORS

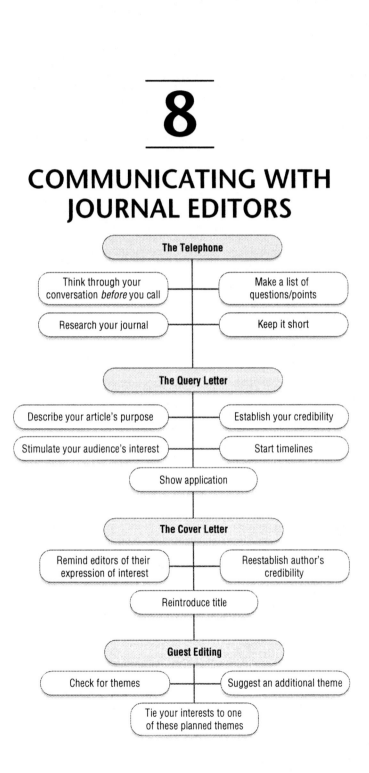

The Telephone

- Think through your conversation *before* you call
- Make a list of questions/points
- Research your journal
- Keep it short

The Query Letter

- Describe your article's purpose
- Establish your credibility
- Stimulate your audience's interest
- Start timelines
- Show application

The Cover Letter

- Remind editors of their expression of interest
- Reestablish author's credibility
- Reintroduce title

Guest Editing

- Check for themes
- Suggest an additional theme
- Tie your interests to one of these planned themes

THE AUTHOR–EDITOR RELATIONSHIP

Successful writing for publication has two requirements. First, authors must learn how to write correctly and they must discipline themselves to do just that in order to produce a quality manuscript. Second, writers must learn how to communicate with editors. Just as good manuscript writing involves mastering certain techniques, *learning to communicate with editors requires mastering specific skills.* Basic to mastering those skills needed to communicate effectively with editors is understanding the editor's role and the relationship between writers and editors.

Beginning writers often perceive editors as their adversaries. Only a few rejection letters are needed to convince many aspiring writers that the editor's main job is to pass negative judgment on the author's work. A few more rejection letters may convince the beginning author that editors are really sick people who derive their life's pleasure from rejecting and putting down writers. Some successful novices, however, pick themselves up, shake themselves off, and conclude that this is really a competition between the author and editors. To these individuals, the editor becomes the major opponent, and this sense of competition is all they need to succeed.

But you can do better. Begin by accepting the fact that *all editors would rather receive good manuscripts than poor ones.* Most editors get no pleasure from rejecting manuscripts but they get much satisfaction from the time they spend accepting manuscripts. Realize that editors and writers are not natural enemies. On the contrary, *the successful author–editor relationship is symbiotic. When authors succeed, editors succeed.* Authors and editors share the same goal. That goal is to produce a high-quality article for the readers on a topic the readers find relevant. The article must give the readers something they need and want, and it must present this information so that the readers can easily understand the author's message. There are many possible channels of communication between the author and editor; some of these are much more effective than others. The choice of communication channel should be based on knowledge about the editor's preferences and knowledge about the advantages that each communication channel offers the writer.

The Telephone

Some beginning writers go directly to the telephone and call the editors of those journals to which they wish to submit manuscripts. Some editors welcome and actually prefer this channel of communication even for use by unknown writers. Other editors prefer not to get phone calls. Should you choose to call, remember that editors are very busy. Keep your call brief and to the point. Think through your conversation *before* you call, and know exactly what questions you wish to ask. Be able to describe your manuscript clearly and specifically.

Successful writers determine the preferences of the editors of their target journals. They often research their journals to learn the editors' preferences. Sometimes journal articles tell the requirements and preferences of their editors. For example, a recent issue of *Training and Development Journal* contains an article that gives the communication channel preferences for several business journals. Appendix A contains a chart that lists the preferences of these journals—information that was derived from a questionnaire the authors sent to the editors of these journals.

You can gather many important facts about these business journals. First, notice the key at the bottom of the chart. Identifying the journals in terms of these nine categories can prove useful to authors. For example, suppose you want to write for journals that publish experimental results. A quick glance down the column under Types of Research lets you quickly identify all of the journals that publish your kind of writing.

Scanning the column headings, you will quickly learn such important facts about each journal as its acceptance rate, whether it is refereed, the number of subscribers, and how long it is likely to take to get a response from your query letter or your manuscript. You will also learn a lot about the journal's requirements, which will be a great help in preparing a better manuscript. Using this chart can help you significantly improve your acceptance rates in these journals.

Also included in Appendix A is similar information about education journals which appears periodically in the *Phi Delta Kappan* (December 1984, April 1986, April 1988, June 1990, June 1993, June 1995, June 1997, June 1999, June 2001, and June 2003). The most recent results of a biennial survey of some 50 education journals show that there is much disparity among the preferences and requirements of the editors of these journals. You should learn the requirements of the particular journals to which you wish to submit manuscripts.

The most interesting and important information found in Appendix A includes:

- Two-thirds of the journals have circulations of 5,000 and fewer.
- Nearly all of the journals report on research of some kind.
- Ninety-three percent of the journals are at least partially refereed; 52 percent are fully refereed.
- The acceptance rates among these journals range from 5 percent to 90 percent; two-thirds of these journals reject two-thirds of the manuscripts they receive.
- One-fifth of the journals reject at least 90 percent of the manuscripts received, but one-fifth accept at least half of the manuscripts received.
- Annually, four-fifths of these journals dedicate one or more issues to a theme.
- Writing for theme issues increases a manuscript's likelihood of acceptance by 300 percent.

- The average time required to accept or reject a manuscript is 2.5 months; the average time from acceptance to publishing is about 8 months.
- Three times as many journal editors prefer query letters as prefer phone calls.
- When authors revise at the request of editors, the resulting manuscript is accepted 85 percent of the time.

The same survey was sent to journals of allied health and nursing, behavioral and social sciences, and library science. Those results are also shown in the charts in Appendix A.

Another way to learn about the preferences of journals in your own field is to go to the reference room of the local library and consult such reference books as those listed in Chapter 1. Most of these books are quite comprehensive and give information about preferences and requirements of their journals.

Perhaps you noticed that the editors of some of these journals prefer that writers use letters to inquire about their preferences and requirements. Actually, four-fifths of the editors of the education journals prefer not to receive letters from prospective authors. But, before dismissing the query letter as a tool to use to communicate with editors, consider what letters can do for you.

The Query Letter

A query letter asks for permission to send in your manuscript. A well-structured query letter provides you a chance to:

- Accurately describe the purpose of your article.
- Stimulate the editor's interest in your article.
- Establish your credibility as someone qualified to write on this topic.
- Establish timeliness of your topic.
- Show how the information can be applied in various settings.

To ensure the full benefits from your query letters, follow these 10 steps:

1. Address the editor personally, accurately.
2. Use the editor's correct title.
3. Make sure that you have the name of the current editor.
4. Type the exact title of the journal in UPPER CASE letters.
5. Explain the subject.
6. Establish credibility.
7. Establish currency.
8. Show application (tell how the reader can use it).
9. Obligate the editor to respond.
10. Be concise.

Most editors have extremely demanding jobs. Like our high school English teachers, the only reason most editors could offer to explain why they work so hard is their total commitment to their jobs. One editor was so involved in his desire to have people communicate clearly and accurately that, when the owners of a nearby laundry misspelled a word on their marquee, he went to the shop and asked them to correct the error. To many editors, grammatical errors, spelling errors, and punctuation errors are virtually obscene. (This should tell us something about our need to avoid such errors in our query letters!) Because of such high levels of commitment to high standards, editors are often accused of being picky, cranky, and idiosyncratic. For in-

FIGURE 8.1   A poorly received query letter.

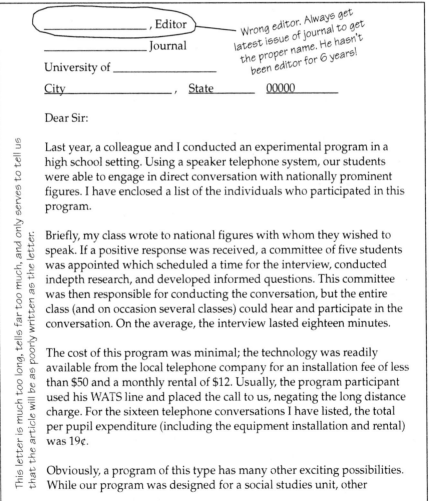

_____ , Editor

_____ Journal

Wrong editor. Always get latest issue of journal to get the proper name. He hasn't been editor for 6 years!

University of _____

City _____ , State _____ 00000 _____

Dear Sir:

Last year, a colleague and I conducted an experimental program in a high school setting. Using a speaker telephone system, our students were able to engage in direct conversation with nationally prominent figures. I have enclosed a list of the individuals who participated in this program.

Briefly, my class wrote to national figures with whom they wished to speak. If a positive response was received, a committee of five students was appointed which scheduled a time for the interview, conducted indepth research, and developed informed questions. This committee was then responsible for conducting the conversation, but the entire class (and on occasion several classes) could hear and participate in the conversation. On the average, the interview lasted eighteen minutes.

The cost of this program was minimal; the technology was readily available from the local telephone company for an installation fee of less than $50 and a monthly rental of $12. Usually, the program participant used his WATS line and placed the call to us, negating the long distance charge. For the sixteen telephone conversations I have listed, the total per pupil expenditure (including the equipment installation and rental) was 19¢.

Obviously, a program of this type has many other exciting possibilities. While our program was designed for a social studies unit, other

This letter is much too long, tells far too much, and only serves to tell us that the article will be as poorly written as the letter.

stance, they may get angry—and rightfully so—if correspondence is addressed to a former editor. The query letter shown in Figure 8.1 was actually sent to a journal editor. The handwritten comments show the editor's reaction. This editor, like most, is protective of his journal. Should this author follow up by sending the manuscript, it undoubtedly will be met with hostility, putting the novice author at a distinct disadvantage.

Another common and equally damaging mistake is any error in the journal title. The letter in Figure 8.2 shows that the editor in this case was greatly offended by the author's failure to recognize that "The" is part of the journal's title.

Too often, editors receive outdated manuscripts written by individuals who haven't the expertise to contribute to the reader's understanding of the topics. The query letter offers an opportunity to convince the editor that your manuscript is current and that you have the expertise to write such a manuscript. Use it to achieve these goals. Whenever possible, you should let the editor know that your manuscript will explain how the reader can apply the information found in your article. Figure 8.3 shows a successful query letter. Use the 10 steps described earlier as guidelines to examine the query letter in Figure 8.3. Does this letter adequately explain the subject? Yes, "The purpose is to identify recent changes in school law. . . ." Does it establish credibility? If so, how? (Here is where most beginning authors trip.) The most common

FIGURE 8.2   Another poorly received query letter.

> ,The
>
> Editor,/Journal of _____
> University of _____
> <u>City</u>_____ , <u>State</u>_____ <u>00000</u>_____
> Gentlemen:
>
> I would appreciate receiving a copy of the guidelines for authors to follow if they submit a manuscript for review and possible later publication in Journal of _____
>
> The ——
>
> A current area of interest with me is student educational self-evaluation as it relates to self-directed learning. What I hope to submit is a manuscript that will show classroom teachers how they can design and use a student self-evaluation tool with their learners.
>
> Cordially,
>
> *Why tell us this if he doesn't ask us whether we are interested in it?*

FIGURE 8.3   Sample of a successful query letter.

_____ , Editor

Journal of _____

Street Address

City, State 00000

Dear _____ :

I would like to share with you a manuscript which will report the results of a study under way at Eastern Kentucky University. The purpose of the study is to identify recent changes in school law that affect middle school administrators. The manuscript will give explicit examples of how the American middle school administrator should adjust school discipline codes to better comply with the new laws.

I shall look forward to hearing whether you are interested in this work. Thank you.

Sincerely yours,

response is that the author's title (such as dean, senior architect, civil engineer, D.M.D., or Ph.D.) establishes credibility for the author. In fact, titles and degrees are very weak evidence that the author is qualified to write the article. Being told that this article "will report the results of a study" is much better assurance that the author is qualified to write the article. Direct experience is also a good source of credibility. For example, an author of an article titled "Baking Christmas Cookies" might begin the query letter by saying, "As the head chef at a major bakery for the past 12 years, . . . " or an article on "Interstate Auto Repair Rip-offs" might be signed by Robert Grimes, Mechanic.

Which part of the letter in Figure 8.3 establishes that the article content is current? One phrase removes any suspicion that this article might be a two-year-old manuscript that has been rejected by 20 other journals. The key phrase is "*under way.*"

This letter also tells that readers of the article will be able to apply and use the information in it. It will "identify changes in school law" and will "give explicit examples of how the American middle school administrators should adjust school discipline codes to better comply with the new laws." What do you think about the relevance of this topic to the audience, school administrators? With the recent rise in lawsuits aimed at high school administrators, it is likely that this topic would capture the interest of even the most confident administrators.

The letter ends by asking the editor to respond: "I shall look forward to hearing whether you are interested in this work." Without this specific request, the editor may assume that the manuscript is already in the mail and might not respond to the author's query. Notice that all of these goals were achieved in only three sentences. Because editors are so busy, and because they receive so many manuscripts, a good guideline is to *always limit your query letter to one page or less.*

The Cover Letter

Most authors believe it is to their advantage to include a cover (or covering) letter with their manuscripts. Correctly written, the cover letter can achieve at least three important purposes. It can:

1. Remind editors of their prior expression of interest in this manuscript.
2. Reacquaint the editor with the title of the manuscript.
3. Reestablish the author's credibility.

The cover letter should be limited to just a few sentences. Its purpose is to "sell" the manuscript, not to repeat it. Figure 8.4 shows a sample cover letter. Examine it to see if you can identify the specific parts that achieve the three objectives. It reminds the editor of his prior expression of interest ("which you asked to see in your letter of January 3, 2004"). It reacquaints the editor

FIGURE 8.4 Sample cover letter.

_____ Editor

Journal of _____

Street Address

City, State 00000

Dear _____ :

Enclosed please find the manuscript "New Discipline Laws and the Middle School Principal" which you asked to see in your letter of January 3, 1985. Thank you for your interest in our research which has culminated in the writing of this manuscript.

I look forward to hearing your response.

Sincerely yours,

with the manuscript by mentioning the manuscript's title. Finally, it reestablishes the author's credibility ("our research which culminated in the writing of this manuscript").

GUEST EDITING

One avenue for establishing yourself in the writing profession is guest editing. Because this effective method is used by relatively few writers, you will do well to consider this approach. Here is how I learned about the tremendous power of guest editing.

At the time, I had served as guest editor of a special theme issue of the journal *Contemporary Education*, a journal published by my own employer at that time, Indiana State University. I mention this because the chances are excellent that either your current employer publishes one or more journals, or you have an alma mater that does.

I simply went to the editor of this journal and asked to plan and edit a special issue on earth science, because I had received my master's degree in this field. Having participated in a National Science Foundation Academic Year Institute, I knew some 20 other people in the field who had returned to their own universities throughout the country.

My next opportunity to guest edit—the one that taught me the most—came totally by accident. I had always wanted to publish in *Theory into Practice*, a scholarly journal written for professors and graduate students. So I sent a query letter to its editor, Charles M. Galloway, describing my manuscript. A few days later the phone rang, and it was none other than Dr. Galloway, who said, "You know, Ken, we don't accept unsolicited manuscripts." Actually, I didn't know that. This was some time ago, and at that time I knew very little about the vast differences among journals. In fact, I was as ignorant as a rock concerning their procedures, but I didn't let a little obstacle like that stand in my way. "However," he continued, "we like your topic and we wondered if you might wish to put together such an issue."

He said there were two ways that they let their guest editors work. I could choose to title all articles and identify some good authors, then let the in-house editorial staff do the rest. Or I could do that plus have all manuscripts sent to me for my editing. Either way, I knew that I already knew one of the authors—me. That was my first benefit.

Then I looked for the best known experts inside and outside the United States. I learned that, because of the journal's reputation, I could get an article from almost anyone I asked, so I chose the most highly acclaimed experts. This put me in a one-on-one working relationship with these renowned scholars. This was my second benefit.

In about three months, I received another phone call from the editor. This time, he asked me to consider planning and editing a subsequent issue of this journal. I gladly obliged and have since planned and edited several issues. Each experience provided additional benefits.

When the journal was approaching its twenty-fifth anniversary, I was asked to review 25 years of articles in my field, choose the three best articles, and use them to write an article for a Silver Anniversary Issue. This benefit was topped off by a distinguished service award given jointly by the journal and The Ohio State University.

From conducting surveys to editors of journals in the disciplines of Business, Behavioral and Social Sciences, and Nursing, I learned that over half of all articles in these journals are part of a theme. This means, that, whatever your field, you probably have journals that plan themed issues. I suggest that you consider planning a theme issue on an exciting topic. If the first editor you choose declines, go to another one.

Perhaps the greatest benefit from my experience—and certainly yours, too, should you choose to do this—was that all this required editing, and editing was the best writing teacher I've ever had. Good editing is good writing and vice versa.

RECAPPING THE MAJOR POINTS

As you prepare to communicate with editors in the future, remember:

- Authors and editors share the same goal, to produce an article that is relevant and helpful to the readers.
- Several communication channels are available to authors.
- Many editors prefer not to receive query letters.
- Correctly designed, the query letter and the cover letter work for the author.
- Editors are very busy; therefore, all phone calls and letters should be kept short.
- To work, query letters and cover letters must be correctly written.
- Authors should never miss an opportunity to tactfully establish their credibility with editors.
- Guest editing is a little used but highly rewarding entree into the publishing world.

REFERENCE

Henson, K. T. (2005). *A brief guide to writing for professional publication.* Fastback (monograph) No. 538. Bloomington, IN: Phi Delta Kappa International.

9

QUESTIONS WRITERS ASK

Questions Writers Ask

What suggestions can you give to aspiring writers?

Have you a favorite success story?

How do you handle rejection?

What distinguishes highly successful writers from less successful writers?

Is it acceptable to send manuscripts to multiple publishers simultaneously?

Does collaborating have advantages?

Should I collaborate long-distance?

Should I write articles before writing books?

Exactly what is a refereed journal?

Is using vanity publishers wise?

What about self-publishing?

If asked, should I pay journal-publishing expenses?

Should I be a specialist or a generalist?

How can authors learn to use the library more effectively?

Are colloquialisms and clichés acceptable?

What should I do when an editor keeps holding my manuscript, delaying a publishing decision?

Whose name comes first on an article?

Who is listed first when professors and graduate students collaborate?

If I furnish my dissertation or thesis for a collaborator to shape into an article, is that an equitable exchange?

If I share a book idea with a publisher, how can I be sure it won't be turned over to a more experienced author?

What does it mean when an editor asks the author to rewrite and resubmit a manuscript? Should I do that?

Should I use a computer?

What should I list on my résumé as publications?

Can you give advice for establishing a discussion group?

All beginning writers can be put into two categories: those who ask questions and those who want to ask questions, if only they were brave enough to do so. All writers—beginners and experienced writers alike—have questions to ask. *Successful writers are bold.* This does not imply that they are pompous, arrogant, or egotistical. Boldness in successful writers means that they are confident, determined, and persistent. Those who ask questions are likely to grow much faster than those who have questions to ask, but wait, hoping that someone else will ask their questions for them.

In previous chapters we have addressed some of the most frequently asked questions: How do you find the time to write? What tools do writers use? Should I use query letters? When is the best time to write? Where is the best place to write? and How do you identify topics? In this chapter, I will ask—and answer—some of the remaining questions you may have.

WHY DO YOU WRITE?

All writers have their own reasons for writing. Many successful writers offer two reasons for writing. First, they are compelled to write. Apart from any tangible benefits—and far more important—they have a personal need to write. A psychology professor and practicing psychologist told the following story to impress on his students the importance of an individual's perceptions and the way these perceptions determine the individual's world.

> *I walked into the private ward of the hospital to see a patient. Mr. Jones was screaming at the top of his lungs. I asked him what was wrong.*
> *He shouted, "They're killing me! They're killing me!"*
> *I said, "Mr. Jones, who's killing you?"*
> *"Those little devils on my chest! They're stabbing me with pitch forks! Can't you see them?"*
> *I responded, "No, but I can see that they are hurting you."*

As workshop participants talk about their reasons for writing, sometimes their reasons sound so bizarre that they are almost unbelievable; then I remember the patient and the pitch forks. To him the devils were real. *People have different reasons for writing, and they have a right to these reasons—whatever they are.* Some people write only because their job requires them to publish; these people may never understand how others could ever feel compelled to write. The fact remains that this compulsion is the major force that motivates many people to write.

Most successful writers also say that they write because they immensely enjoy writing. Given the choice between writing or watching television or going to a movie, they will take writing every time. Perhaps it's a combination of creating something, completing a task, and knowing that someday it will be read by others.

Recently, I was attending a workshop conducted by Kurt Vonnegut, and someone asked him: Why do you write? Vonnegut answered that there is only one justifiable reason to write. He said that some people have a burning desire to be published, and, although this is getting close, this is not an acceptable reason for writing. Vonnegut said the only justifiable reason for writing is because you have something that is so compelling that it must be said. Certainly, such passion provides the internal motivation that writers must have to hone their manuscripts while honing their writing skills.

WHAT SUGGESTIONS CAN YOU GIVE TO ASPIRING WRITERS?

First, write. If you want to become a *successful* writer you must become a *good* writer. The best way to do this is to write. Write often and much. Make mistakes. Don't worry about it. First, get your ideas on paper. That's what counts. Then edit your work, and rewrite it. Set some goals; then set yourself a schedule. Give your goals some deadlines. Then watch your writing activities move forward.

Second, if for some reason you forget or choose to ignore all that you have read in this book, remember this one thing: you can succeed as a writer *only* if you think you can. I have yet to hear anyone say that for years they have really tried to learn how to write well but have failed to reach any of their writing goals, but I do receive many letters containing passages like this one:

> *I can't believe it. Once I finally took that first bold step and learned a few basic techniques, then I learned how easy it really is. I've had an article accepted in that journal that I always wanted to have publish my material. Not only have I had one article published in it, I've since had others accepted and it's easy.*

One way to learn the basics and then continue to expand your ability is to attend writing workshops. Appendix D contains detailed information about workshops.

HAVE YOU A FAVORITE SUCCESS STORY?

Yes. My favorite story happened to a friend. It's full of coincidences. In fact, it has all the earmarks of a fisherman's lie; I can understand if you don't believe it.

I walked into a trophy store in a large mall. There on display was a desk-top nameplate with the name of an old army buddy. Let's call him Wayne. It is such an unusual name that I decided to check the phone directory to ver-ify my discovery. I found the number and dialed it. For the first time in 25 years, I heard my friend's voice. I asked him to have lunch with me at a local club. We set a date. As I drove up to the club, I noticed that my friend (who hails from a background that rivals my own for being humble and un-known) stepped out of a new limousine. As we ate, we reminisced about our experiences as enlisted men in Uncle Sam's army. Wayne was the outdoors person who actually enjoyed bivouacking and sleeping on the ground, eat-ing K-rations, and, in short, roughing it. In school Wayne was never consid-ered a star pupil. By his own admission, he was lucky to get through freshman English composition. Although he did well in his major (wildlife), his writing skills were so limited that he had to repeat freshman composi-tion. Twice!

As we ate, Wayne told me that he was sitting at home one day bored be-cause the rain was keeping him inside. To cope with his boredom, he decided to write an article to share some of his personal experiences in the out-of-doors. He modeled his article after those in a leading national wildlife jour-nal. To his utter amazement, the journal accepted his article, and with his letter of acceptance he received a substantial check. This whetted his appetite; so he wrote a second article, then a third, and fourth. In summary, this person who, in his own words, was lucky to ever pass freshman composition wrote a string of 15 articles for wildlife magazines—and, with the acceptance of the 15 articles, he had never received a rejection!

Equally amazing, Wayne began to write books, experiencing the same degree of success. He disclosed that he had just signed a contract for his eleventh book, a cookbook for campers, for which he received an advance of $85,000. He and his wife had been conducting writing workshops, but even for an enormous fee he could no longer afford to take time from his writing to conduct the workshops. With their writing and workshop earnings, Wayne and his wife had purchased their own publishing company and two hunting and fishing lodges. They had recently bought a summer house in Montana and a winter house in Georgia.

Several lessons can be learned from the experiences of this writer. Even with his bleak school record, Wayne was able to succeed; nevertheless, Wayne would be the first to agree that better composition skills would have made his writing much easier. What contributed most to his success? Wayne loved the out-of-doors. Since childhood, he nurtured a passion for hunting, fishing, and trapping. As he grew older, this passion gradually shifted from killing animals to preservation and conservation. He even took a job as a wildlife ranger on a national game reserve, a job which he loved from the first moment and grew to love even more.

Wayne was fortunate in that he was a modest person who was able to see his weaknesses and even admit them to others. He explained that he was astonished by the acceptance of his articles. "I just wrote about what I enjoyed doing. My articles were nonfiction, focusing on my own experiences." *A key to success for many writers is writing about a subject for which they care passionately.*

HOW DO YOU HANDLE REJECTION?

As an experienced writer and teacher of writing, I always want to respond to this question with fatherly advice and say something like, "I view rejections as evidence of growth." But to the novice, such fatherly advice may sound like "Eat your spinach; it's good for you." Well, as many parents will attest, spinach is good for you—but only if it doesn't cause you to throw up. Similarly, getting rejections may be good for you, but only if they don't cause you to give up. Greg Daugherty, editor of *Money* magazine (1996, p. 28), says that if you haven't been rejected lately, it may mean "you simply aren't trying hard enough."

Perhaps a better response is that *all successful authors get rejections.* Successful writers grow as a result of rejections because they learn from experience. Some aggressive novices ask the editors for advice. They ask the editors of refereed journals for copies of the reviewers' evaluations of their manuscript. With this feedback in hand, rejections can become painful blessings.

Perhaps the best advice for dealing with rejections is to *study the rejections immediately, make the necessary improvements, and promptly send the manuscript to another publisher.* If no feedback is received, either ask for it, or quickly examine your returned manuscript for editorial marks. Then make the needed corrections, put the manuscript and a self-addressed stamped envelope in an envelope, and send it to another publisher. Remember, *sometimes the reasons behind rejections are unrelated to the quality of the manuscript.*

There are two reasons for handling rejections hastily. If you leave the rejection on your desk, you will dwell on it—even if only in your subconscious—and it seems to grow. Second, by promptly sending the manuscript out again, you decrease the time between acceptances, and this increases your number of publications. If your manuscript has any value at all, there is likely to be some correlation between your number of acceptances and the time that your manuscript spends on an editor's desk.

After twenty years of writing, I still get rejections, and each one has a little sting. But each rejection brings a smile as I think, "That's O.K. I've been rejected before, and I can take pride in knowing that I've been rejected by the very best."

Experienced authors know that some of their time is better spent planning to avoid rejections. Jesus Garcia uses an approach that is both preventive and objective. He has worked out a method to reduce rejections and a method to deal with rejections objectively.

Rejection should not be the most difficult part of writing, but it is. I suspect potential authors do not write for publication because they do not wish to deal with rejection. I learned early in my writing career that I would need to develop my own mechanism for addressing rejection. After a few rejections, I sat down and developed a process.

First, I always attempt to develop quality manuscripts. Usually, when I have a manuscript rejected, it is not because it is poorly written or poorly put together. Nor is it because my idea was not well thought out.

Second, I target the manuscript for at least two journals. If one rejects it, I send it to the other.

Third, when I receive a rejection I read the cover letter and file the manuscript for a week.

Fourth, after the hurt has subsided, I return to the manuscript and read the cover letter and the constructive criticism provided on a rating sheet or on the manuscript. (If no constructive comments are provided, I send the manuscript to the second journal).

Fifth, when constructive criticism is provided, I weigh the comments and make those changes I feel are warranted. I then send the manuscript to the second journal.

Individuals wishing to write for publication should not copy my approach but develop a mechanism that is reflective of their own personalities.

Garcia's effort to develop a quality manuscript before sending it to an editor saves time and disappointment. His process of carefully scrutinizing and using criticisms to improve the manuscript is wise. This may be difficult when readers are unkind, but remember that, left unchanged, the manuscript might affect others in equally negative ways. Garcia's concluding advice is the voice of experience; individual authors must develop their own systems for dealing with rejection.

WHAT DISTINGUISHES HIGHLY SUCCESSFUL WRITERS FROM LESS SUCCESSFUL WRITERS?

Apart from their degree of commitment to learning the basics of good writing and applying them with diligence, *highly successful writers usually have several projects going simultaneously.* At any time, highly successful writers have a couple of investigations under way, two or more manuscripts partially completed, and several manuscripts being considered by editors. In contrast, the novice writer often uses a linear approach to writing, writing one draft, then

correcting and revising the draft, then polishing it, then sending a query letter, then waiting for a response, then sending the manuscript, and then waiting for months or years for a response. For this type of writer, the highest
success rate possible is one or two acceptances a year.

IS IT O.K. TO SEND A MANUSCRIPT
TO MULTIPLE PUBLISHERS?

Simultaneous submission of article manuscripts to multiple publishers is
nothing short of Russian roulette. The desperate writer who plays this game
never considers the possible adverse consequences. Put simply, multiple submissions can produce multiple acceptances. Then, the writer must decide
which journal to reject. Editors like rejections even less than writers do—for
editors invest not only their own time but also their reviewers' time evaluating manuscripts. Editors also plan issues so that manuscripts complement
each other. When one of these manuscripts is abruptly withdrawn, a unique
piece of the jigsaw puzzle is missing. Because most journals operate on a tight
schedule and may operate behind schedule, there simply isn't time to locate
a satisfactory replacement for a withdrawn manuscript.

Despite the problems created, multiple submissions is a frequent occur-
rence. It has caused such a problem that some publishers and societies have
written codes forbidding this practice. For example, the American Sociological Society has a written policy published in its journals to remedy the situation (see Figure 9.1).

An author who refuses to let a publisher print an accepted manuscript
should be prepared to have this door of opportunity closed in the future, and

FIGURE 9.1   Statement of ASA policy on multiple submission.

Submission of manuscripts to a professional journal clearly implies commitment to publish in that journal. The competition for journal space requires a
great deal of time and effort on the part of editorial readers whose main
compensation for this service is the opportunity to read papers prior to
publication and the gratification associated with discharge of professional
obligations. For these reasons the ASA regards submission of a manuscript to a
professional journal while that paper is under review by another journal as
unacceptable.

Section 11, B4, ASA Code of Ethics

no serious writers can afford to shut out any possible markets for their manuscripts. The alternative is even worse; allowing different publishers to publish the same manuscript would be professional suicide. The bottom line for writers is: *don't make simultaneous submissions to journals.*

This advice applies to journal manuscripts only. For books, multiple submissions are acceptable and they are recommended, but only when used according to the process described in Chapter 10.

ARE THERE ADVANTAGES IN COLLABORATING?

If you find the right partner, collaborating can offer several advantages. *The most important quality to seek in a partnership is similar personality.* For example, if you have a Type-A personality and feel compelled to get your work done on time, you should never work with a Type-B who thinks a deadline is the sign that it's time to start working on the job. Such an arrangement is equally painful for both partners.

When personalities are compatible, collaborating can bring out the best in all. Each partner stimulates the other. The unique expertise of each writer complements that of the others. For academicians who are required to publish, collaborating can accelerate the rate of publishing of all partners. But, even under the best of circumstances, all writers should go solo part of the time; otherwise, they become vulnerable to the criticism that they let others write for them. A few articles of your own can nullify such a charge.

Should you decide to collaborate, you will need to produce a product that is consistent and coherent. A good method to achieve these goals is to have each collaborator edit the entire manuscript. Each edit will remove some incoherence and inconsistency.

I asked Tom Good if he would share some of his insights on collaborating. Here is his response:

I have had the pleasure of publishing a lot of my work with coauthors. This experience, although sometimes awkward (why must my coauthor be in Tibet or at the condo when page proofs arrive?) has provided an important context for learning. Differences of opinion (theoretical values; what constitutes a good example; what represents valid evidence) have to be seriously confronted and negotiated successfully. Hence, issues one might "conveniently avoid" become opportunities for new learning. For example, I have learned much about Piagetian theory from Jere Brophy, my long-time coauthor who teaches at Michigan State University, and I have learned much about socially situated learning and Vygotskian theory from Mary McCaslin, who teaches at Arizona University.

SHOULD I COLLABORATE LONG DISTANCE?

Some special advantages and limitations can be realized when authors collaborate over long distances. Perhaps the limitations are more obvious. For example, there is the delay in sending manuscripts through the mail. Facsimile machines and electronic mail are improving these conditions and making long distance collaboration more feasible. But in some fashion collaborators should read, edit, and rewrite their partners' work. Otherwise, the manuscript is likely to lack a uniform tone and consistent style.

A second limitation of collaborating long distance is the increased likelihood of miscommunication. As an author who has collaborated long distance on about a dozen books, I will share an example of this limitation. On one of my book projects, one of the coauthors wrote a chapter and sent it to the others as a model. Receiving the chapter, one of the authors took great care to ensure that his drafted chapters had the same pedagogical subheadings. Later, when we met to go over their chapters, the coauthor who sent the sample chapter explained that the subheadings were optional and perhaps should differ according to content. His purpose for sending the sample chapter had been to show the other authors the length that his chapter set for certain parts—a feature that some authors had not thought important.

But, with care, these difficulties can be handled. An advantage of collaborating long distance is that it brings to the work a broader range of perspectives, which improves the product and allows each collaborator to develop awareness and insight that can only be gained through long-distance collaboration. Whether the advantages outweigh the disadvantages depends on the collaborators, their differences in expertise, and the topic of the book. A look at the number of textbook authors who collaborate over a long distance is testimony that for many the process does work, and for many it works extremely well.

SHOULD I WRITE ARTICLES BEFORE WRITING SHORT STORIES OR BOOKS?

The best answer to this question is probably "yes." Article writing is excellent preparation for writing nonfiction books, and writing short stories is good preparation for writing fiction books. Article writing provides the opportunity to develop important writing skills. For those who wish to strengthen their ability to get a new job and for those who need to fill their résumés to earn merit pay, promotion, or tenure, article writing is usually a far better investment of their time than book writing.

WHAT IS A REFEREED JOURNAL?

At institutions of higher education, no term is more common among faculty members than "refereed journal." The extent of its use is exceeded, however, only by the degree to which it is misunderstood. Although to everyone the word *refereed* reflects scholarship, when cornered, even among those who so readily use the term, few could accurately define it.

Although the academic world disagrees on the many definitions of *refereed journal,* most academicians would readily agree that journal refereeing has three common characteristics: *where, how* and *by whom* the refereeing occurs.

Generally, the jurors or referees are considered to be peers in the profession (see Figure 9.2.) At some journals, referees are carefully chosen for their reputations and because they are recognized throughout their field as experts. Some journal editors who claim refereed status for their journals would argue that they themselves are qualified referees. Another aspect of refereeing is location. Some people think that all refereed processes must be nationwide because it ensures a national viewpoint as opposed to a provincial perspective; others consider the location of little consequence. Many professional journals are published on large university campuses. Some of the editors of these journals send each manuscript to a colleague in the appropriate department on their campus. Others would even argue that refereeing can and does occur in the editor's office.

Perhaps a more important criterion than either *who* evaluates the manuscripts or *where* the manuscripts are reviewed is *how* the manuscripts are evaluated. The most loosely conducted evaluations consist merely of the reviewers' subjective opinions. Some evaluators use rating scales to make their judgments. The most rigid evaluators provide evaluation instruments to referees across the country and conduct the reviews anonymously.

FIGURE 9.2   **Refereeing occurs in degrees.**

	Criteria

Third Degree
    meets all three
    criteria
	Is refereed by experts throughout the country.
	Editor provides a rating instrument.
	Referee process is conducted anonymously.

Second Degree
    meets two of the
    three criteria
	Is refereed by experts throughout the country.
	Editor provides a rating instrument.
	Referee process is conducted anonymously.

First Degree
    meets only one of
    the criteria
	Is refereed by experts throughout the country.
	Editor provides a rating instrument.
	Referee process is conducted anonymously.

IS IT WISE TO USE VANITY PUBLISHERS?

Vanity publishers are those who require their authors to pay all or part of the publishing costs. Sometimes this type of publisher may be a good choice; usually it is not. Suppose you have something important to say in a book, and you have tried several commercial publishers but all of these publishers have declined to publish your work. Suppose the content is accurate but the market for the book is too small to make it profitable. So, you cannot get a contract from a commercial publisher. One alternative is to turn to a vanity publisher. (You could also choose to publish it yourself.) But suppose you don't have the money that is required to pay for the printing and materials; and suppose the vanity press requires only that you use the book in your classes. Vanity publishing might provide your only option.

Under most circumstances a vanity publisher would be a poor choice. For example, suppose your main motive for having a book published is to accrue academic prestige or academic rewards. Most academic institutions place far less value on works that are published by vanity presses. Some colleges even refuse to recognize vanity publications. The reason is clear; unlike other publishers, vanity publishers seldom send the manuscript off to be evaluated anonymously by experts, and, for a fee, some vanity publishers will publish almost anything. Likewise, if your goal is to produce a very successful book, one that is recognized as a leading textbook or a leading professional book, many vanity publishers would not have the marketing capabilities needed to make their books highly competitive with those published by other publishers. Indeed, most vanity presses provide very little marketing support for their authors' books.

WHAT ABOUT SELF-PUBLISHING?

Like vanity publishing, the self-published author must bear the expenses—and like vanity books they seldom prove to be a route to professional recognition, fortune, or fame.

The self-published author is always subject to suspicion. This suspicion may or may not be warranted. For example, suppose Professor Jones writes a book and later discovers that she cannot find a recognized publisher who is willing to publish it. Many colleagues will conclude that it is because the book is shallow or that it is full of errors. This could be true, but there are other reasons for rejections. For example, the decision to reject a book proposal is often based solely on the publisher's perception of the market size. Sometimes the publisher knows that the market for the book is so small that, even if the book were bought and used by everyone in this specialized field, the sales of the book would not be large enough to make it profitable for the publisher. This introduces my second favorite story.

In the late 1960s two professors at a Midwestern university developed a prospectus for a book aimed at a new market. They contacted several publishers and were consistently told that such a market did not exist. Convinced otherwise, these authors went to a local press, designed a layout, and paid to have 2,000 copies of this new book printed. Using a small mailer which they also designed and paid a printer to produce, they quickly sold the 2,000 copies and immediately printed a second 2,000 copies. The success of the book prompted the authors to write and self-publish a second edition. The second edition was more successful than the first. As you might guess, the second edition led to a third edition. The book is now in its tenth edition and its sales have exceeded 40,000 copies, all mailed directly from the home of one of the authors. Obviously, these authors are pleased with their decision to self-publish. Such success stories make self-publishing sound attractive, yet such success may be more a product of the authors' own capabilities and commitment than of the merits of the self-publishing process itself.

If you have a book inside you that must come out at any expense, self-publishing may be a viable option for you to consider; however, the odds against a self-published book reaching this level of success are gigantic.

IF ASKED, SHOULD I PAY A JOURNAL PUBLISHING EXPENSES?

For decades journals in some disciplines, particularly some of the sciences, have required their contributing authors to pay for certain publishing expenses such as the costs of graphs, charts, and page proofs. In recent years, additional disciplines (such as education) have begun charging such costs to their contributors. Because some professional journals do not sell advertisements, charging expenses to contributors is often considered acceptable—but as an incentive to get faculty members to publish, many colleges and departments pay part or all of these expenses.

A few journals charge their contributors a reading fee. Many professionals find this practice unacceptable, unprofessional, and a contrivance to make money.

SHOULD I BE A SPECIALIST OR A GENERALIST?

As many aspiring authors think about their futures, they are uncertain whether they will benefit more from becoming a specialist or generalist. This decision is tough. It depends on the author's writing goals. If your purpose is to earn recognition in a particular field, the nature of the subject may restrict you to publishing in only one or two specific journals. If your field of expertise does not restrict your publishing so severely, there may be much benefit in your writing for a wide array of journals. The wider the range of your topics and audiences, the greater the number of outlets you will have for your manuscripts. Writing for a wide range of journals also enables you to reach more varied audiences and to indulge in different kinds of writing. You may have knowledge that can benefit groups outside your own academic major, and because they do not read your journals, the only way to reach them is through publishing in their journals.

Still another benefit of being a generalist is the opportunity it gives you to learn about the knowledge bases in other fields. This is important in that you can enrich your own knowledge base by studying several fields. For example, all administrators need to understand principles of leadership, and all fields have studies that contribute significantly to the understanding of leadership theory. Those who write for publication on this topic should at least review the leadership literature in other disciplines.

QUESTIONS REGARDING COPYRIGHT

1. Exactly what is meant by copyright? Copyright is the legal right that all authors and other artists have to prohibit others from copying their work. Some of the copyright laws have changed, making the author's job of keeping up with them challenging.

2. How long is the copyright valid? The time of endurance of copyright has changed. The length of coverage depends on the date of the copyright. To determine whether a work is still under copyright protection, first check the date to see if it is before 1950. If so, the work will be under protection for 75 years beyond the copyright date.

For works published between 1950 and 1977, the copyright will endure for 56 years. For works published since 1978, the copyright extends throughout the life of the author plus 50 years.

3. Are all published works subject to copyright laws? No. Works such as government documents are under public domain. This means that you can use them as you wish, but to help the reader locate these works and to show professional courtesy to their authors, you should always cite the source.

4. Can I ever quote copyrighted works without securing permission? Yes. Fair-use guidelines permit you to quote up to 300 words from a book.

You can also quote up to 10 percent of an article. But should you wish to quote from a poem or song, be careful; the laws are more restrictive for these works. Diagrams, charts, and photos also require permission, regardless how small or how few you are using. Photos also require signed releases or permission from each recognizable person. Children's photos require signatures of the child's parent or guardian. At best, most of the copyright laws are "fuzzy," leaving you the responsibility to use your own judgment to determine what is honest and fair.

5. Does this mean that I should avoid using ideas and facts that I have discovered in books and journals? No. Facts and ideas themselves are not copyrighted. Many beginning authors limit themselves unnecessarily because they are afraid to use ideas that they may have read in a book, magazine, or other printed material.

For example, suppose you are writing about the water cycle: Rain turns into runoff, which eventually evaporates, later condensing to form clouds, which in turn condense to form rain. This is a well-known process, and you need not quote any source or ask for permission to use it. But if you wish to lift a description of the process verbatim from a book or magazine, this would require permission.

You could also draw a graphic representation of the water cycle without seeking permission, but if you want to copy an existing diagram, you will need to seek permission.

6. To whom should I write for permission? First, notice who holds the copyright. If you can tell that it is the publisher, write the publisher. If it is the author, you still may need to write to the publisher to secure the author's address.

7. How can I get my works copyrighted? There are three ways a writer can get copyright protection. You could write the copyright office at:

> Register of Copyrights
> Copyright Office
> Library of Congress
> Washington, DC 20559

A second way to get copyright protection is to put a small c inside a circle, followed by the date on your new work.
Example: © 1994 by Hilda Monza

A third way to get copyright protection is just to write down your ideas and then do nothing. As soon as you put your ideas into writing, the writing itself automatically becomes subject to copyright laws.

HOW CAN AUTHORS LEARN TO USE
THE LIBRARY MORE EFFECTIVELY?

Because I am no expert in this field, I turned to someone who is, Dr. Toby Graham, who offers the following help.

Over the past decade, information technology has changed the environment in which researchers work. While a visit to the local library to check out a book, leaf through a reference work, or photocopy a journal article remains a common activity, even more common is the use of virtual information resources on computers within the library, in classrooms and offices across campus, and on desktops across the globe. Researchers use these digital resources to identify the information they need for their work, and in many cases the full text of relevant items also is available online.

Most research libraries now provide access to a massive—and sometimes bewildering—array of online information, including indexes, books, journals, newspapers, inventories of archives and manuscripts, digitized holdings of special collections, lists of useful Web sites, and library catalogs. Much of this is licensed content provided by commercial vendors and, thus, requires special authentication (such as a personal identification number or password) to use outside of the library building.

The key to making sense of the universe of information available at or through the modern research library is connecting with the librarians who select, organize, and support access to these resources. Librarians are trained information professionals with accredited degrees in information studies, and authors should take time to become acquainted with them. Whether in the form of a formal consultation, an informal conversation, or even an electronic mail exchange, serious researchers benefit when they communicate with librarians regarding their information needs. Electronic mail provides an expedient and low-cost opportunity to contact librarians and archivists at repositories across the country or across the world who are experts on a particular subject or may know where key pieces of information to support a research project may reside.

Early on in their research, writers should identify the reference materials most appropriate to their topics. The online catalog of a local university or other research library is a good place to start, as it will provide comprehensive coverage of the books, journals, and other materials held within a particular institution. Increasingly, the records in library catalogs also provide hyperlinks to online information, such as electronic books and journals. Another type of library catalog is WorldCat, a database covering the holdings of libraries across the United States and, to a lesser extent, internationally. Most research libraries provide access to this valuable resource, which can help researchers identify relevant books, journals, archives and manuscripts, audiovisual, and other sources regardless of where they are held. Many of the resources described in WorldCat are available for interli-brary loan.

Research libraries provide access to print indices and electronic data-bases that index the literature of discrete scholarly areas. These reference sources help writers locate journal articles and other information on their topics. For example, ERIC *covers the literature on education, and* America: History and Life *does the same for U.S. history. Using the electronic ver-sions of these publications saves time, and librarians and technologists con-tinue to find sensible ways to connect the citations in these databases to full-text versions of the materials wherever they may reside. Often, this con-tent appears in the electronic versions of scholarly journals to which the li-brary subscribes. Most research libraries also provide access to the JSTOR database, a collection of full-text articles from back issues of journals in the humanities, sciences, and social sciences.*

The World Wide Web is another important source of information for writers. Researchers often approach the Web through commercial search en-gines such as those at www.google.com and www.yahoo.com. The uncon-trolled nature of this vast resource requires that Web researchers become careful and critical consumers of online information. Consulting sites pro-vided by reputable and established organizations or institutions is an impor-tant way to assure that the information derived from the Web is authoritative and reliable. Also, many research libraries provide lists of sites checked by li-brarians and classified by subject matter and discipline.

Web-based academic networks are another helpful information source for writers. Sites such as the Humanities Network (H-Net) and services like the Community of Scholars (COS) alert researchers to grant and fellowship pro-grams in their fields of study as well as offering a venue to connect with po-tential research collaborators.

Successful academic writing is a product of quality research, which, it-self, is tied to the effective use of information resources provided by libraries. Information needs are unique to individual writers. Common to all, how-ever, are the need for a working relationship with librarians, a familiarity with the print and online library resources relevant to researchers' areas of study, and the commitment to continually update information-seeking skills that are required by the evolving information environment in which writers work.

ARE COLLOQUIALISMS AND CLICHÉS ACCEPTABLE?

Colloquialisms offer skilled fiction authors a way to provide authentic descriptions of their characters. But for nonfiction authors, colloquialisms are like inside jokes. They invite miscommunication, leaving the outsider feeling estranged. A good rule for nonfiction writers is to avoid using colloquialisms.

Clichés seldom offer anything that brings quality to a manuscript. They are popular because they are convenient. Frequently, authors use clichés as substitutes when they cannot find the appropriate words to express their ideas. Because of their overuse, clichés soon become objects of boredom. They may identify you as a weak writer.

SHOULD I USE TABLES AND GRAPHS IN MY ARTICLES?

Because tables and graphs are more expensive than words, they should not be used unless they are needed to enhance understanding and unless at least some of the articles in a recent issue of the intended journal use them.

WHAT SHOULD I DO WHEN AN EDITOR KEEPS HOLDING MY MANUSCRIPT?

At one workshop I conducted a participant said, "This editor has promised to give my coauthor and me a decision several times but always misses the deadlines. My coauthor wants to choke him. What should we do?"

My first advice was "Don't choke the editor." I realize that this editor has been unfair, and fairness is definitely a two-way street; yet, nothing would be gained from squaring off against the editor. On the contrary, something would be lost; you would eliminate one target journal for your future manuscripts. Perhaps one thing would be gained; you would have your manuscript back and would be free to go to another publisher. But you can do that without shutting off this one.

Calmly write a letter saying something like, "If I haven't heard from you by (include month and day), I will assume that you are no longer interested in this manuscript and will pursue this project with other publishers. Thank you for your continuing interest in this manuscript." This course of action should reclaim your manuscript and leave you on good terms with the editor. Should the editor fail to respond, soon after the designated deadline, go ahead and resubmit the manuscript to another publisher. Be careful to file a copy of this correspondence with your manuscript to be used as evidence of your innocence, should you end up with two acceptances.

WHOSE NAME COMES FIRST?

If your collaborators are colleagues, the person who initiated the manuscript should have the privilege of being listed first. If I asked you to join me in writing a manuscript, I would probably generate the first draft or at least an outline, and I would probably specify exactly what I considered your work role in this project. With your approval, I would even set deadline dates for the completion of the various stages of the project. These actions would make me the originator, organizer, and manager—and would entitle me to the placement as first author.

I have developed a system of collaboration that eliminates the possibility of conflict—I do not ask anyone to collaborate with me on just one article. When I initiate one idea, I make it clear that I expect the collaborator(s) to come up with an idea for a second article. For that article, the originator would be the first author. Remember, the sooner you specify what's expected of all parties, the fewer misunderstandings you will have.

WHO IS LISTED FIRST IF THE COLLABORATORS ARE PROFESSORS AND GRADUATE STUDENTS?

Some graduate advisors encourage their students to write for publication. Even more admirable, some professors collaborate with students. If an article reports a student's research performed in support of the thesis or dissertation (which of course, belongs to the student), fairness dictates that the first article generated from the study also belongs to the student. Therefore, I would insist that the student be listed as first author.

Many theses and dissertations have enough data for more than one article. Should the professor collaborate with this student on a second article, the professor would usually take the lead in writing the second article and should be listed as the first author.

IF I FURNISH MY DISSERTATION OR THESIS FOR A COLLABORATOR TO SHAPE INTO A MANUSCRIPT, IS THAT AN EQUITABLE EXCHANGE?

I don't believe I know anyone who would be willing to undertake the interpretation of someone else's work. I wouldn't feel competent to do the job unless perhaps I had served as the committee chair for the study. The first article from a study should be drafted by the student who conducted the study.

As to the question of equity, beginning authors often perceive the difference between a dissertation and an article to be small, only requiring a few adjustments here and there. I know this because as a guest editor I have received theses that have had only minor tinkering. But, these papers seldom, if ever, are accepted for publication. Actually, the task of converting a thesis into an article is tantamount to writing an article from scratch. The study provides the data; that's a lot, but it isn't enough to justify getting your name on an article.

IF I SHARE A BOOK IDEA WITH A PUBLISHER, HOW CAN I BE SURE IT WON'T BE TURNED OVER TO A MORE EXPERIENCED AUTHOR?

This suspicion raises its head in almost every workshop I teach. My first response is to share my own personal perception, which is based on 20 years of submitting book prospectuses. Most editors are too honest to try such a stunt. Publishing houses need to retain credibility with authors, and the potential gain in such shady dealings would be outweighed over the long haul by loss of reputation with potential authors. Most publishing companies are in business for the long run.

But as I give this response I see that worried look on the questioner's face, and I remember how important this question is to an individual who wants to protect a really great idea, so I offer the following advice. If you are still worried that the editor might give your idea to an experienced author, before sharing your idea, begin to develop it. Begin working on some of the chapters so that when you do approach an editor you are far enough ahead in the project that you can finish it long before anyone else could write it.

WHAT DOES IT MEAN WHEN AN EDITOR ASKS THE AUTHOR TO REWRITE AND RESUBMIT A MANUSCRIPT? SHOULD I DO THAT?

Occasionally editors neither accept nor reject a manuscript. Instead, they write or phone the authors and ask them to revise the manuscript. Sometimes authors ask me how they should respond to such a request. I tell them: First, let's determine what this request means, or what it tells us about the editor's view of the manuscript; then, let's consider how rewriting and resubmitting a manuscript affects its chances of being accepted.

According to my latest questionnaire returns, professional journal editors receive about five times as many manuscripts as they have undesignated space in their journal. This means that most editors probably have enough good manuscripts to fill the next several issues of their journal. If that's so, why don't they just reject your manuscript instead of asking you to rewrite it? The answer is probably one of the following:

1. They see a good "fit" between the manuscript topic and the journal (which is to say that your topic is of interest to their readers).
2. The editor believes that your manuscript offers a worthwhile contribution (which is to say that the editor believes that you have something important to contribute).

The next essential consideration is how a resubmitted manuscript's chance for acceptance compares to that of an original submission. For that information let's consult the survey responses.

Contrary to some people's suspicions that a resubmitted manuscript will automatically be accepted, most editors indicate that they send the resubmitted manuscripts for review. Sometimes the author is asked to rewrite the manuscript a second or third time. But the good news is that 75 percent of all resubmitted manuscripts are eventually accepted, compared to a 15 percent acceptance rate for original submissions. This means that rewriting a manuscript to meet the requests of the editor improves its chances for acceptance by 500 percent. For me, the answer is clear; I usually honor the editor's request by making as many of the requested changes as I find comfortable. So my advice is: gladly accept this offer and give the rewrite close attention to meet all of the editor's requests.

One editor responding to the survey (Henson, 1993) said, "A revise and resubmit recommendation indicates interest in eventual publication. If possible, look at recommended revisions as positive attempts to improve the manuscript. The most successful authors are those who revise well."

SHOULD I USE A COMPUTER?

This is a question that must be answered by each writer. Since I cannot think as freely and clearly with typing as I can while writing, I prefer to put the first draft in script. But, I have known individuals who, I am convinced, can think more clearly when they have their fingers on the keyboard. I suggest that you decide which system affords you the opportunity to think clearly, and then use that system.

I asked a couple of authors for their views on using computers. Robert Maddox, Associate Professor of Business at the University of Tennessee, says:

There is, I believe, no way to write except by using a computer. Legal pad and pencil or typewriter just do not work. The ability to load tons of files of notes in the computer, to move around in these notes, and to switch from these notes to the document on which you are working (carrying some of the material with you) is invaluable as a time saver. I think that using a computer also helps me overcome the problem of having to discipline myself to write. I used to find it difficult to put words on paper when they had that permanent quality of going on paper. However, using a computer, I feel freer to get words down, knowing that poorly thought out or stated ideas can easily be deleted or changed.

WHAT SHOULD I LIST ON MY RÉSUMÉ AS PUBLICATIONS?

Academic writers have a difficult job deciding what to list in their résumés under the heading "Publications." Obviously, some find this decision very easy; they use the same process that many academicians use when applying for promotion or tenure. The rule seems to be, if it fits in a pickup truck, include it.

For those who are a bit more selective, several questions arise. A common question concerns "in press" publications. This is a great camouflage term. Some evaluators are willing to believe that "in press" means the manuscript has been accepted and is sitting suspended on a launching pad about to blast off. But others are more skeptical. Professor Allen Berger (1985) of Miami University teaches Writing for Publication courses, and he says that to him "in press" means only that the person knows his way to the post office and is able to buy stamps.

Writers also ask if they should list meeting proceedings. The answer depends on the discipline. Some disciplines place considerable weight on meeting proceedings, but others do not. For example, in education, meeting proceedings have little meaning as evidence of scholarly achievement because usually they are not evaluated and therefore are not weighted heavily as evidence of scholarship.

My advice is, unless you know that it can significantly add to your credits, do not list it. By including questionable evidence, candidates run the risk of discrediting their complete résumé.

DO YOU RECOMMEND USING SUPPORT GROUPS?

I like this idea. In fact, when giving writing workshops on college campuses, I always recommend this to the audience. I believe beginning writers need support, which is unlikely to come from outside. If conducted properly, other benefits can come from such an organization. Consider the following guidelines:

First, be systematic and set aside the same day(s) for such meetings, say the first Monday in every month. Second, keep the meetings short. Brown bag luncheons work well for most groups. Third, have a designated speaker and topic for each meeting. Some speakers can be members of the group, but invited guests can also contribute significantly. For suggested topics, check the chapters of this book. You might ask a successful author from any department on campus to give a 20- to 30-minute presentation on "Why I write for publication" or "How I find topics" or "How I choose my target journals." Or you might ask a researcher to speak on developing and using questionnaires. A prolific English professor might be willing to speak for 20 to 30 minutes on "Writing lead sentences" or "Getting the reader's attention." Also, other departments on campus have some book authors. I would hold an occasional meeting aimed at motivating and reinforcing the desire to write.

RECAPPING THE MAJOR POINTS

Most questions that plague writers are perennial. For years these questions have baffled and impeded the success of writers, and they will continue to present problems for writers. Simply try to remember:

- Most successful writers immensely enjoy writing; they are compelled to write by a need to say something that they feel must be said.
- To become a successful writer, you must believe in your abilities, and you must write often.
- The best way to handle rejections is to repair the rejected manuscript and immediately send it to another publisher.
- Highly successful writers have two or three manuscripts under way while two or three others are being considered.
- Authors should never simultaneously submit a manuscript to multiple journals.
- Collaborating on writing projects with colleagues can provide needed motivation and opportunities to learn from your colleagues, while expediting your writing program. Such success depends on finding partners with similar personalities and work habits.
- Tables and graphs are more expensive to print than words and, therefore, should be used only when the journals to which you submit manuscripts use them and only when they communicate messages clearer than written comments.
- For the beginner, time is best invested in writing for national journals.
- There are several definitions of *refereed journals*. To make your writing program pay off, learn how your institution defines "refereed," and act accordingly.
- Vanity publishing is seldom a good choice for authors.
- Self-publishing is usually a better choice than vanity publishing—but only if you can both afford it and tolerate the risk involved.

REFERENCE

Daugherty, G. (1996, January). Get motivated . . . and stay motivated. *Money Magazine*, pp. 28–29.

10

GETTING BOOK CONTRACTS

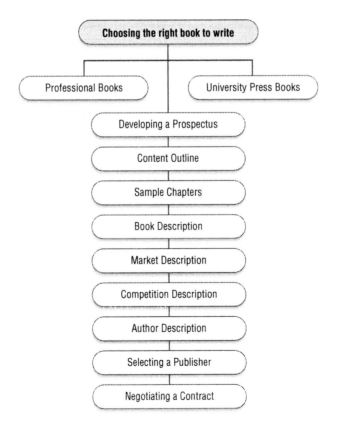

For most people, the act of getting a contract for a book has always been a chore; it's getting harder. Before the economic recession of the 1970s, many editors couldn't seem to find enough authors. Although in some fields, editors still vigorously pursue authors to write specific nonfiction books, such as college textbooks, an aspiring textbook author should not wait for an editor's knock on the door. The economics of publishing has made acquisitions editors cautious. If you have an idea for a book, carefully plan a strategy to pursue the publishers, rather than hoping they will pursue you. Writing a book is enormously time consuming, with no success guaranteed. If you still are determined to write a book, take the time needed to do it right. You can do it.

CHOOSING THE RIGHT BOOK TO WRITE

Some people decide to write books but go no further than making the decision. Others write complete manuscripts and never succeed in getting them published. Some of the major obstacles include procrastination, striving for perfection, and ignorance about the roles of authors, editors, and agents.

Before putting pen to paper or fingers to keyboard, take a moment to reflect on the type of book you wish to write. Is it fiction or nonfiction? Is it a how-to book or a self-help book? Is its major function to inform or to entertain? Is it a professional book or a textbook? If it's a textbook, for what grade level is it intended? Generally, the larger the general market for a book, the harder the writer must work to beat out the competition.

WRITING PROFESSIONAL BOOKS

An overlooked market that is available to all professionals, regardless of profession or content expertise, is the professional book market. Usually written by individuals who have considerable experience in the workplace (although the length of experience varies), these books are often written by scholars of scholars and leaders of leaders. In psychology, Joyce Brothers is a leading author. In business, one readily thinks of Tom Peters, or in pediatric medicine one thinks of T. Berry Brazelton. All of these authors have been exceptionally successful, although it did not occur overnight. Most writers of professional books do not gain such recognition, but no one should be discouraged from writing professional books. Those who succeed in getting contracts in this market usually combine the expertise gained from coursework with new insights gathered from research, surveys, or on-the-job experience.

In a sense, writing professional books is an extension of writing for professional journals. Both outlets provide opportunities to advance the profession while establishing professional credibility for the author. Like writing for university presses, the professional market offers opportunities for reaching particular markets that are difficult or impossible for other publishers to reach.

Before choosing a publisher for your professional book manuscript, be aware that only a few publishers can reach this specialized market. For example, university professors and business people write many professional books. One might assume that college textbook publishers would be a good choice for targeting these manuscripts, but usually they are not. Textbooks are sold in multiple adoptions. A professor might order enough copies for one or more sections of a course or a committee may adopt several hundred copies for multiple sections of an introductory course.

In contrast, professional books are marketed for single copy sales. Since very few textbook companies can afford to advertise for single sales, you should be sure your intended publisher publishes and sells to a single adoption audience. *The Writer's Market* is an excellent source for identifying publishers of professional books and other particular types of books.

WRITING BOOKS FOR UNIVERSITY PRESSES

University presses can be an excellent outlet for certain books—but you must take time to learn the nature of these institutions. First, the royalties earned on these books are generally less than on commercially published books. Although the royalty rates of some of these books may equal that of their commercial counterparts, the dollars received do not. At least three factors work together to make this so.

First, university presses publish for specialized markets that are usually smaller than the markets for trade and other nonfiction books. Second, most university presses do not have the financial support needed to market books as extensively as do commercial publishers. Most university presses do not have full-time sales representatives in the field nor do they depend on sales profits for all of their funds. Third, although many university presses are not insensitive to sales earnings, most have other sources of support; therefore, they are not forced to sell large numbers of books. When commercial publishers fall short on sales, they have no alternative sources of funds on which to draw.

The fledgling author may ask, "Then why do authors ever seek to have their works published by university presses?" This question has more than one good answer. Because some authors' topics are so specific, the university press is their only hope of getting their book manuscripts published. With small markets, even self-publishing is seldom a good alternative. For example, a professor who wishes to publish a book on the history of native Americans could not find a more likely publisher for this work than the University of Oklahoma Press. For publishing a book on gambling and gaming, the University of Nevada Press would be an excellent choice. For a manuscript on archaeology, a writer might query the University of Michigan Press or the University of Pittsburgh Press. For a book on anthropology, an author might contact the University of Arizona Press, the University of Iowa Press, the University of New Mexico Press, or the University of Pittsburgh Press. Many of the university presses focus on books that are of interest to their own geographic region. Several publish books on Americans. Appendix E contains a listing of university presses and the subject areas in which they specialize.

The point here is to avoid sending a manuscript or query to a university press until you first know the topic on which the particular press generally publishes. In addition to finding the university presses to be your best chance for some topics, professors and other professional scholars often prefer these presses because most of them stress scholarship. Some have as their main mission the advancement of particular academic fields of study.

DEVELOPING A PROSPECTUS

Having decided to write a book, the next decision that confronts you is whether to first write the book and then seek a publisher or to begin by seeking a publisher. Writing a book requires an enormous investment of time and energy. To avoid the risk of having the investment result in an unpublishable manuscript, a plausible alternative is to develop a prospectus. Because it also saves time for the editors, most publishers require a prospectus. A good prospectus contains the following parts:

1. Contents outline
2. Sample chapters
3. Book description
4. Market description
5. Competition description
6. Author description

Content Outline

Moving from the would-be-book-writer category to that of a published author begins with getting an overall mental picture of the book you want to write. Begin by making a list of all the major topics (chapters) you plan to include. Then fill in the subtopics you intend to cover within each chapter. How-to books and self-help books might require only tables of contents because of the degree of detail and structure. Chapter outlines are usually much more detailed than tables of contents, and therefore more appropriate in some cases.

For example, Figure 10.1 shows the contents page in James J. Kilpatrick's book *The Writer's Art*. Notice that some of these titles give clues about the contents. We might suppose that Chapter One will offer some analysis and criticism of the English language and that Chapter Two will emphasize the need for clarity in writing, but only the author knows what Chapter Three is about. Because most of these titles just sort of make the reader feel good, they are inviting and functional. But the acquisitions editor will want more. Some acquisitions editors ask to see the entire manuscript.

Compare Kilpatrick's contents section (Figure 10.1) to Dale Baughman's contents page for *Baughman's Handbook of Humor* shown in Figure 10.2. As you can see, even the contents section for nonfiction how-to and self-help books can be detailed and descriptive; each entry is succinct. Robert Hochheiser achieves the art of entertaining while informing the reader with the contents page in *How to Work for a Jerk* (see Figure 10.3).

Other types of nonfiction books, such as textbooks or professional books, have formal chapters. These books demand a more detailed chapter outline. Figure 10.4 shows one chapter outline from each of two college textbooks.

When you consider that the education textbook has 20 chapters and 510 pages, and some other books have well over 1,000 pages, the need for detailed chapter outlines becomes obvious. Detailed chapter outlines help writers conceptualize and organize the enormous quantity of information in these books so it is comprehensible to their readers. Content outlines also help acquisitions editors understand the overall purpose and nature of the book, in addition to assuring the editor that the author has fully planned the project.

FIGURE 10.1   Sample chapter outline for a how-to book.

Contents

Foreword

Introduction

1. How Fares the English Language?
2. Faith, Hope, and Clarity
3. Beyond the Toothpaste Tube
4. The Things We Ought Not to Do
5. The Things We Ought to Be Doing
6. The Tools We Live By
7. My Crotchets and Your Crotchets
8. The Games We Play

FIGURE 10.2 More detailed content outline for a how-to book.

The Practical Value of Humor in Education

Section 1: Types of Humor and Application in Education
The pun • The limerick • Comic verse • The gag • The joke • The anecdote • Rustic humor • One-liners • Riddles • Boners • The tongue twister • Publication bloopers • Fun with words • Report-card-day shock • Seasonal and holiday humor • Communications humor • Teacher dilemmas • Adolescent dilemmas • Kindergarten kapers • Student masterpieces • Examination humor • The double blunder • Parent perplexities • PTA humor • The fable • Satire • Plain nonsense

Section 2: How, When and Where to Use Humor in Education

The Nature of Humor

The Functions of Humor
Social lubricant • Safety valve • Therapy • Tonic • Sixth sense • Survival kit • Motivation and cognitive challenge

The Phenomenon of Laughter

Laughter and Learning

Laughing at One's Self

Joy in the Schools

Sources of Humor

The Many Ways to Use Humor in Education
Diagnosis • Humanizing • Democratic living • Variety and unpre-dictability • Tension reducer • Openers • Preoccupied minds • To make a point • Holidays and vacations • The mischief of language

References

Sample Chapters

The first chapter serves as a foundation for the following chapters; thus, many publishers specifically ask to see the first chapter. So you should begin by writing Chapter One. Then peruse your content outline and choose another chapter or two you think will be the best and most representative of the whole book. When you have written and polished Chapter One and one or two additional chapters, they will become the significant part of your prospectus.

FIGURE 10.3   Contents section that both entertains and informs.

CONTENTS

1. They Do It on Purpose
Why bosses act like jerks, and how they get away with it.

2. The Cast of Characters
Identifying the type of boss you have and determining how to deal with him.

3. Dilettantes, Fops, Experts, and Other Meatheads
Assorted losers do reach the top. Here's how to get the upper hand with them.

4. Corporate Dinosaurs
Entrepreneurs as they evolve from fearless to fearful.

5. Inhuman Resourcefulness
How jerks get hired. The schemes bosses use to avoid rewarding us. Counterattacking those schemes.

6. Politics
An assortment of unprincipled principles for dealing with uncooperative bosses, colleagues, and subordinates.

7. If You're Also a Boss
Motivating your people to work for you, not against you. Mutual indispensability and how it works. The importance of compatibility. How to hire good people.

8. It's Only a Job
Putting your job in perspective as a means to an end. Controlling your ego. Dealing with egocentric bosses. Creative selfishness. When and how to be assertive. Setting goals. What to do when nothing works.

Book Description

You must describe your book clearly and succinctly. For example, "This is a general secondary and middle school methods textbook for undergraduate classes." Then tell the major features of the product. I used the following strengths to "sell" a book that is now in its sixth edition (Henson, 1996), *Methods and Strategies for Teaching in Secondary and Middle Schools:*

> *It is comprehensive [it has all of those chapters commonly found in secondary and middle school methods texts]. It is timely [it has those new chapters that are not commonly found in methods texts]. For example, it contains a chapter on educational reform, a chapter on educational technology, an annotated bibliography on simulations and games (complete with addresses of sources), and a resource list for teaching thinking skills.*

FIGURE 10.4   Detailed chapter outlines for textbooks.

Chapter 7: Effective Schools
    Objectives
    Pretest
    Introduction
    Defining Effective Schools
    School Climate
    Positive Discipline and Control
    The Role of the School Principal
    Providing for Staff Development
    Monitoring of Clearly Established Goals & Objectives
    The Importance of Autonomy
    Parent Involvement
    Recapitulation of Major Ideas
    Summary
    References

Chapter 8: Helping People Change
    Objectives
    Regional University EEC Case
    Leadership
    Resistance to Change
    Barriers to Change
        Failure to Use Research
        Teachers Are Classroom Bound
    A Need for Involvement
    Ways of Involving Teachers
    The Use of Incentives
    Teachers as Researchers
    Staff Development
    NCSIE
    Consortia
    School Culture and Climate
    Forces That Promote and Impede Change
    Group Leadership
    Using Power
    The Future of Educational Leadership
    Summary
    Questions
    Suggested Further Activities
    Bibliography

Sources: Chapter 7 from Armstrong, D. G., Henson, K. T., and Savage, T. V., *Education: An Introduction*, 3rd ed. New York: Macmillan, 1989. Chapter 8 from Kenneth T. Henson, *Curriculum Planning: Integrating Multiculturalism, Constructivism, and Education Reform*, 2nd ed. (New York: McGraw-Hill, 2001). Reprinted in 2003 by Waveland Press: Long Grove, Illinois.

Since evaluation has become a topic of great reform interest, the prospectus for the next revision of this book will announce that it has two separate chapters on evaluation and testing.

Because I thoroughly update all the chapters and cite the latest research studies with each revision of this book, I am careful to say so. For example, "This book reports the findings of over 300 research studies." If your book is a textbook, pay close attention to pedagogy, and stress this strength in your prospectus. For example, in the *Methods and Strategies* book prospectus I say:

> *Each chapter has a list of objectives, a pre-test, a post-test, a recap of major ideas, suggested further activities, and suggested further readings. Throughout each chapter, "Let's Ponder" sections cause the reader to interact with the dialogue. An "Experiences" (or case study) section at the end of each chapter shows the major principles being applied.*

To determine the expenses or capital needed to publish a book, the acquisitions editor will need some information about the book's physical characteristics. For example: "The book length will be approximately 450 pages (or 750 manuscript pages). The book will contain about 25 photos and approximately 25 line drawings. Present plans include a Teacher's Manual of approximately 64 book pages. Present plans do not include supplementary aids for students."

Market Description

Of paramount interest to the editor is the market for which your work is intended. This market must be large enough to support the project, and it must be attainable, which means that it must be specific. Although authors may be tempted to think of their work as having application to many markets, editors know that few works are used by multiple audiences. An old adage expresses the dilemma: "The only thing that is wrong with a book that is written for everybody is that it is used by nobody."

In addition to being specific, the market description should provide examples of specific contexts in which the book might be required. For a college textbook prospectus, examples of particular university courses that would use this book should be provided. Most university libraries have college catalogs; it takes only a few minutes to look up the courses and jot down their names, numbers, and descriptions.

Description of the Competition

The worst mistake a military commander can make, they say, is to underestimate the potential of the enemy. Equally so, authors who fail to know and acknowledge the strength of the competition ensure their own defeat. Because you are writing a textbook and it is in your field of study, you will have expertise on the subject, and you will be aware of some of the competition. But you may fall short unless you are aware of all of the viable competing texts. Furthermore, you must be more than aware of these books; you must be closely familiar with each competing book. Only then can you use their strengths and weaknesses to improve the design of your own product.

All editors want assurance that your book will contain those chapters that professors who teach the course expect to cover. Also, they want your book to be superior to, not equally good but *superior to,* the competitors'. Two items are needed to communicate these features. First, you should submit a very detailed and very comprehensive chapter outline of competing titles—detailed enough to contain all of the major topics in each chapter. Second, you should create a content comparison chart that clearly demonstrates the superiority of your book. A sample content comparison chart is shown in Figure 10.5.

Such a chart allows the editor to readily identify chapter topics that are common among the major textbooks used in the targeted course. In Figure 10.5, your book is in Column H. About two-thirds down the chart are two chapters that you chose to delete in favor of other chapters (listed at the bottom of the figure). The content comparison chart can help *you* design a superior book by helping you identify the chapter topics that you must cover, by helping you identify important and relevant topics for new chapters, and by helping you communicate these coverages to your editors.

Author Description

Finally, include a brief statement that clearly establishes your competence in writing this work. If your credibility emerges from your own research, say so. If you have had unique experiences that contribute to the quality of this work, the editor should know this. Also include a statement about your previous, relevant publications. Say when you will complete the manuscript.

Contrary to popular belief, an author's degrees and titles are of little importance unless they assure that the contributor has the expertise needed to write a superior book. For example, "department chair" is a significant title only if you are writing a book on leadership or administration. Much more convincing would be your experience in conducting research, surveys, or other investigations on the subject of this book.

SELECTING A PUBLISHER

Once the prospectus is complete, it is time to approach a publisher. You will want to *choose only publishers publishing books in your subject area.* For example, if you send your textbook prospectus to a publisher who does not publish textbooks in your field, you have wasted valuable time. This can be avoided by checking your own professional materials to see who published them, or better yet by making a trip to the library. At the library, check the current

FIGURE 10.5 Content comparison chart.

Chapter Topics	Book A	Book B	Book C	Book D	Book E	Book F	Book G	Book H
Adolescence and Learning	X	X	X	X	X			X
Planning	X	X	X	X	X	X	X	X
Classroom Management	X	X	X	X	X	X	X	X
Evaluation	X	X	X	X	X	X	X	X
Teaching Styles	X	X	X	X	X			X
Motivation	X	X						X
Multicultures of Disadvantaged		X		X	X			X
History and Aims		X						X
Audiovisuals		X		X				X
Teaching Special Pupils		X	X					X
Communications		X						X
The Professional Teacher/Getting a Job		X	X					
Student Teaching		X	X					
Educational Reform								X
Effective Teaching								X
Using Technology								X

reference book, *Books in Print*. In the "Subjects" volume of *Books in Print*, you will see listed all of the books according to particular subjects. Make a list of the publishers of these books. Then check the current *Literary Market Place* and the current *Writer's Market* for a detailed description of each publisher. You may wish to develop a chart such as the one in Figure 10.6, which was designed to help me identify the best possible publishers for a book on reading. A column heading was included for collecting each type of information that I believed important for this type of book and what I wanted to accomplish by writing this book.

FIGURE 10.6 Chart of publishers.

PUBLISHER	Royalty	Titles/ Year	Printing	Hard/ Paper	Advance	Report Time	Pub Time	How-to	Self-Help	Other Important Features
Andrew, McMeel, and Parker	R	30		H,P				X		4-1-04 Rejected 4-15-04
Arbor House	S	55		P			9 mos			
Avon		300						X	X	
Donning	7–15%	38		H,P	Y	2 mos	1 yr	X	X	
Berkley	6–10%	900		P	2,000	2 mos	18 mos	X	X	
Little, Brown		100		H,P	Y	3 mos		X		4-5-04 Rejected 4-15-04
Prentice-Hall	10–15%	150		H,P	3–5K	3 wks	8 mos	X	X	4-1-04
WW Norton		213			Y		1 yr	X		4-5-04
Prima	15–20%	30+	5,000	H,P	Y	1 mo	6–9 mos	X	X	
Ten Speed Press		40	10,000	P	Y	1 mo	10 mos	X	X	
Ashley	10–15%	30		H,P	1,000	2 mos	20 mos	X		
Menasha Ridge	10%W	13	4,000	H,P	Y	1 mo	8 mos			
Jeremy Tarcher		30		H,P		2 wks	1 yr	X	X	
Wadsworth	5–15%	600		H,P		2 mos		X	X	Speech & Communications
Writer's Digest	10%	45					1 yr			4-1-04
Dodd, Meade	10–15%	200			Y	6 wks	9 mos			
Crown		250		H,P		2 mos		X	X	4-5-04
Random House		120				3–6 wks				
Ballantine	8–10%	20		H,P		6 wks	1 yr	X	X	4-5-04
Contemporary	6–15%	100		H,P			10 mos	X		
Fearon Education		110				1 mo				
Focal Press	10–17%	45		H,P	1,500	3 mos	1 yr	X		Communications
Stephen Greene		30		H,P		3 mos		X	X	College of Ed. graduates
Metamorphous	10%+	10	2,000	H,P	N		8 mos	X	X	Query letter sent
PAR, Inc.	5–10%	8	5,000	H,P		1 mo	1 yr			Developing Writing Skills/Community College

Royalty Rate: Most academic projects provide 10 to 15 percent of the net sales to the author(s). For further information, please see Appendix B.

Number of Titles: The number of titles this publisher publishes per year tells you the size of the company.

Size of Initial Printing: Large initial printings give some assurance that the publisher will work hard to market the book to avoid being stuck with unsold copies.

Hardcover/Paperback: The number of charts in this book makes a hardcover book much preferable, but if the company also publishes paperbacks, this may mean that instead of having the short shelf life of a hardback, the book might be reprinted in paperback at a later date and sold in mass at a lower price.

Advance: A large nonreturnable advance can help assure the author that the publisher will not back out on the agreement and can assure that the publisher will work hard to sell enough copies to cover the advance.

Report Time: Helps the author track multiple submissions of the manuscript.

Publishing Time: Is important if the author needs the book for merit pay, promotion, or tenure.

The next two columns, How-to and Self-help, are important to this book because it falls under these categories. The final column is left open to write in any peculiar features of these publishers important to the author.

Send Query Letters

After you have identified several good prospective publishers, select five or six of the most appropriate ones and simultaneously send them query letters asking whether they are interested in seeing a prospectus for a book of this type. Give them a brief description of your project, but no more than one page. Be direct, letting each editor know that you are contacting other editors. This will avoid the possible embarrassment of having two or more editors accept your work and then having to turn down one or more editors. It will also encourage editors to respond to your letter without unnecessary delay. Figure 10.7 contains a sample query letter to book publishers. (See also suggestions given in Chapter 8.)

NEGOTIATING THE CONTRACT

Once you succeed in getting a publisher to offer you a contract, it is time to negotiate. But if this is your first book, don't overplay your hand. My advice is to ask for a fixed percentage of the sales. I recently read in a local newspaper that a professor at a Midwestern university wrote a book for which he received a flat fee of $200. The book has now sold at least 35 million copies. It doesn't take a mathematician to figure that this professor made a big mistake.

You can do better. Avoid commercial publishers offering straight, one-time fees. I make exceptions for nonprofit professional associations in which I hold memberships. For example, I received a nominal fee for writing a monograph for *Phi Delta Kappa* (Henson, 2005). Phi Delta Kappa offers a standard fee for its monograph authors. Although the fee itself is nominal, many other benefits can come from such writing. For example, national associations offer tremendously large exposure. Your association with these organizations can boost your reputation. When strangers say, "I know your name. You work for *Phi Delta Kappa*, don't you?," then I know that my investment of time and energy was well directed.

In an article published by *The Chronicle of Higher Education* (Henson, 1990), I advised authors to ask for an advance, but I warned against feeling disappointed if the publisher refuses to pay an advance. I also said that you should read the contract carefully and look for hidden expenses to the author such as costs of photos and permissions. If the publisher says that their authors always bear these expenses, then ask for a ceiling to be set on these expenses. Otherwise, you could write a book that is highly profitable to the publisher but one that brings no income at all to you.

RECAPPING THE MAJOR POINTS

This chapter is included to help you in your search for a publisher to produce your future books. Remember:

- Getting book contracts is highly competitive.
- A well-prepared prospectus can save you considerable time should publishers consider the target market for your proposed text too small.
- Each book prospectus should contain information about the book, the market, the competing books, and the author.
- When submitting a prospectus, include content outline, Chapter One, and at least one additional chapter.
- Multiple submissions of a book prospectus are acceptable, provided the author notifies each editor that the prospectus is being shared with other publishers.
- To succeed, your prospectus must convince the publisher that your book will be superior to other books on that topic already on the market.

FIGURE 10.7   Sample query letter to book publishers.

_____, Editor

_____, Inc.

Street Address

City, State 00000

Dear _____ :

Would you be interested in reviewing a prospectus for an undergraduate secondary and middle school methods text? This book will have those chapters commonly found in methods texts.

> *You might want to list those essential chapters that are found in existing texts.*

As a former junior high school teacher, I find that other chapters are needed which are not found in current texts. This book will fill that gap. Three of the chapters that are unique to this book are "Using Microcomputers," "School Reform," and "Effective Teaching Research."

> *This answers that paramount question that editors always ask: "How is your book superior to the existing texts?"*

Since I am contacting other publishers, I hope that you will respond at your earliest convenience and that you will specify if you require additional information beyond the chapter outline, the prospectus, and two sample chapters. Thank you.

> *This tastefully tells the editors that they can't put you on the back burner.*

Sincerely yours,

REFERENCES

Armstrong, D. G., Henson, K. T., & Savage, T. V. (1989). *Education: An introduction.* New York: Macmillan.

Baughman, M. D. *Baughman's handbook of humor in education.* New York: Parker Publishers, 1974.

Henson, K. T. (1990, October). When signing book contracts, scholars should be sure to read the fine print. *The Chronicle of Higher Education,* pp. 132–133.

Henson, K. T. (1993). *A study of the requirements of education journals.* Richmond, KY. For details of the results of this study, see Henson, K. T. (1993, June). Writing for successful publication: Advice from editors. *Phi Delta Kappan, 74*(10), 799–802.

Henson, K. T. (1996). *Methods and strategies for teaching in secondary and middle schools.* 3rd ed. New York: Longman.

Henson, K. T. (2001). *Curriculum planning: Integrating multiculturalism, constructivism, and education reform,* 2nd ed. New York: McGraw-Hill. Reprinted in 2003 by Waveland Press: Long Grove, IL.

Henson, K. T. (2005). *Writing for publication,* 2nd ed. Fastback (monograph) No. 538. Bloomington, IN: Phi Delta Kappa, International.

Hochheiser, R. (1987). *How to work for a jerk.* New York: Random House, 1987.

Kilpatrick, J. J. (1984). *The writer's art.* New York: Andrews, McNeel, & Parker, 1984.

Thompson, A., & Strickland, L. (1987). *Strategic management: Concepts and cases,* 4th ed. New York: Macmillan.

11

PLANNING FOR SUCCESS

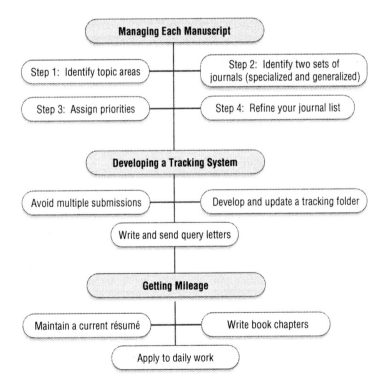

Managing Each Manuscript

Step 1: Identify topic areas

Step 2: Identify two sets of journals (specialized and generalized)

Step 3: Assign priorities

Step 4: Refine your journal list

Developing a Tracking System

Avoid multiple submissions

Develop and update a tracking folder

Write and send query letters

Getting Mileage

Maintain a current résumé

Write book chapters

Apply to daily work

Many variables work collectively to determine an author's degree of success. Among these variables is—no doubt about it—luck. For example, at times editors receive several manuscripts that are so good that they want to select more than one; yet, these manuscripts are so similar that only one can be used. Those authors whose manuscripts are rejected just because they happen to arrive when similar, equally good (but not better) manuscripts arrived were unlucky.

There are also times when writers have *good* luck. For example, often an editor has more than enough excellent manuscripts to fill an issue, but to make the desired journal size, the editor needs one very short manuscript. These editors may be forced to reject some superior manuscripts because they are a little too long to "finish out" this issue. An author who submitted a very short, mediocre manuscript may find the article accepted when the longer but better manuscripts are rejected. This author is lucky.

One of my colleagues, a seasoned author, says this of his early writing efforts:

I remember when, as a junior faculty member at a major university, I wanted desperately to have an article appear in a particular journal. My college had a wonderful media center and an equally wonderful laboratory school. I asked the director of the media center for photos taken of teachers and students at our laboratory school, promising to give the university and the media center credit for any photos used in the article.

The media center director led me to three file cabinet drawers filled with glossy black and white photos, offering me my choice and as many as I could use. I chose a couple of close-ups that showed teachers and students actively involved in projects. As I closed the drawers, I thought, "If a couple of good photos would help get my manuscript accepted, four or five good photos should do twice as well." Then, I thought, "If four or five would help, a couple of dozen should make my article a shoe-in." After an hour of searching, I left the center taking about two dozen excellent photos with me. I then sent all of them along with my very short manuscript to my favorite journal.

A few weeks later as I checked my mail, I noticed a package from this journal. This wasn't uncommon; I'd received many returned manuscripts from the editor, each accompanied with a letter complimenting the manuscript but saying that it didn't meet the journal's current needs. But this package was thicker. A message flashed—complimentary copies! Sure. My manuscript had been accepted, and as with most professional journals this one paid the author by giving a few free copies of the journal carrying the author's article.

My hunch was correct. I quickly checked the contents section. Sure enough, there was my name. I immediately understood why actors fight over top billing. This table of contents was like a Las Vegas marquee. I quickly turned to my article and read it. It read well. Yet, it was very brief, and it didn't report any research. Rather, it reported some observations that I had made while living abroad, identifying some characteristics of American schools that seem to work against minority students.

Then it dawned on me that there were other articles in this issue; I wondered who wrote them. Maybe there were some well-known authors. Quickly checking the table of contents, I found several former presidents of the national association that published this journal. Here I was, a junior assistant professor listed with some of the biggest names in my field. My chest swelled. But as I scanned through the other articles, I sensed a familiar déjà vu. Then I realized why. Each of those manuscripts had one or two of my photos. They still carried our media center's name. Then a disturbing idea struck. I realized that my manuscript wasn't accepted on the basis of its merits at all! It was accepted because the editor wanted to use all of these photos. But that was ok. I had made the big-time journal, and at that moment anything else paled in importance. I knew I was lucky, but I was also very pleased.

Good luck is always welcomed. But it is an overrated variable in writing for publication. Successful authors do not depend on good luck to bring them success; nor do they use bad luck to explain or excuse their lack of success. Successful authors plan for success. This chapter is written to help you plan a systematic writing program. Use it wisely, and you won't need to rely so heavily on luck to make your writing program succeed.

MANAGING EACH MANUSCRIPT

The chances of writers reaching their goals can be dramatically increased when they not only have an understanding of their goals but also have a sense of the relative importance of each goal. Only then can the most appropriate journal for reaching each goal be identified.

In Chapter 8, I described the wide variance in journal characteristics. For example, some journals are read primarily by researchers while others are read almost exclusively by practitioners. Some journals have audiences of only a few hundred; other journals are circulated to hundreds of thousands of readers. You need to search out your own major reasons (goals) for writing and then select those journals that can best help you reach these goals. You can use Figure 11.1 to: (1) list and order your reasons for writing, (2) list and order those journals in which you would most like your work to appear, and (3) develop a profile for these journals.

Sometimes writers are unsure of which journals they want to publish their manuscript. You can use the following steps to identify and order your preferred journals:

FIGURE 11.1 Journal profile.

Reasons for Writing: Rank Ordered
    Most Important:
    Second Most Important:
    Third Most Important:
    Others:

Journal Criteria: Rank Ordered
    Most Important:
    Second Most Important:
    Third Most Important:
    Others:

Journals That Score the Highest

Name of Journal	Refereed	Acceptance Rate	Months Required for Decisions	Number of Readers	Prestige (High, Average, Low)	Other	Other	Other

.
.
.
etc.

1. Identify several topics that you enjoy.
2. Identify two sets of journals—specialized and general.
3. Match these journals to these goals.
4. Prioritize your list of journals.
5. Refine your list (delete all unsatisfactory journals).

Now, let's take a closer look at each of these steps:

Step 1: Identify Topic Areas

You should identify several topic areas that appeal to you, areas on which you would like to write. Consider those areas that you know best. As explained in Chapter 2, you can use a reference book such as *Reader's Guide* or *Education Index* to quickly identify those journals that are publishing articles on this topic. Following are six hints you can use to identify good topics:

1. Consider your undergraduate majors/minors.
2. Examine your dissertation or thesis *carefully*.
   a. Examine the content.
   b. Who would be interested?
3. Consider other theses and reports.
4. Examine your job.
   a. Your major role as a teacher, administrator, supervisor, etc.?
   b. Your grants.
   c. Other accomplishments.
5. Examine your life.
   a. Unusual experiences.
   b. Interests or expertise in other fields.
6. Examine your future.
   a. What kind of job would you like to have in five years? In ten years?
   b. What are your retirement plans?

Step 2: Identify Two Sets of Journals— Specialized and General

Many beginning writers insist that there are only one or two journals in their subject field. It's true that some fields are much more limited than others. Generally, the more highly specialized the field, the fewer the journals in that field. For example, a marine biologist would find fewer marine biology journals than a general biologist would find biology journals. But just because your field is limited *you* don't have to be limited. A good solution for many subject areas is to identify a set of journals with general emphasis. For example, a marine biologist might have a list of one or two marine biology journals as well as a list of general biology journals.

Step 3: Assign Priorities to the Journals You Listed

Because your goals continuously change, you should rerank your journal list periodically. You may find it necessary occasionally to delete some of the journals and add new ones. When ranking your list of journals:

1. Consider your employer's expectations.
   a. Level of journal accepted (Does your employer recognize journals whose circulations are national? Regional? State? Local?)
   b. Refereed or non-refereed (Many employers, particularly higher education institutions, give credit only for refereed journals.)

   c. Research based (Some employers recognize only articles that report the author's research.)

2. Consider the journal's own characteristics.
   a. Acceptance rate (Would several short articles appearing in practitioners' journals serve you better than, say, one scholarly article placed in a more prestigious research journal?)
   b. Preferred topics
   c. Costs to author (Does the journal charge the author a reading fee? Page fees? Would your employer pay these fees for you?)

3. Consider your own needs.
   a. Prestige
   b. Uses in classes you teach
   c. Promotion, tenure, merit pay
   d. Other needs

4. Plan your publications to achieve other goals.
   a. Grant writing
   b. Books
   c. Workshops
   d. Others

Each time you have an article accepted, immediately add it to your résumé, and always attach a copy of your résumé when applying for a grant. This way, the articles give support and credibility to the grant proposals. (It works!)

Step 4: Refine Your Journal List

Some of your old goals give way to new ones. You may find that those journals that match the obsolete goals may no longer be appropriate for you. Don't be reluctant to delete these journals from each of your lists.

PROFILE

Bonnidell Clouse was born to missionary parents in Costa Rica, and she grew up in California and Arizona. She received her B.A. degree in Psychology at Wheaton College, M.A. degree in Psychology at Boston University, and Ph.D. in Educational Psychology at Indiana University. Her first professorship was at Bryan College in Dayton, Tennessee. Since the 1960s, she has taught educational psychology at Indiana State University.

Writing for publication is a tool that all professors can use to reach important professional goals, but for some individuals writing for publication becomes an extension of their personalities and souls.

It began with the doctoral dissertation. After months of wondering what topic you will write on, you come up with what turns out to be the most interesting and important of all subjects known to humankind. You must, of course, share this with the world. It is your contribution to society and a way of paying back, at least in part, what others have contributed to your education. So, you write and rewrite until the dissertation is but a shadow of its former self and becomes one of the hundreds of articles to appear in academic journals the following year.

With that out of the way you begin teaching. You think you are free, only to be told that if you wish to be considered for promotion or for tenure or for merit or for membership on the graduate faculty or for whatever, you must put pen to paper (or fingers to the keys). So, you're off and running again, this time with new insights and new data and a prayer that it will be accepted by someone, somewhere. And sure enough, several rejection letters later, there it is, in print and absolutely beautiful.

So great is your joy that you begin the same painful process all over again—and again—and again. You watch the list of publications grow longer and longer. You update your vita twice a year instead of once. You get the promotion and the tenure and the merit and a place on the graduate faculty. You have found your place in the sun. Now you can relax and watch the rest of the world from your ivory tower.

But then the unexpected happens. You begin getting invitations to write for this journal or that magazine or the other book. No longer do you have to go begging for someone to notice your work.

Someone has noticed and is asking for more. Publication is assured and may be accompanied by a check in the mail. Your resolve to "just say no" weakens as the prospect of thinking through another idea or doing another piece of research stimulates your senses, and your brain starts outlining and sorting it all out. Again, you are off and running, thanking the powers that be that you have something that occupies your time that is far more intriguing than the soaps or a shopping spree.

But far more important than getting the dissertation in print, and far more important than being promoted, and far more important than keeping your brain in gear is being able to fulfill a long-standing ambition. In my case, what I wanted to do was to integrate Christianity and psychology. This could best be done by writing for publication. Fortunately, this area is popular with many other scholars as well, as is seen in such publications as *Journal of Psychology and Theology* and *Journal of Psychology and Christianity*, and other journals and magazines that carry articles on the same subject.

My area of expertise is that of moral development and moral education. My latest book is *Teaching for Moral Growth: A Guide for the Christian Community* (Victor, 1993). Will I stop with this? As I tell my students, "The best predictor of future behavior is past behavior."

So, it appears I will continue writing. I know that through the printed page I will reach a larger audience than those who sit in my classes each day. And perhaps God in His grace will see fit to use what I write to encourage others in truth and justice.

DEVELOP A TRACKING SYSTEM

The absolute necessity of getting several manuscripts in the mail was clearly emphasized in Chapter 9: "What distinguishes highly successful writers from less successful writers?" The answer is that highly successful writers write more, and they keep their manuscripts in the mail.

As you increase your number of manuscripts, two things will happen that can complicate your life. At any point, you may find it difficult to remember which journal is currently considering one of your manuscripts, and you may have trouble remembering the location and status of a particular manuscript. Have you sent a query letter? To whom? When? Has the editor responded? Was the response negative or positive? If positive, did you send the manuscript? When? Has the publisher acknowledged receipt of the manuscript? The life of each manuscript has many stages.

All prolific authors have several manuscripts under consideration at any one time, and the logistics of tracking a half-dozen can become quite complex. What if you were to forget that you had already sent a particular manuscript to a publisher and then sent a second manuscript to that same publisher? You may raise suspicion that you have tried all of the other publishers and that no other journals will accept your manuscripts. No editors want their journals to be used as dumping grounds, so you should try to avoid sending manuscripts to an editor who is already considering another of your manuscripts. Worse yet, think of the embarrassment of sending an older manuscript that was rejected once back to the same editor—or of sending the same manuscript to be considered simultaneously by two different journals.

To avoid these unpleasant and damaging situations, you need two types of tracking systems. First, for each of your manuscripts, create a file folder. This folder provides a convenient place to keep early drafts and the notes used during the writing process. In addition to providing a way of locating your latest copy of the manuscript and all related information, the file folder can become an excellent system for tracking the manuscript through its publication life.

On the inside of each folder, begin the tracking form recommended in Figure 11.2. Enter the names of those journals to which you plan to send this manuscript, listing them in order of preference. Because the manuscript is now fresher in your memory than it will be at a later time, making a ranked list of appropriate journals for this manuscript will be easier now than later. Should the manuscript be rejected by the first choice, knowing immediately where to send it next will save much time and will decrease the amount of time that the manuscript stays on your desk.

Now that you have a method of tracking each manuscript individually, you must develop a way of tracking all of your manuscripts simultaneously.

Upon completion of each manuscript, I immediately send a query letter, recording the date sent on a chart as shown in Figure 11.3. When a response

FIGURE 11.2 Sample individual manuscript tracking form.

Article Sent to:	Date	R/A*	Query Letter Sent	MS Sent
The Clearing House	12/1/04	R	7/15/04	7/21/04
Contemporary Ed	4/2/05	A	12/2/04	12/18/04
Educational Horizons				
College & University Teaching				
The High School Journal				
*Rejected/Accepted				

is received (assuming that it is positive because most responses to query letters are positive), I immediately send the manuscript, recording the date sent. The names of the journals are listed in the far right column so that, at a glance, I can see if I already have a manuscript at a particular journal.

In Chapter 6 I recommended that you identify a few journals in your area and become familiar with each. In time, that list will grow. A list of your manuscripts, such as the one in Figure 11.3, will enable you to see at a glance which of your manuscripts you have pending at each of your target journals.

For example, the practical benefit of this list and the ease with which it can be used are readily obvious. Just a quick glance reveals some duplications at two of the journals. You will remember that generally this is a poor practice. But, both of these instances involve *invited* manuscripts. This makes a big difference; have no reluctance to send more than one manuscript to a publisher if the second manuscript is requested by the editor.

As manuscripts are rejected, mark through that journal title and, looking at the manuscript tracking form, query the next journal. If you receive a positive response from a query letter, then send the manuscript to the next journal.

GETTING MILEAGE

Once you've experienced the thrill of having a manuscript accepted for publication, you must choose between one-time success or ongoing success. I

FIGURE 11.3 Sample of multiple tracking system.

Author(s)	Manuscript	Date Query Letter Sent	Date of Response to Query Letter	Date Manuscript Was Sent	Journal
Henson	Inquiry Learning: A New Look	11/1/04	1/7/05	1/8/05	Contemporary Ed.
Henson	Corporal Punishment: Ten Myths	1/2/05	1/11/05	1/9/05	The High School Journal
Balantine & Henson	Back to Basics: Skills Needed	1/3/05	1/11/05	1/11/05	Contemporary Education
Henson/ Buttery/ Chissom	Middle Schl as Prevd by Cntmpry Tchrs	1/28/05	2/4/05	2/2/05	Middle School Jnl
Block & Henson	Mast Lng & Middle Sch Instruct	1/31/05	2/4/05	2/3/05	American Middle Jnl
Henson/ Chissom/ Riley	Impro. Instr in Middle Schools	1/31/05	2/4/05	2/5/05	AMSE
Henson	Publishing Textbooks & Monographs	2/25/05	3/2/05	3/3/05	Thresholds in Education
Henson & Morris	Prospectives, Insights & Direction	2/29/05	5/7/05	3/8/05	Thresholds in Education
Henson/ Coulter/ Harrell	The UA Summer Inst for Physics Tchrs	2/30/05	5/7/05	3/8/05	The Physics Teacher
Henson/ Saterfiel	How to Get Good Research Data	3/1/05	3/9/05	3/10/05	Amer Sch Board Jnl
Henson/ Buttery/ Chissom	Middle Schl Tchr as Mbr of Cmty	3/27/05	4/2/05	4/2/05	Middle School Jnl

believe that spending some time to make the article serve you is a wise investment. Here are some ways to get more mileage from your work.

Maintain a Current Résumé

To ensure that an article acceptance is not a one-time success, you should immediately add this entry to your résumé. Using the referencing style most commonly used in your discipline, add the title to your résumé under a heading, "Publications." Each time you make a new entry you should also note the date on the résumé.

Every new article on your résumé enhances your credibility. Each article raises your level of expertise on the particular topic. By keeping your résumé current, you can use it to further your career. It also serves in a variety of additional ways. For example, attach the résumé to grant proposals to assure the judges that you have expertise that merits the trust that is involved each time a proposal is funded.

Also include your résumé each time you submit a book prospectus. Getting book contracts is highly competitive in our current economic climate. I use my vita to convince the publisher that I have the expertise needed to write accurately on the subject. What better evidence could I offer than a nationally refereed article?

Write Book Chapters

Anyone who is capable of writing a published article is also capable of writing a publishable book chapter. I use articles to do this. Recently, I wrote a book titled *Curriculum Development for Educational Reform*. One chapter in this book begins with an article titled, "The Little School That Grew," which is a satire on curriculum development. Because satires don't age like other topics, I was able to go back in my résumé and pull out this 15-year-old article. It sounds as though it were written to address current education reform practices.

In another current textbook, I used no fewer than a half dozen articles to write a heavily researched chapter. The articles supply the research and framework for the chapter, and they keep the chapter current. I have revised this 1974 book five times. Each revision contains new articles. The book motivates me to write new articles on these same topics, and the new articles keep the book current.

Many authors write chapters for collaborative textbooks that are edited by others. Some authors are invited to write professional yearbook chapters. Invariably these authors use their articles when writing these larger works.

Apply to Daily Work

Many writers are professors who have heavy teaching responsibilities. I do not know of any professors who separate their writing and their teaching. On the contrary, most professors who write for publication use their articles and books in the classroom. This practice was mentioned as a reason for writing for publication; it gives a teacher the confidence and reassurance needed to deliver lessons that are meaningful and enjoyable to both the instructor and the students.

RECAPPING THE MAJOR POINTS

When carefully planned, writing for publication enables authors to reach many professional and personal goals that they could not otherwise reach. But the setting and reaching of these goals require careful planning. Whether or not each of your goals will be reached will be determined in part by the types of manuscripts you write, the topics you choose to write about, the journals to which you submit your manuscripts, and *especially* by how many manuscripts you write.

As your number of manuscripts increases, so does your need for a system to track them. Making a folder for each manuscript is a must. Equally important, you need a system to show you where all of your manuscripts reside at any one time. This chapter has presented and discussed the preparation of an example of each of these systems. These systems are simple to construct but very useful—they work! Your professional and personal goals are unique, so you should either modify these systems to work for you or develop your own personalized systems.

Success is achieved when you reach your goals. This chapter has provided information to help you use writing to reach these goals. The following points are worth remembering:

- Writing can help you reach professional and personal goals, but only if your goals are clear and your writing program is consistent with these goals.
- Success through writing requires extensive writing. As your number of manuscripts increase, your need for a system to track your manuscripts increases.
- A simple manila folder can provide a safe place for your manuscript and related information. A log sheet inside the folder provides an easy system for tracking that manuscript.
- Use your goals as criteria for choosing article topics and for choosing the journals to which you send your manuscripts.
- Identifying several journals for a manuscript at the time it is written can save turnaround time should the journal that was your first choice reject the manuscript.
- Simultaneously placing two manuscripts at the same journal can jeopardize the acceptance of each; simultaneously placing copies of the same

manuscript at two different publishers can destroy your relationship with one or both of these publishers.

- Luck can play an important part in an author's success, but without planning, *good* luck can be a stranger to a writer.

REFERENCE

Henson, K. T. (2005). *A brief guide to writing for professional publication,* 2nd ed. Fastback (monograph) No. 538. Bloomington, IN: Phi Delta Kappa International.

12

GRANT PROPOSAL WRITING

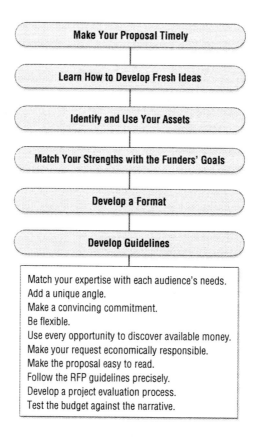

Make Your Proposal Timely

Learn How to Develop Fresh Ideas

Identify and Use Your Assets

Match Your Strengths with the Funders' Goals

Develop a Format

Develop Guidelines

Match your expertise with each audience's needs.
Add a unique angle.
Make a convincing commitment.
Be flexible.
Use every opportunity to discover available money.
Make your request economically responsible.
Make the proposal easy to read.
Follow the RFP guidelines precisely.
Develop a project evaluation process.
Test the budget against the narrative.

Economic constraints place severe limits on many businesses and other institutions—public and private, large and small. Organizations from small colleges to major university systems, from small family-owned businesses to major conglomerates, and from small county and town offices to major city, state, and national governments can be severely affected by scarce resources.

"Do more with less" becomes the motto that expresses the economic reality of such periods of recession, but stretching resources can go only so far. One alternative to doing more with less—or doing *less* with less or learning to do without—is grant proposal writing. Grants from foundations and other institutions provide recipients with resources and opportunities that otherwise would not be available.

But in a nation with free enterprise, the law of supply and demand is always at work. The consequence is that with money in short supply there are more people who are ready to work hard and creatively to take it. In more practical terms, this means that grant money is getting much harder to get. Yet, it is still there for the taking, and all that is required to get it is to learn how to prepare a highly competitive grant proposal. This chapter is designed to help you do just that. The examples given in this chapter, though simplistic in tone, are tested and proved—they have earned over $2 million. By following the guidelines that are set forth, you will be capable of producing a highly competitive proposal, one that will edge out 95 percent of the competition.

Robert Louis Stevenson once said that, "[The essence of good writing] is not to write but to write what you mean, not to affect your reader but to affect him precisely as you wish." This is true of successful grant proposal writing. Money can and does buy accountability. Most people who have money to give away are astute enough to know this and will demand concrete evidence to ensure that they will get their money's worth. For example, if one writer says, "There is a critical need for a safety project" and another applicant conducts a survey of the number of accidents over a given time, the data will be more convincing than words.

Money is an important reason for writing grant proposals, but it's not the only reason people choose to spend their professional time writing proposals. A few years ago I had the pleasure of meeting and working with a person who impressed me with her level of commitment to proposal writing.

Over the past eight years, Olga Ramirez, Associate Professor of Mathematics and Computer Science at the University of Texas–Pan American, has written 15 funded Eisenhower math and science education grants. When I asked her why she put so much time and energy into grant writing, she responded:

> *Writing these grants is my professional and personal contribution to a community where I was born and raised. These grants bring to elementary*

This chapter is based on the author's book: *Grant writing in higher education: A step-by-step guide*, with permission from Allyn & Bacon, 2004.

teachers necessary mathematics instruction and support materials; hence, the grants contribute greatly to enhancing mathematics instruction and in eliminating the shortage of qualified mathematics teachers.

Although grant projects involve extensive work, they afford some benefits that otherwise would not be as accessible or pronounced. These benefits include: (1) establishing public school and university education partnerships; (2) working side-by-side with colleagues; (3) implementing and discovering new and exciting teaching ideas with teacher in-service audiences; (4) visiting teachers and students in classrooms; (5) collecting data pertinent to teacher training research; and (6) gaining administrative and people skills.

Most important, I write these grants because the teacher audience makes me feel needed, wanted, and appreciated. I like to see and document their attitudinal and cognitive growth. Altogether, the grant-funded projects provide many fun opportunities and much room for my own professional and personal growth.

Perhaps you are ready to try your "luck" at proposal writing, or you may wish to improve your odds in the grant proposal writing game. Such repeated success as that experienced by Olga Ramirez involves more than luck; it requires learning how to do it right. Even in a strong economy, if you are to be successful you must produce proposals that are among the best 5 percent. And, in case you are wondering if you can reach this goal, the answer is yes; you can operate at this level of success, but only if you demand of yourself your very best. Following are some suggestions that can put you in the top 5 percent of proposal writers.

MAKE YOUR PROPOSAL TIMELY

To write a successful grant proposal, that is, one that will be funded, you must have a good, *timely* idea. A topic that was a good idea a few years or even a few months ago may be a very poor idea today. The power in acting on a good idea at the right time is shown in a single example. During the 1970s our nation experienced one of its greatest energy shortages, and a creative principal in Minnesota thought of a way to heat his school building at half the regular cost. This idea was received so enthusiastically that special efforts were taken to ensure the proposal's success.

LEARN HOW TO DEVELOP FRESH IDEAS

Sincere proposal writers usually start their work by asking where others get such good ideas. Unfortunately, most struggling proposal writers get their ideas from reading newspapers and magazines, watching television, or listening to the radio. What's wrong with that? After all, those are the main sources of news. There are two problems with these sources: (1) they belong to others and (2) they are old news. Even the next day, they are old hat. Such is the nature of news. So, you ask, how can I get ideas that are fresh? Ideas that are mine?

You can *learn* how to develop fresh ideas through a simple process that requires the same skills required to work a jigsaw puzzle. If you have ever spent any time working jigsaw puzzles, you know that the mind can train itself to look for patterns. Instead of going to your office and sitting down with a pencil and paper, or sitting at your computer just waiting for creative inspiration, pick up a newspaper, or better yet, a magazine or journal in your field. Notice the topics that are getting the attention. Now, see if you can relate two or more of these topics to form a new idea. The ability to generate an original idea does not require ignoring all existing ideas. Sometimes a highly successful idea is no more than seeing how to apply the parts of two or more existing successful ideas.

IDENTIFY AND USE YOUR ASSETS

Too often, grant proposal writers think that they must start with no existing knowledge and use only their imaginations to create grant proposals. But starting from zero places an unnecessary burden on the proposal writer. Exacerbating the problem, these proposal writers are afraid that they will break some type of copyright or patent laws or violate some professional ethics code if they use any existing information, which restricts their thinking even further. Successful grant proposal writers know better than to restrict themselves unnecessarily. They know that, so long as they use existing knowledge creatively, get written permission when necessary, and give credit where credit is due, they are not being dishonest.

For example, for economic reasons, most higher education institutions have increased their number of part-time faculty members. This has caused some grave concerns over the quality of instruction; many are worried that the use of too many part-timers will diminish the institution's quality of instruction so much that ultimately both the institution's reputation and quality will suffer. Virtually every higher education institution has a developmental program for helping tenure-track faculty members improve their teaching effectiveness. But how much is being done to develop and support the instruction of part-time faculty members? Probably far less than for tenure-track faculty. A grant proposal combining the two concepts—improved instruction and part-time faculty—would be timely and perhaps tempting to the right donor.

GATHER THE NECESSARY MATERIALS

A good way to start your grant proposal writing program is to gather the necessary materials. One document that many consider indispensable is the *Catalog of Federal Domestic Assistance* which is available for about $50 from:

Superintendent of Documents
U.S. Government Printing Office
Washington, DC 20402

Ask for stock #922-014-00000-1

Another useful document is the *Federal Register,* a booklet that is published daily giving deadlines for requests for proposals. A subscription to the *Federal Register* is too expensive for most writers, but this document is available at most libraries. Figure 12.1 shows a sample entry from the *Federal*

FIGURE 12.1 **Sample entry from the *Federal Register.***

Federal Register
Monday, September 21

PART II: DEPARTMENT OF EDUCATION

Direct Grant Programs and Fellowship Programs; Notice Inviting Applications for New Awards for Fiscal Year 1993.

84.061C Planning, Pilot and Demonstration Projects for Indian Children (Planning Projects)

Purpose of Program: To provide grants for projects designed to plan effective educational approaches for Indian children.

Eligible Applicants: State educational agencies: local educational agencies; Indian tribes; Indian organizations; Indian institutions; and federally supported elementary and secondary schools for Indian children.

Applicable Regulations: (a) The Education Department General Administrative Regulations (EDGAR) in 34 CFR parts 74, 75, 77, 79, 80, 81, 82, 85, and 86; and (b) The regulations for this program in 34 CFR parts 250 and 254.

Note: The regulations in 34 CFR part 79 apply to all applicants except federally recognized Indian tribes.

Project Period: Up to 12 months.

For Applications or Information Contact: U.S. Department of Education, 400 Maryland Avenue, SW., room 2177, Washington, DC 20202-6335. Telephone: (202) 401-1902.

Program Authority: 25 U.S.C. 2621(a)(1), (b).

Register. By studying these headings, you can become familiar with the nature of projects for which funding is available.

A particularly good source for identifying grant sources to fund small projects is the *National Data Book of Foundations.* Since the federal government requires anyone who gives money to file an IRS Form 990, you can look up any grant and learn what groups have been funded by a particular party and the amount of each grant.

MATCH YOUR STRENGTHS WITH THE FUNDERS' GOALS

Grant proposal writers can choose either a shotgun approach or a rifle approach to writing their proposals. Both approaches require the writer to understand the nature of the funder, the proposal writer's own strengths, and the strengths and needs of the writer's institution and community (see Figure 12.2). Using the shotgun approach, some writers prepare their proposals and then seek a funder or funders. (This approach is usually more effective when seeking small grants.) The rifle approach—tailoring the proposal to a particular request—is almost essential to capturing large awards.

FIGURE 12.2   Matching strengths with the funders' goals and practices.

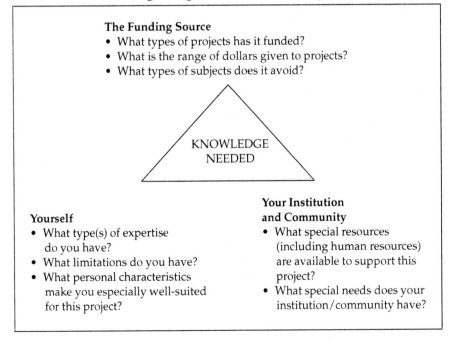

Grant writing is like playing the stock market; there is seldom a guarantee that your efforts will be rewarded, but the more you know about the process and the more you use this knowledge, the greater the probability for success. So, if you see that a particular proposal request will result in only a small amount being awarded over the year, skip this request and select one with better odds. There is an exception to this advice, however. It's been said, "Most corporations fund only in the shadows of their smokestacks," so small local grants from religious institutions and other community-oriented organizations represent a realistic opportunity for success.

Deadlines

Most requests for proposals (RFPs) specify deadlines. Suppose you learn about the opportunity just a week or two before the cutoff date. Many novice proposal writers panic and go for the deadline—which is tantamount to racing a train to the crossing; both can be disastrous. A last-minute proposal is usually a poorly conceptualized proposal. You have an alternative. Go ahead and send the RFP, and start your draft for next year. Most RFPs change very little from year to year, so when the new request is available you will already have a first draft of your proposal.

Sometimes people ask how much lead time is required to respond adequately to an RFP. Time is needed to think through the project. Donald Orlich, a professor at Washington State University who has given many grant proposal writing workshops, says that 20 working days is a minimum; but he warns that you will probably need even more time for complex projects and for those projects that you have not already given thought to how you will organize your activities.

A Format for Proposals

The elements that are essential to every proposal are: (1) statement of need, (2) project objectives, (3) statement of procedures, (4) statement of strengths, and (5) a method for evaluating the effectiveness of the program. These basics and other components that enhance proposals are discussed here in detail.

1. **Statement of Need.** A good starting point for any proposal is establishing a need for funds or restating your understanding of the needs as described in the RFP. This need should be specific, not general. A good guideline to follow when establishing the need is to keep the statement narrow and precise. If you do not know the exact needs, you may wish to begin by designing and conducting a needs assessment using one or a combination of the following data sources: questionnaire or survey, test scores, committee reports, or literature reviews. Figure 12.3 (Orlich, 1992) gives a checklist for evaluating a needs statement.

2. **Project Objectives.** Once your need for the funding has been established, you must outline the objectives of the project, describing exactly what you plan to accomplish. Like your needs statement, each objective should be specific. Your list should not exceed five objectives. Write each objective clearly, which usually means that each objective should be succinct and should have a specific, identifiable subject followed by a transitive verb. Each objective statement should be a complete sentence.

   When these few objectives are written, rank them in order of their relative importance. If your proposal is complex and you find that you need more than five objectives, consider writing two or three goals. If you do include goals, each goal should be paired with one or more objectives. This gives your proposal organization, a quality that counts in most evaluation schemes.

3. **Statement of Procedures.** The statement of procedures tells how you will conduct this project. It should be brief and to the point, telling exactly what you and others will do to achieve the objectives. The statement of procedures answers those questions that reporters ask when conducting an investigation: Who? What? When? Where? and Why?

4. **Statement of Strengths.** Although this part is absent from many proposals, it is found in most of those proposals that receive funding. A statement of strengths is an opportunity for you to tell why you or your organization should be awarded this money. What qualifications do you have that will ensure that you will succeed? If appropriate, examine your community, too. What resources does it have that could be used to achieve the proposal's objectives?

5. **Evaluation.** The purpose of the evaluation is to measure the degree to which your project accomplishes the objectives stated. For major projects, consider an external evaluation. Having someone outside your organization to design and conduct the evaluation gives the evaluation objectivity and credibility.

Once your proposal draft is complete, proof it for errors, and then ask a colleague to read it for clarity. If you think there isn't adequate time for this step, consider holding the proposal for a future RFP. A poorly written proposal can be worse than no proposal.

FOUNDATION PROPOSALS

Most foundations fund only small proposals ($5,000 or less). Yet, there are so many foundations that the number of funding opportunities they offer warrants attention as a potential source.

FIGURE 12.3   Sample evaluation of problem or needs statement.

Below is a series of criteria to be used in judging the needs or problem statement. Evaluate each criterion by circling the number to the right of the statement.

4	Very apparent
3	Somewhat apparent
2	Not readily apparent
1	Missing
NA	Not Applicable

1. Appropriate introduction is provided.   4   3   2   1
2. Logical lead to problem or need statement.   4   3   2   1
3. Problem or need is feasible to address.   4   3   2   1
4. Statistical data support statement.   4   3   2   1
5. If a training project, the "target" group has   4   3   2   1
   provided support to the need or problem.
6. Assumptions or hypotheses are clearly stated.   4   3   2   1
7. Need or problem appears to be credible.   4   3   2   1
8. Statement is clearly written.   4   3   2   1
9. The statement is presented in a logical order.   4   3   2   1
10. What is your overall impression of statement?

11. Strengths:

12. Comments for improvement:

Suppose, like many professors, after having received your degree you wish to update your dissertation for publication. A very practical place to look for such resources is foundations. Another advantage of foundation grants is that having no staff to evaluate the proposals, most foundations require and prefer only a one- or two-page statement from the applicant. Figure 12.4 is a model proposal letter.

The following guidelines can be used to write effective proposals for any situation.

FIGURE 12.4   A model proposal letter.

[Use appropriate letterhead.]	
Statement of purpose:	Provide an overview of the project including some general activities. (One brief paragraph)
Balance of letter:	*Situation and Problem.* (One paragraph)
	Capabilities. What your organization has done and its ability to carry out the project if support received. (One paragraph)
	Program Methods and Operation. What you will do, how you will do it, who will be involved—community agencies, other organizations, donors? (Two paragraphs)
	Impact. How will youth, schools, or the community benefit? (One paragraph)
	Evaluation, Reporting, and Visibility. How will success be measured, how will the donor be informed, and what visibility will the donor receive? (One paragraph)
	Budget. The amount being requested. Include when you need the pledge, when you need the contribution, and your IRS number. (Short answer)
	Summary. A brief recap of the significance of this program for people, the community, and the donor. Add telephone number if not on the letterhead. (One paragraph)
Signatory:	Someone needing *no* introduction (e.g., president of organization).
Length:	Keep the entire letter to about two pages.
Best Use:	Companies, businesses, plants, foundations, local family charities, community trusts, individuals.

Guideline 1: Match Your Expertise with the Needs of Various Audiences

Successful proposals don't always require the writer to have the answer in hand. Albert Einstein said that the ability to ask the right questions is more valuable than the ability to find the right answers. Indeed, if you can raise significant, timely questions you may be able to find a sponsor who will pay you or your assistant to research the correct answers.

So, how do you identify timely questions? The same process you use to identify article topics works well on grants. Begin by thinking of your audience. This time your audience is your prospective sponsor. What would this sponsor most want to know? This may be far from what you, yourself, find most interesting. But, if you want the benefits of a successful grant, you may be willing to identify and study a topic that has the only chance of being funded—one that the funder finds interesting.

Keeping the needs of your audience in mind, think about your own expertise—not just the knowledge you have gained from books and courses, but knowledge you've gained from direct experience as well. Don't overlook this valuable source; identify those things you do well, both on and off the job. Ask yourself what your audience wants and needs and then take an inventory of your own unique knowledge and skills.

For example, everybody wants to discover ways of cutting back on unnecessary expenses. A professor of applied arts and technology might have learned how to cut out patterns that will avoid unnecessary waste. Or a mathematics professor might collaborate with a woodworks professor to write a proposal with the purpose of discovering the most waste-free systems for cutting out patterns. If there are no donors who support woodworks, the same type of proposal might be applied to textiles or other materials.

Guideline 2: Add a Unique Angle

Individuals who evaluate grant proposals are impressed by unique features. This is understandable in light of the dozens of proposals that are usually reviewed at a single sitting. Undoubtedly, many of the proposals are very similar, so evaluators are compelled to look for uniqueness among them.

An example illustrates the importance of uniqueness to grant proposals. Facing a national shortage of science, math, and foreign language teachers, the federal government issued a block grant to each state so that each could entice universities to develop summer institutes to prepare qualified teachers in these critical disciplines. More exactly, the purpose of this program was to take teachers who were teaching out of their field (for example, biology teachers who were teaching physics or chemistry, or physical education teachers who were teaching mathematics) and better prepare them to teach in the needed fields. Summer teacher training institutes would be used to lead these teachers toward full certification in the target disciplines. Each state would be granted only one summer teacher training institute in each subject.

In all states, the winning proposals had unique features. For example, in one state the winning physics grant had a feature that received more attention from the proposal evaluators than any other of its features. This unique feature was a course that brought a "master" teacher (i.e., a teacher recognized by colleagues and administrators for expert teaching ability) from a high school classroom onto the university campus to teach a special course. Using the most popular *high school* physics textbook in the state, chapter by chapter, this master high school teacher worked all of the problems for her fellow teachers.

The critical questions are: How did the authors of this proposal hit upon the idea for such a course; and, of all unlikely approaches, why did they propose to use a high school teacher to teach this course when any member of the university physics faculty could have easily worked these problems? The proposal writers anticipated that the grant proposal evaluation team would be excited over this feature because master teachers were the focus of many education reform reports of the day. The writers knew that the team of evaluators would be educators who worked in the state department of education. These people would be familiar with the school reform reports.

A second unique feature in this proposal was a weekly seminar which brought in special guest speakers. The guests included a retired physics professor who continued to research the private lives of physicists, an astronomer who specialized in galaxies, and a robotics professor who brought his self-assembled robot to the seminar for demonstration.

This special course taught by a master high school teacher, and this seminar which tapped unique expertise in the community (expertise which, incidentally, was cost-free to the funding agency) undoubtedly caught the eyes of the evaluators. During the first year this grant money was available, 11 institutions in this state submitted proposals to a team of eight independent evaluators. This particular proposal was selected as the best of the 11 proposals by all eight evaluators.

Guideline 3: Make a Convincing Commitment

Many grants are made on a matching basis. Some RFPs require the recipient to make a dollar-for-dollar matched contribution. Many RFPs that do not specify this requirement outright nevertheless will restrict recipients to those whose proposals show a heavy contribution.

Granting agencies usually have several good reasons for requiring proposal writers to make a commitment of their own resources. Two reasons always prevail. Despite many misconceptions, funding agencies do not have unlimited resources. By getting the recipients to commit their own resources, the funding agency can fund more grants, thus attaining more of its goals. A second reason that agencies require a heavy commitment by the recipient is to assure the funding agency that the resources will be managed judiciously. Even the most wealthy sponsors of grants don't want their money squandered, and a heavy commitment by the recipient guarantees good stewardship and good management.

Many grant proposal writers and their employers cannot afford to make a cash contribution to the project, so they offer an "in-kind" contribution. For example, the company or institution may offer the use of buildings, rooms, equipment, and personnel. Proposal writers may even offer their time as a contribution. The author of the winning proposal in our example offered to codirect the summer institutes at no cost to the funding agency. Furthermore, he offered to drive throughout the state *after each summer institute* ended to visit each participant and see what parts of the institute each teacher was applying in class. By contributing his own time, this proposal writer was able to persuade his institution to supply a car and gasoline. While visiting each participant, the writer conducted a follow-up evaluation of the summer institute, asking what the teacher had found most useful and what else might have been done to benefit the participants.

The evaluators were obviously impressed with this heavy, personal commitment by the proposal writer and with the almost 50 percent in-kind contribution from the grant writer's institution. This proposal outperformed the other 10 competing proposals not once but several consecutive summers. See Appendix F.

Guideline 4: Be Flexible

Abraham Lincoln said that when planning for a debate, he spent about one-third of his preparation time thinking about what he was going to say and about two-thirds of his time thinking about what his opponent was going to say. This principle will apply well to grant proposal writing. The writer must spend some time thinking about what the prospective funder wants and how to deliver in full—not what the *writer* wants to happen but what the prospective funder wants to happen.

Many proposals fail because the authors refuse to shape their proposals to meet the expectations of the prospective grantor. Sold on the greatness of their ideas, these proposal writers think they can stand firm and make demands on the funding agency. This seldom works, and rightfully so. If these unsuccessful proposal writers were paying for services, they, too, would insist on getting what they wanted for their money. The following example illustrates this point.

An education professor at a midwestern university wanted to create a competency-based teacher education program. The state had no available money to create innovative teacher education programs; however, the state did have money designated for use by its K–12 schools to develop innovative programs. Hearing this, the professor wrote a program that had two goals: to create a competency-based teacher education program (a higher education goal for which there were no available funds) *and* to solve a teacher burnout problem which was a timely topic and much in the news (a K–12-level goal which qualified for proposal funding).

By being flexible, this professor succeeded with this grant and received $385,000 to fund his innovative program, which eventually was recognized with an award from the National Association of Teacher Educators.

Guideline 5: Use Every Opportunity to Gather Information about Available Money

The imbalance in supply and demand ensures a wealth of proposals for most announced grant opportunities. Usually, among these many proposals are several excellently written proposals. So, what determines which proposals are funded? Many grants owe their funding to a tip from someone on the inside of the funding agency. The tip may or may not be intentional. For example, the author of the grant for the innovative competency-based teacher education program owes his success to a casual comment overheard in a coffee room. Someone mentioned that the state department of education had funds to support innovative public school programs. The conveyor of this information vaguely remembered that the RFP for these funds said something about teacher burnout. Overhearing this comment, the proposal writer drove to the capitol city and met with officials who were in charge of the funding. By talking to them, he was able to get a true sense of what they wanted for their money. Upon his return home, the proposal for Project ESCAPE (Elementary and Secondary Competency Approach to Teacher Education) retained its title but was altered to focus on teacher burnout.

Another grant that owes its funding to the flexibility of its authors was a technology grant written to the American Telephone & Telegraph Company (AT&T). The writer wanted to acquire a computer network program that would link the education programs in three buildings. An attempt was made to include some benefits for each department in the college and for other colleges at the university. By talking to some of the representatives, the writer learned that the company was highly interested in some of the topics and *dis*interested in others.

The grant proposal writer was keenly interested in two goals: implementing a model distance learning program and providing computers in the offices of all instructors in the college. But the AT&T representatives showed no enthusiasm for these subjects. So, rather than trying their patience by trying to sell them on ideas which held little or no interest for them, the writer refocused his attention on the potential funders to learn what they wanted, quickly tossing out a half dozen other timely ideas.

One of the topics that the writer mentioned was a state-of-the-art computer network system for the college's nursery through twelfth grade laboratory school. Since the company officials seemed intrigued with the institution's large laboratory school, the grant proposal was immediately modified to focus heavily on the lab school. The writer's initiative and willingness to explore several possible areas of interest were rewarded; the grant was funded for the largest amount of any AT&T grant proposal funded during the year.

Guideline 6: Make Your Request Economically Responsible

One of the greatest temptations that face grant proposal writers is the desire to get too much individual gain from the grant. Such attempts seldom succeed. When grant writers get greedy, their greed becomes immediately obvious to most proposal evaluators. Experienced proposal evaluators have a refined ability to sense greed quickly. One of the most common mistakes— perhaps *the* most common mistake—contemporary writers make is throwing in a computer or two, thinking that at the end of the project there will be something permanent to show for all this work.

Because so many writers include a superfluous computer or two, you would be wise to avoid this temptation. Even if the grant activities require a computer and you do not have one available for this purpose, a wise alternative is to rent or lease a computer and build the rental cost into the proposal's budget. This alternative provides you with the use of the computer and it tells the funder that you are not trying to give yourself a gift at their expense. Although you may think yourself beyond reproach, remember that nobody, regardless how innocent their intentions may be, can afford to have others question their integrity, especially prospective funders.

Guideline 7: Make the Proposal Easy to Read

Good proposal writing, like any other good writing for publication, is simple and clear. Use the same advice given in Chapter 7 on writing for journals— avoid jargon, complex paragraphs, and complex sentences. Avoid unfamiliar words. Some experts say that successful proposals must use the "in vogue" words of the day, and sprinkling a few of these words at appropriate places in the proposal might help. Still, it is better to place the goal of clarity above any felt need to juggle the right jargon.

Before submitting your proposal, give it a viewing from a distance. Look at the overall structure and ask yourself how you can alter your proposal to make it clearer and easier to read. Following are three ways to clarify that always work.

First, having written the proposal, now **write an abstract.** Some proposals specifically require an abstract. If your request for proposals requires an abstract, note the length and make your abstract comply. Even if the RFP does not ask for an abstract, make one anyway. If the evaluators don't want it, they can ignore it. But the chances are good that they will read the abstract. Often evaluators are so busy that they just quickly skim over the proposals. A good abstract can focus the evaluators' attention on the major strengths of the proposal. Figure 12.5 shows the abstract that was submitted with the physics proposal.

Second, make a **table of contents.** A succinct table of contents tells the reviewers at a glance what this proposal is all about and helps the evaluators quickly survey the entire proposal or locate any specific part.

Third, write some **objectives.** These objectives should be clear. A simple, short, numbered list works best, leaving a sense that these authors are serious; they know exactly what they wish to achieve, and they know how to conduct the activities specified in this proposal to achieve these goals. Remember that you are asking to be trusted to manage and protect this money as if it belonged to you. It's no wonder that potential funders demand clarity. It's no wonder that they choose to fund proposals that have clear objectives and logical procedures for attaining them.

Guideline 8: Follow the RFP Guidelines Precisely

The RFP is the best single source of information available to most writers; yet, few use it to its full advantage. If you are fortunate enough to have an RFP, follow it to the letter. The RFP is usually written by a team. Often, some or all of the RFP developers are also assigned the task of evaluating the proposals. Each makes sure that the RFP contains some of his or her personal needs or interests. So, by carefully responding to *each part* of the RFP, proposal writers

FIGURE 12.5   Sample proposal abstract.

Responding to the critical shortage of high school physics teachers, the investigator proposes a 10-week summer institute which will better prepare secondary teachers who are now teaching physics or who anticipate teaching physics this fall but who lack certification in the area of physics. Each participant will be given a total of 266 contact hours of physics courses, laboratory experiences, tutorials, and seminars, providing students the opportunity to earn 12 semester credit hours.

During the fall semester, each participant will be visited at his or her own school and provided opportunity to ask further questions and share successes and criticisms of the materials developed in the institute.

help to ensure support from all of the evaluators. Unlike the sample physics proposal, which received an 11 to 0 vote, most grant decisions are based on a very narrow margin. Points are carefully counted and added for each part of each proposal. Often the winner is identified by only a few votes, sometimes by only a fraction of one percent.

Proposal evaluators are usually provided a rating form. By examining a sample rating form you can begin to see the proposals from the evaluators' perspective. Appendix G shows the actual rating form used to evaluate the physics proposals. Do not be reluctant to ask the funding source for an evaluation form.

Guideline 9: Develop a Project Evaluation Process

Most RFPs require a project evaluation process as part of every proposal. To provide impartiality, most RFPs require that such evaluations be conducted by outside evaluators who have expertise in conducting evaluations and who are positioned to conduct the evaluation impartially and objectively. The purpose of this requirement is to assure representatives of the funding agency that they are getting complete value from their investment.

When correctly designed, the project evaluation can serve the proposal writer, too. For this reason, you should always include an evaluation component in your proposals, even when it is not required. By doing so, you give the funding agency an assurance that most of the competing proposals won't offer. This, alone, gives your proposal some advantage. Perhaps even more important, the evaluation can help your proposal remain competitive when you apply for repeats if you address the weaknesses identified by the evaluation. The followup visits with the built-in evaluations undoubtedly played a significant role in the physics proposal which beat all of the competition for several consecutive years. The more closely you follow the RFP, the more support you garner.

Project evaluations should appraise both the process by which the study was conducted and the product or outcome. For example, the hypothetical proposal (mentioned earlier) to improve instruction skills of part-time faculty members would be evaluated by focusing on the steps used and by assessing how smoothly and exactly each step was implemented. The product evaluation might measure the performance of students in a control group of part-time teachers' classes and the performance of a similar group who participated in the program.

Guideline 10: Test the Budget against the Narrative

When you have finished writing your proposal and have developed a budget, test this budget against the narrative part of the proposal. A sensible budget must include costs associated with personnel, equipment, and travel.

When complete, the budget should mirror the narrative. This means that the major objectives and the major parts of the project should incur the largest expenses. This happens best when you write your budget last. An imbalance between your proposal narrative and budget can be corrected by adjusting the budget so that it will reflect the narrative. (See Section VI of the physics teachers' institute proposal contained in Appendix F.)

The two largest items in the budget for the physics teacher institute were support for the participants and the coursework that the participants take. Together, these two items account for a significant percent of the total budget for this proposal. This parallels the importance of these two elements. Suppose that the combined budget for these two items had totaled only 20 percent or 30 percent of the total budget. The proper way to correct this imbalance is not to change the text, nor is it to compromise and tone down the importance of these items. Rather, the correct way to adjust for this discrepancy is to change the budget, increasing the amounts allocated to these two major goals until their allotments accurately reflect the relative importance of these two goals to the importance of the total project.

RECAPPING THE MAJOR POINTS

In summary, grant writing offers a way to obtain resources and opportunities for your organization or institution—resources and opportunities that otherwise would not be available, especially during an economic recession. But the competition is getting stronger all the time, and this means that you must develop and refine your grant proposal writing skills so that you can produce the best proposal submitted. The following elements are essential:

- **Excellent Timing:** Combine two or more highly popular ideas. If needed, consult the research.
- **Unique Angle:** Give your proposal a quality of its own, but be practical.
- **Heavy Commitment:** Get your organization to make a strong in-kind contribution. Match this with a personal commitment of your own time and expertise.
- **Flexibility:** As a proposal writer, your job is to please the funder. If you are very lucky you can please yourself, too; however, the importance of your own desires must be a distant second to those of the funder. Use inside information when you can get it, but never give up hope just because you don't have an inside source.
- **Responsibility:** Don't ask for too much, and never use the grant to get individual gifts for yourself or your own office.
- **Clarity:** Write simply. Include an abstract, a list of clear objectives, and a table of contents.

- **Attention to the Guidelines**: If an RFP is available, follow it precisely and completely.
- **Evaluation**: Always develop a method to evaluate your proposal. Include both process and product appraisals and have them conducted by external evaluators. Remember to test the budget against the narrative.

Perhaps the best guideline you can follow when writing a grant proposal is to think of yourself as the potential funder. Knowing that you would want to get the most possible for your money, design every part of the proposal, especially the budget, accordingly.

REFERENCE

Henson, K. T. (2004). *Grant writing in higher education: A step-by-step guide*. Boston: Allyn & Bacon.

13

PARTS OF A PROPOSAL

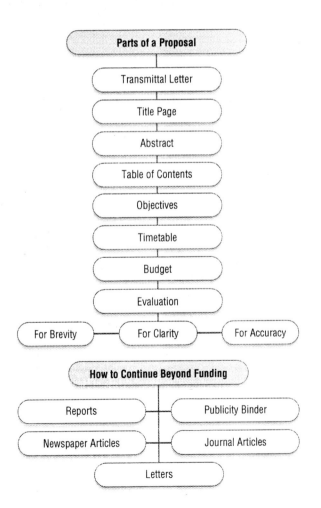

Novice grant writers often find the task of writing grant proposals daunting because, although it can play an important part in the lives of today's professionals, few college programs prepare their students for this responsibility. Through the years, grant writing has mysteriously remained a major responsibility in many professions; yet it has not managed to become part of college curricula, and new professionals are expected to develop the necessary grant writing skills on their own. With the absence of any leadership, most novice professionals don't even know what parts to include in their proposals. It is little wonder that without any grant writing training in most programs, students can earn the highest degrees in their disciplines, graduate, and begin their careers totally bewildered over the grant writing process. But it doesn't have to be that way, and it shouldn't be. This chapter is written to help you decide what parts to put in your proposals and to provide guidance in the writing of each part.

Some RFPs specify the parts their evaluators expect to find in the proposals they read. For grants that specify certain parts, these specifications, like all requirements stated in RFPs, should be adhered to rigorously, No guideline is more important than this: Always address part of the proposal as directly, clearly, and convincingly as you can.

Unfortunately, most RFPs do not specify the exact parts their proposals should have, and for those RFPs, the decision as to exactly which parts to include is somewhat subjective. For example, while one might argue that all proposals should require a budget or transmittal page, it is less certain that all should contain an abstract or a title page. When written correctly, each of the proposal parts can become an opportunity to sell your proposal to the readers; therefore, when you are in doubt as to whether to include one of the parts, include it.

This chapter introduces those parts of a proposal that have proven successful in applying for more than thirty grants, therefore, while some of these parts are not offered as prescriptions, each has proved to be important and should be given close consideration. You can think of the parts as tools that you can use to enhance the acceptance of your proposals. These parts include a (1) transmittal letter, (2) title page, (3) abstract, (4) table of contents, (5) purposes, goals, and objectives, (6) timetable, (7) evaluation, and (8) budget.

TRANSMITTAL LETTER

The transmittal letter is a short, one- or two-page letter written by the senior officer at a company or institution. Its purposes are to introduce the proposal and to assure the potential funders that the institution supports the proposal. By signing the transmittal letter, the senior officer agrees to stand behind the promises and commitments made by those who wrote the proposal.

The importance of keeping the transmittal letter short can be appreciated by remembering the last time you saw a guest speaker or keynote speaker being introduced by a windy introduction that turned out to be as long as the anticipated speech. If your proposal's transmittal letter is too long, the evaluators have the power to put your proposal in the rejection file and go to another proposal. So, when you ask your senior officer for a transmittal letter, you might wish to ask for a short transmittal letter. An even better approach is to draft the letter and ask the senior officer to make the necessary adjustments in the letter and then put it on his or her letterhead. Like the rest of the proposal, the transmittal letter should be written in a clear, straightforward style.

At a minimum, the transmittal letter should contain the following.

- The president's phone number
- The president's fax number
- The president's address
- A statement of purpose

Notice that the sample transmittal letter shown in Figure 13.1 immediately defines the problem that the investigators plan to address. The letter also answers an important question, "Why us? Why should we be the ones to study this problem? What special skills or resources do we have that suggest we would be more successful than others who are responding to this RFP?" Notice too, that this letter uses recent data from a credible source to substantiate its claim that the problem really is significant.

> Using the sample transmittal letter shown in Figure 13.1, you can develop your own generic transmittal letter template. Your template letter should include some of your special needs and some of your unique strengths that you can use in all types of proposals.

TITLE PAGE

A title page is a sparse page that resembles the top page of a business report or the top sheet on a college research assignment. See Figure 13.2. At a minimum, the title page should include the following:

- The project's title
- The name of the company or institution submitting the proposal
- The date

The title page may include additional information, such as the amount of money requested or the names, phone numbers, and fax numbers of the

FIGURE 13.1 Sample transmittal letter.

Mr. Robert P. Anderson, Executive Director
Southwest Foundations, Inc.
108 Holly Hill Drive
P.O. Box 55
Lubbock, TX 79493

Dear Mr. Anderson:

A recent study released by the U.S. Department of Health has reported obesity as the number one health problem of America's youths.

The Nurse Practitioner Program in the School of Allied Health and Nursing at Southwest University seeks support for the enclosed proposal, titled the Ashley Obesity Reduction Program for America's Youths. We have taken a holistic approach to this problem because we believe that most of today's weight problems result from a change in lifestyle. Our proposed program begins at the pre-elementary school level because this same report says that poor eating habits and sedentary lifestyle begin at this early age.

We have chosen to send this proposal to you because we know that your organization is committed to improving the health of individuals at all ages, especially teenagers and children.

Because our state has the highest rate of obesity in the nation, we believe that our need for addressing this issue is acute; however, our decision to attack this problem is based on an even greater factor: Our organization has studied health practices among youths and has experimented with developing health foods for over one hundred years. We have accumulated a knowledge base to build upon.

Please let us know if further information or explanation is needed. Thank you for considering this proposal.

Sincerely,

Jania K. Worley, President
Southwest University
301 University Avenue
Lubbock, TX 79493
Phone: (704) 822-5186
Fax: (704) 822-5102

FIGURE 13.2   Sample title page.

A Proposed Method for Enhancing the Purity of Steel

Submitted to: The Vulcan Foundation

by

The Rocky Mountain Bureau of Mines

July 21, 2004

investigators. But, since the title page serves as a graphic organizer, enabling easy and quick identification of your proposal, and because your proposal is likely to be one of many proposals being evaluated, brevity is essential.

If you are responding to an RFP, check the RFP to make sure that your title reflects the purpose(s) described. If you are not responding to an RFP, check the mission statement of your targeted funder. You might literally pull some key words from this statement to use in your title, giving your proposal a closer-than-average similarity to the major concerns and goals of the targeted funding agency.

Although you want to avoid using jargon unnecessarily, using a few key words to give focus to the proposal is another matter, because it suggests to the reader that you understand and intend to serve the funder's mission.

ABSTRACT

An abstract is a short description of the proposal. Some funders require an abstract; others do not. Check your RFP. If an abstract is required, follow the specifications precisely. Most RFPs that require abstracts specify required lengths (for example, *Include a 250-word abstract*). Other RFPs that require abstracts specify maximum lengths (for example, *Include an abstract, not to exceed 500 words*). These common restrictions reflect the purpose of abstracts, which is to enable the evaluators to make a quick assessment of all the proposals received. The evaluators may begin the evaluation process by conducting an initial screening, and to make this screening, they may read only the abstracts. Many grant proposal evaluators receive so many proposals that they have to find a way to reduce the number of proposals they must deal with to a small fraction of all the proposals they receive. This makes the abstract extremely important.

Other RFPs do not require or, indeed, even mention an abstract, leaving the choice to you. If your proposal is longer than two or three pages, seriously consider preparing an abstract. Carefully written, the abstract will highlight your proposal's major features. To ensure that your proposal works to its maximum potential, examine the RFP to learn the most important purposes and goals of the funder. Extract a few of these key concepts for your abstract. Then, think about your own reasons for writing the proposal and the unique qualities of your proposal. Include some of these unique features. Think of the abstract not as a requirement but as an *opportunity* to sell your ideas to the evaluators, and construct it accordingly. Once you have drafted your abstract, edit it until it reads smoothly. As you may recall from Chapter 12, a proposal abstract should resemble Figure 13.3, the sample abstract for the physics proposal.

FIGURE 13.3   Sample proposal abstract.

Responding to the critical shortage of high school physics teachers, the investigator proposes a 10-week summer institute which will better prepare secondary teachers who are now teaching physics or who anticipate teaching physics this fall but who lack certification in the area of physics. Each participant will be given a total of 266 contact hours of physics courses, laboratory experiences, tutorials, and seminars, providing students the opportunity to earn 12 semester credit hours.

   During the fall semester, each participant will be visited at his or her own school and provided opportunity to ask further questions and share successes and criticisms of the materials developed in the institute.

TABLE OF CONTENTS

Some RFPs specify a table of contents as a requirement, but most RFPs leave the decision to include or omit a table of contents to their writers. Like the title page and abstract, the table of contents is a visual tool that can work for you and, therefore, is too important to omit. Furthermore, the table of contents can be constructed easily and quickly. For example, see the table of contents shown in Figure 13.4.

   Begin by titling your table of contents. Then, using Roman numerals, list the major parts of the proposal. On the right-hand side of the page, insert the page numbers. When you have completed filling in all of the parts, check your list and make certain that you have not overlooked any parts. A simple omission can be interpreted as carelessness and can lose the confidence of funders, who may generalize and conclude that you will be equally careless with the implementation of your proposal.

PURPOSES, GOALS, AND OBJECTIVES

Purposes are global statements used to explain the general expectations of the funder. For example, a purpose of a grant proposal might be to reduce the pollution in a particular part of the city. This is a little vague. It doesn't tell what types of pollution, how great the need is to reduce pollution, or how the forthcoming reduction of pollution is to be measured.

   Goals are used to break the purposes down into parts. One goal might be to reduce the number of pollutants in the air; another one might concern the water. But neither of these goals answers the question, What types of air pollutants or water pollutants? Or, How much does the funder want these to be reduced? So, goals are broken down into objectives, which are much more specific. For example, one objective might be to reduce the amount of sulfur in the air to one part in each 10,000 parts. Each objective should be a short statement with an action verb written in present or future tense.

Get a copy of your institution or company's mission statement. Examine it for goals. For each goal, write one or two specific objectives telling how you can help reach each of these goals.

TIMETABLE

Funders always want to know the different stages in the project, when you can begin implementing the project, and how long each stage will take. If the project has several steps or phases, it is the investigator's responsibility to

FIGURE 13.4   Sample table of contents.

Physics Teachers Summer Institute Proposal
Table of Contents

I. PROJECT SUMMARY	Page	1
II. PROJECT DESCRIPTION		2
A. Objectives		2
B. Participant Selection		4
1. Number of participants		4
2. Policy for admission		4
3. Selection procedure		5
C. Program Content		6
1. Physics 110		6
2. Physics electives		7
3. Integrated laboratory		8
4. Seminar		9
D. Additional Components		9
1. Follow-up activities		9
2. Evaluation		9
III. STAFF		10
IV. FACILITIES		11
A. Instructional Facilities		11
B. Housing Facilities		12
V. INSTITUTIONAL SUPPORT		12
VI. BUDGET		14

make a clear distinction between each phase and inform the funder as to when each phase will start and end. Because funders often have so many proposals to consider, failure to communicate the different phases and the time frame for each can be disastrous; unclear proposals simply get put aside and end up in the rejection pile.

The flow chart is an excellent tool to use to show your sequence of events and the times you expect to begin and end each event. As you assign the time for each phase, remember that funders give their support because they have a job that they want to get done. If there is an urgency to get the program into operation, the evaluators will be sensitive to the urgency and may be highly influenced by the ability of some investigators to complete the job sooner than others. This suggests that you should be ready to immediately begin putting the first implementation phase of your project into action as soon as you learn that your project has been funded. But remember also that the funders demand quality work; allow the time you believe will be required to do a good job. The goal here is to present a timetable that shows that you are ready to begin implementing your project and that, once you begin, you will move the project forward from one phase to another until it becomes operational. See Figure 13.5. Notice that it lists all of the steps in chronological order and also includes specific beginning and ending dates for all phases of the project.

FIGURE 13.5   Sample timetable.

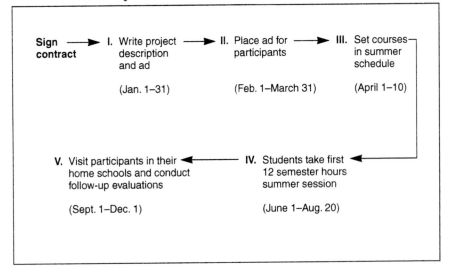

Source: From "Debunking Some Myths About Grant Writing," by K. T. Henson, *The Chronicle of Higher Education*, Vol. 60, No. 3, June 26, 2003. Reprinted with permission.

In retrospect, it is easy to see that this timetable has a major omission. It fails to include plans to disseminate information. At the beginning of the first summer session (June 1), plans to have a news reporter on hand should have been included. Most funders like to have publicity on their programs showing their generosity and commitment to the causes they support. The publicity can also be filed and used in future years to strengthen applications for further grants.

Make a list of at least three or four strategies you can always use to publicize your grants. Write these strategies down, including the addresses and phone numbers of consultants and news reporters. You might also want to include the editors and addresses of journals to which you would like to target articles you write to help others use these new programs.

Another factor to consider is extending the timetable to show your plans to continue the program *after* the funder's support is withdrawn. Obviously, not all grant proposals are written to establish programs, so providing information on how you plan to sustain your program once the funds dry up was not listed as a proposal part on the checklist provided later in this chapter. If, however, your proposal does involve establishing a program or an ongoing service, having a clear statement explaining how you propose to keep your program alive could be one of the most influential parts of your proposal. Grant funders know that a very high percentage of funded programs immediately die once the funding ends.

As you know, hindsight offers opportunities to discover omissions that were not noticed earlier. Examine the sample timetable shown in Figure 13.5 and see if you can find other events and dates that could improve the project.

EVALUATION

Most RFPs require the investigators to arrange for external evaluations to make comprehensive assessments of their programs. Others permit investigators to conduct the evaluations themselves. When given the choice between conducting the evaluation yourself and hiring an external evaluator, seriously consider the latter choice. Regardless of how objective and accurate your own evaluation might be, it is always subject to suspicion; therefore, it is usually far better to commission a third party to perform the evaluation. Always select a company or evaluation consultant who has no connections with your company or institution.

Although you decide to use an external evaluator, you should consider collecting your own data. These data can be quickly and easily gathered. The grant whose timetable is shown in Figure 13.5 won over the competition five years running. The continuing success can be attributed to a very simple annual evaluation. Each year, *after* the summer institute was over, the investigator drove to see the participants and ask them two questions: *"What did you get in last summer's institute that you have been able to implement?"* and *"What might we have done in the institute that would have helped you even more?"* Having the proposal win over the competition for five consecutive years was a great payoff for asking two simple questions. (Of course, each year we used the answers to these two questions to rewrite and improve the proposal.)

BUDGET

Be Reasonable

Virtually all RFPs require budgets, to show how much money they will be asked to provide and how that money will be spent. Naturally, a major concern is always the need for the investigator to be a good steward of funds. Two principles should be remembered at the onset of constructing a budget. First, do not succumb to the common temptation to purchase a computer or other items that are not absolutely essential to perform the responsibilities of the grant. Even if a computer is essential, to avoid suspicion of the evaluators, consider renting one instead of purchasing it. Second, treat the grant money as though you were spending your own money. Ask for enough money to do a good job, but don't be overly generous with someone else's money.

Some grant writers argue that the budget should be the first part of the grant-writing process because by developing the budget first and then writing the body of the grant, they are able to stay within the limits specified in their budget. Others find this process too restrictive and prefer to spell out all other parts of the program and, then, as a final step, prepare the budget. The order is a personal choice. Regardless of when the budget is written, however, it must reflect the mission of the proposal. This means that the items that cost the most should be the most essential parts.

Begin by listing the most costly, tangible items. Then list the most costly intangibles. Salaries are often among this latter group. Don't forget to include overhead expenses. If you work at an institution of higher learning, check with your grants office for the exact amount to ask for overhead. If your institution, business, or organization is small and does not have a grants and contracts office, your administration can provide this information.

Make In-Kind Contributions

A part of the budget that has become increasingly important over the years is in-kind contributions. These are noncash contributions that your institution or company makes to the project. In-kind contributions have become increasingly more important because funders have expected investigators to make larger and larger contributions. Indeed, many grants of recent years require an even dollar-for-dollar match.

The investigator can use in-kind contributions to make this match. These include such items as portions of salaries of employees who spend time working on the project. The investigators themselves may offer to spend a portion of their time codirecting the program and therefore should list the percent of their salary that is reflected in the percent of their working time spent on the project. Don't forget to also count the time that secretaries and other clerical employees might spend on the project. The cost of building space required to house the project can be calculated and counted as an in-kind contribution. The space includes buildings and rooms rented especially for the project, and it also includes buildings and space that your employer already owns. Don't forget to include the cost of utilities and photocopying.

Once your budget is drafted, review it for missing items and to see that it mirrors the body of your proposal. For example, the most expensive items should not include expendable items.

Remember that once the program is in operation, you may not be able to adjust the budget for at least a year. Furthermore, it is conceivable that the funder may wish to negotiate for a smaller budget. Desperate to have their proposal funded, some investigators accept cuts in their budgets that are so severe that they cannot conduct the project effectively. This is a common mistake. One way to plan to cushion against possible forthcoming negotiations is to plan an extra dimension into the proposal, perhaps a service that would be a nice feature but not an indispensable one. So, when the funder says you must cut the budget by 10 percent or 20 percent, for example, this could be done by eliminating this expendable feature, without damaging the rest of the proposal. Most funders like this feature because it gives them an opportunity to exercise caution against padded or inflated budgets without sacrificing the quality of the overall project.

CHECKLIST

To guard against omissions, some grant writers make a checklist of all the major parts in their grant proposals. They use this as a first *and* last step. This is an easy task if you list each part of the grant under a subheading. It is further simplified by putting each subheading in italics or bold letters. The checklist might contain the following parts:

- Transmittal letter
- Title page
- Abstract

- Table of contents
- Purposes, goals, and objectives
- Timetable
- Evaluation
- Budget

SUMMARY

Grant writing can be made easier by knowing exactly what parts your proposal should include. Many RFPs list the parts the evaluators will expect to see when they examine and evaluate the proposals. Some evaluators are given evaluation guides or rating sheets with instruction to give each proposal part a numerical rating. When the scoring is complete, these evaluators simply add the scores and award the grant to the proposals with the highest scores. Therefore, it behooves the investigator to (1) follow the directions and include every part that is listed in the RFP and (2) ask whether a proposal evaluation score sheet is available for use in preparing the proposal.

For the many RFPs that do not specify the exact parts they wish to have in their proposals, remember that each part can be a tool to sell your proposal to the evaluators; therefore, you should seriously consider including all of the parts discussed in this chapter.

Because many evaluators receive an unmanageable number of long, poorly written proposals, brevity and clarity should be the goal when writing each part. Include just enough in each part to do the job, and the job, of course, is to communicate clearly and persuasively. Putting quality above everything else is an equally important principle to use as a guideline when preparing proposals. While it is to your advantage to be both economical and expedient, promising to deliver too much too soon can be disastrous. Common sense and good judgment should temper your temptation to overcommit.

Credibility is an indispensable quality for all grant writers. Experienced grant writers who have written previous grants and have successfully implemented them have an advantage over novice grant writers, but only if they have collected data and maintained records to substantiate their success. Novice grant writers can offset this advantage by keeping careful records and by using their first grant and each succeeding grant to establish their own record of credibility.

For novice writers, it is possible to put credibility into that first proposal by citing the literature. Funders expect to see evidence of need for the proposed program or product, and they expect to see data to support any claims that the investigators make, including their claims to have expertise or other resources such as the facilities and human power needed to support their proposal. Locating and citing studies that support your generalizations can be tantamount to taking that extra step to ensure acceptance of your proposal.

When your proposal is complete, check it against your parts checklist to see that no part was inadvertently omitted. As incredible as it may sound, sometimes investigators become so wrapped up in the writing of their proposals that they leave out some of the most important parts, including the budget, when they are mailing; therefore, you should use this checklist again when you are literally putting the proposal in an envelope to mail.

A final check is also needed to remove any grammatical or mathematical errors. Simple errors give the impression that the investigator is careless, leading the evaluators to believe that anyone who makes errors in the proposal would be equally careless in overseeing the grant, if, somehow, the flawed proposal were eventually funded.

RECAPPING THE MAJOR POINTS

- Some RFPs specify the parts the evaluators expect to see in all proposals. Evaluators frequently assign points to each part of the proposal and total the scores to determine which proposals will be funded.
- Clarity and brevity should be the goals for preparing each part of each proposal.
- Each part of each proposal can be used as a tool to garner support for the proposal.
- Most funders value the ability to deliver a quality program or product over the needs of the investigators; therefore, do not emphasize need over ability.
- Investigators should avoid including extra equipment purchases, such as computers.
- Investigators should be prudent but realistic when preparing their budgets.
- RFPs should always be followed meticulously.
- Investigators can strengthen their proposals by citing reports and articles.
- Each proposal should include a method for publicizing the program.
- Investigators should explain how their programs will be continued after support from the funder is discontinued.

14

THREE WINNING PROPOSALS

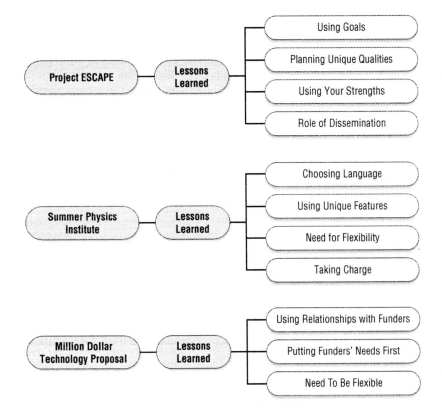

PRELUDE

Grant writing is a slippery business. The nature of grant writing is such that you can write about it or talk about it at great lengths without causing the audience to understand how to do it successfully. Sometimes what is needed is a good example of a real grant proposal, one that was carefully crafted, submitted for evaluation, and chosen above its competitors for funding. Each of the following three sections focuses on a separate grant proposal that has met all of these conditions. Each section will point specifically to the strengths of each of the proposals—unique features that are responsible for that proposal's having been selected above its competition. Each of these unique strengths is a quality that you can include in your proposals. To make these experiences more realistic, each of these sections is written in the first person.

Many grant-writing workshop participants say that they need to see some proposals that have been funded. While this is clearly helpful, participant's often need explanations for particular features in the proposals and the writer's techniques for getting the proposals funded. Put another way, participants find it helpful to have someone walk them through the process, explaining the reasons for particular features in the proposals and pointing out the steps followed in getting the proposals funded. This chapter will introduce three different proposals and will explain the features of each and the steps followed in getting each funded.

PROPOSAL ONE: PROJECT ESCAPE

It was early December and I was barely out of my doctoral program. I had moved 500 miles to take my first higher education teaching position at a Midwestern university, choosing this position over several others because it provided ready access to a mainframe computer, a half-time editor for the faculty's use, and the opportunity to work with a nationally known professor in the department, a prolific writer who enjoyed sharing his expertise by teaching a course to the faculty titled "Writing for Professional Publication."

Purpose of the Proposal

Having received a doctoral degree in curriculum and research, and having the level of optimism that characterizes most recent graduates, I was determined to create a better teacher education program than anyone had ever seen before. I wanted a very different program, and if my wants were granted, this program would be totally field based; all of the pedagogy would occur not on the university campuses but in elementary and secondary classrooms. A second major condition for this new program is that it would be totally performance based.

I checked with the university's office of grants and contracts to locate a potential funder for a performance-based, school based, teacher education program. The news was disappointing; no known source was currently funding program designs for higher education programs. So, I talked to my colleagues, who found my idea interesting but who also knew of no possible funding source for such a program.

Our school had a nice teachers' lounge where we often retreated between classes for a quick cup of coffee to prime ourselves for the next class. As I sat quietly, enjoying a moment of silence and a good cup of coffee, two colleagues entered the room, barely acknowledging my presence because they were engrossed in their own conversation. One was telling the other about a new teacher burnout program that he had heard was coming to the local schools. As this colleague talked, I sipped my coffee and listened. The purpose of some forthcoming grant money was to design programs to rejuvenate teachers who were experiencing emotional burnout.

As the discussion continued, I thought about my desire to create a performance-based, school-based teacher education program, wondering whether the new teacher burnout program and my personal dream for a model teacher education program might, in some way, be connected. Being an early riser, I was fortunate to have my teaching load in the mornings, freeing my afternoons for conducting research, preparing lessons, and handling other professional responsibilities, including grant writing. So, the next morning I taught my classes, went directly to my car, and drove to the state capital where I began asking about the proposed teacher burnout program. I wasn't professionally mature enough to solicit the help of my legislators, but I had one force on my side: persistence. I was determined to have my model teacher education program.

The State Department of Education office had both good news and bad news. The good news was that the rumor I had heard was true; money had been appropriated to support teacher burnout research. The bad news was that the money was earmarked, not for universities, but for elementary and secondary schools. The further less-than-good news was that the request for proposals (RFP) had already been issued and it had a short deadline. The job was too big for one individual to do alone in the short time available. In retrospect, for an inexperienced group of writers, quickly creating a proposal wasn't very realistic. But, fortunately, I was too inexperienced to realize the odds, and even had I known of the slim chances for success, I was probably too determined and self-assured to respect these odds. All I knew for sure was that if I didn't try, I was certain not to have my dreams become a reality. Even with an outside chance, the only way to meet this challenge was to locate some interested partners who were willing to work through part of their Christmas break. Still determined, I located three equally inexperienced colleagues who agreed to spend part of their holidays preparing a grant proposal. Following is a description of that proposal.

Examine your own workplace. Do you have a coffee or a lunch group; a golf, racquet ball, or other exercise group; or a civic club where you can gather ideas for research project topics? Or as in this case, do you have a place where you might learn of funding opportunities? Choose one of these group gatherings to routinely discuss your creative ideas and keep an ongoing record of the positive or negative reactions of your colleagues. Should you choose to collaborate on a proposal, this record will help you identify colleagues who share your commitments.

Putting the Funder's Goals First

Our program was not created to replace the existing, traditional teacher education program; rather it was aimed at a small cohort of exceptionally bright students who sought to escape the traditional route to teacher education, students who would prefer to develop their pedagogical skills in elementary and secondary classrooms. As with all successful grant proposals, our own professional and personal goals had to become secondary to the potential funder's goal. According to this RFP, the funder's goal was to reduce the level of teacher burnout in elementary and secondary schools throughout the state. So, to be competitive, our proposal had to proclaim reducing teacher burnout as its paramount goal, and we had to devise a method to convince the evaluators that our proposed program would meet this goal.

Unique Features

Our program would not purport to erase all teacher burnout in the state; rather, we proposed to identify a manageable number of highly competent teachers who just happened to be experiencing burnout: We decided that a manageable number of participants would be fifty teachers, so we settled on twenty-five elementary school teachers and twenty-five secondary school teachers.

We wanted to believe that the best proposals are always the ones that are selected for funding, but we knew that this is not always true. Although we did not know why this happened, we knew that often some of the best proposals are overlooked. The most important thing we knew was that each proposal that is accepted for funding is selected because it is different from the other proposals; it has one or more qualities that make it stand out above the many other competing proposals. We knew that we had better use this knowledge well to enhance the chances that our proposal would be accepted. All we had to do was to make certain that our proposed program had some unique features that the evaluators would consider strengths.

In a sense, our program would be unique because it was performance based. This was a uniqueness, and we knew that the evaluators would probably consider it desirable because performance-based programs were becoming popular and performance-based assessment was being proposed for all schools. But we knew that this uniqueness might not be enough; after all, some of the other proposals might be performance based.

> *Just as it is important that grant writers remain willing to put the goals of the potential funders ahead of their own goals, it is equally important that grant writers have their own professional and personal goals identified and in mind at all times. Take a few moments and jot down some of your professional and personal goals. Make each of these goals time specific by giving it a deadline. By this time next year, I will have done such and such.*

When choosing unique qualities for your own proposals, it is important that you *keep your attention on the purpose of the program, as it is stated in the RFP.* My own personal purpose for this proposal was to develop a superior, performance-based model for a teacher education program, one that our college and other colleges could use to prepare future teachers. But, to my knowledge, the evaluators for this program weren't interested in my goal; they wanted a program that would eliminate some of the teacher burnout pervasive in elementary and secondary schools throughout the state. They wanted to jump start those teachers who had emotionally burned out.

USING THE LITERATURE

We researched the literature that related to the funder's goal—teacher burnout—and discovered that there was agreement—we found at least two supporting articles—that the point at which most teachers experience the most burnout is during their sixth or seventh year. We said so, citing these articles. Citing current journal articles, books, and research has value in itself; it earns the evaluators' confidence, reassuring them that they are entrusting their money to individuals who are knowledgeable and current in their field, individuals who are willing to put forth the energy required to substantiate their work. Citing references also suggests that the proposal writers are thorough, reassuring the evaluators that if their proposal is chosen for funding that these writers will make the extra effort needed to ensure that their project succeeds.

> *Check a few of the journals in your field, some that you may choose to target some of your own articles and note the referencing style used in these journals. Most disciplines have a preferred referencing style. By examining a few of these journals, you can determine the preferred or most frequently used style in your discipline. Get a copy of the style manual—the latest edition—and add it to your grant-writing library. (For further instruction in establishing a grant-writing library, see Chapter 12.) Reading this manual*

from time to time should become routine behavior in your ongoing grant-writing program.

Keeping the potential funder's central purpose in mind, we decided to design a program that would rejuvenate teachers who were experiencing high levels of burnout. We were careful to specify that the teachers chosen would be exceptionally talented teachers. This served our grant proposal well because while many of our competitors were building a case based on their *needs* (a common mistake among grant writers), we were basing our program, not on our needs, but on our strengths. Some investigators (grant writers) believe that the prize goes to the institution or individuals with the greatest needs. I don't. People like to identify with winners, and people like to invest in winners; so we wanted our proposal to have the markings of a winner throughout.

Dealing with Disagreement

So far, it sounds as though we collaborators were in perfect agreement on all issues. Actually, nothing could be further from the truth, we were the clumsiest collection of individual thinkers imaginable, and this will be revealed later; but, we were a congenial collection of individuals, and we used our disagreements to strengthen our program.

Too often, teams fall apart when they learn that they do not agree on all issues. Actually, disagreement can be helpful if it is managed appropriately. Once a decision to collaborate has been reached, the leader should immediately call a meeting to plan and organize the strategy for this group. During this first meeting, all members should agree to express their feelings and beliefs and then *go with the majority;* unanimity is not necessary. If the group has a member who is known for being argumentative, or a member who has a record of writing minority reports, eliminate that member. Remember that regardless of how excited that member may be over the proposed grant topic, the best predictor for future behavior is prior behavior; get rid of that member or get out of the group yourself. From the onset, we agreed to let all members express their preferences on every issue but to let no member impede the progress of the proposal.

Using Modules

Through surveying the literature, we learned that other performance-based programs used modules to develop the desired skills. We knew that modules were an effective way to develop teaching skills, so we, too, chose to use modules in our program. Modules provide a way to ensure that the program has clear objectives and that it has activities to cover all objectives. To teach our teachers and students about modules, we even wrote a module on modules. We also knew the value in shared ownership; people work harder when they perceive the project as their own, not a job to be done for somebody else. Because we had chosen to use the best teachers, it seemed to make sense to give them a lot of leadership. These were the brightest of the bright and the best of the best, so we wanted to use their talents and, at the same time, give them ownership in the program.

Unlike other performance-based programs, which were written by professors and research and development (R and D) experts, we decided to entrust our teachers to write the modules. We went a step further. Unlike all other performance-based programs that we found in our review of the literature, whose objectives and topics were chosen by professors and R and D teams, we decided to let our teachers choose the topics for their modules. In a sense, this plan was flawed because most of the teachers had far less writing skill than we had envisioned, yet, putting teachers in charge of writing their own modules was one of the best decisions we made because it gave them ownership and commitment. We simply began by telling the teachers that they had been chosen for this program because their respective principals had identified them as being among the best of the best teachers in their respective schools. We asked them to reflect individually on their teaching and tell us what one or two areas they might choose if they could improve even more. Would they improve their classroom management? Testing skills? Motivational skills? For their module topics, teachers could choose an area of individual weakness or they could choose to develop a model that focused on and taught future teachers their greatest strengths.

To avoid duplication, we made a comprehensive list of all areas identified and matched individual teachers with one of their top preferences. Each topic would become a learning module, which would immediately improve the skills of the teacher who developed it and we would develop a dissemination plan to ensure that these models would eventually impact teachers throughout the state.

If it is, indeed, true that people hire to be associated with winners, it will behoove any serious grant writers to assess their own strengths. In his 1994 inaugural address, Nelson Mandela wrote,

Our deepest fear is not that we are inadequate. Our deepest fear is that we are powerful beyond measure. It is our light, not our darkness that most frightens us. We ask ourselves who am I to be brilliant, gorgeous, talented, and fabulous? Actually, who am I not to be! Your playing small doesn't serve the world.

There is nothing enlightened about shrinking so that other people won't feel insecure around you. We were born to manifest the glory that is within us. It is not just in some of us; it's in everyone. As we let our own light shine, we unconsciously give other people permission to do the same. As we are liberated from our own fear, our presence automatically liberates others.

Without being overly modest, take a few minutes to make a list of your own strengths. Consider both your personal and professional qualities.

After some six months had passed, news that our proposal had been selected for funding arrived. Unfortunately, I was teaching a three-week-long comparative education course in London, England. I returned on a Saturday, checked my mail, and found both good and bad news. The good news was that our proposal had been selected above all the competition for funding; the bad news was that the program was to start full-time at 8 A.M. Monday, leaving us only one day to prepare. Naturally, we panicked. Our naysayer voices spoke: "There's no way we can do this on such a short notice." "We don't even have a room to meet in." "Half of these teachers are probably on vacation; how will we reach them?" "We don't even have a program to follow."

An important and often overlooked advantage of grants is that they provide opportunities to do things differently, things that otherwise would be impossible. Another overlooked advantage is that every funded grant is loaded with learning opportunities. The common expression "Every grant you write is easier than the one before" is true, at least for alert participants who note and record their successes and failures.

Each graduate of our program was promised teacher certification. The summer would be spent writing modules. Each teacher would carefully compute an estimate of the number of hours required to complete the module. The module would then be assigned a number of credits. For example, modules that require forty-five or more hours to complete would earn three credit hours of coursework.

Some modules were required of all students who participated in this program because they were based on content that was either required for graduation or for teacher certification. For example, all students in this program had to successfully complete the module on classroom management and the module on testing. The state also required a minimum number of credits in pedagogy; so our students had to complete enough modules to earn the minimum number of credits. Having completed these required modules, the student could then choose the modules preferred to earn the remaining credits. This enabled the students to ESCAPE the normal routine on campus, thus the acronym ESCAPE (Elementary and Secondary Competency Approach to Performance Education).

Disseminating the Grant

When grant money is appropriated by federal, state, or local governments the *evaluators look for assurance that the funded programs will serve the largest number of individuals possible.* Knowing this, you can give your proposal a boost by explaining how large numbers of people will benefit from your proposed program. We wanted our project to benefit more teachers than the fifty who were directly involved in writing the modules, so we put stipulations on each module they produced. Because we knew that many teachers would be bored by a lot of reading assignments, we limited the amount of reading and required each module to have a corresponding videotape. These videotapes were eventually made available to all teachers throughout the state. So that other teachers would be tempted to use these modules, we required each module to have a flowchart, providing easy-to-follow steps for its application. Notice that the sample flowchart in Figure 14.1 guides each student, step-by-step through the program.

This flow chart was designed for the module titled, "A Module on Modules." This particular flow chart provides its unsuccessful users an opportunity to recycle again and again until they succeed. This is a strong quality that can be planned into any module.

As mentioned earlier, one of the favorite modules, "A Module on Modules," was created to help these teachers develop the other modules. Now this same module would be the first module required of all students who

FIGURE 14.1   Sample flowchart.

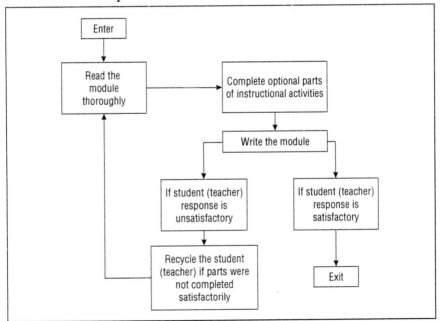

would participate in the ESCAPE Program. It served as a guide to prepare them to follow and use the other modules.

Lessons Learned from Project ESCAPE

Although a good proposal can never be guaranteed funding, the grant writer who uses the tips set forth in this book can significantly improve the probability of acceptance and can learn from the successes and failures associated with each proposal. Following is a list of lessons learned through writing the Project ESCAPE grant:

- Flexibility is essential.
- The desires of the funder must take precedence over the proposal writer's needs.
- Grant writers should remain alert at all times, listening for new funding opportunities.
- The probability of a proposal's acceptance can be increased by including unique features.
- Persistence can turn road blocks into highways of success.
- The roles of collaborators should be spelled out clearly before the project begins.
- To be competitive, each proposal must have unique features.
- Citations from recent books and journals can and will strengthen proposals.
- Demonstration of exactly how the product will be disseminated for the use of others enhances the chances of a proposal's success.
- Disagreement among collaborators can improve a proposal *if* the partners can express their differences and move onward.

PROPOSAL TWO: THE SUMMER PHYSICS INSTITUTE

Grant writing has many benefits, and these benefits differ from one grant writer to another, depending on the professional and personal goals of each grant writer. Successful grant writing requires knowing what benefits you most want to derive from each grant. A major benefit, perhaps even the most important of all, is the self-satisfaction grants can provide by helping you to help others.

The Role of Passion

Having grown up in a rural area, I attended a small, two-room elementary school with three grades in each room. Since then, having worked in hundreds of schools in this country and abroad, I am convinced that my elementary schooling was second to none. The smallness of the classes, the integrated program, and the outstanding teachers made a perfect combination.

By today's standards, the school I attended for my next six years of schooling was also small, with only forty-six students in my graduating class. Unlike my elementary school years, the smallness of my high school had a serious disadvantage: the curriculum was extremely limited. As a lover of both sports and music, I found the absence of a football team and the absence of a band a major handicap. Later, in college, I would discover that for a student who preferred science and mathematics over other subjects, the absence of a foreign language, particularly Latin, was a major disadvantage. The proverbial straw was broken when, in my senior year, I was told that the limited curriculum offerings in my small high school would not enable me to take both advanced science and advanced mathematics. At the beginning of my senior year, I refused to choose between taking advanced science and advanced math, and, instead, transferred to a larger school with a more diversified curriculum.

After becoming a teacher of science and mathematics, and later returning to my home state to work as a teacher educator, I began writing grants to help improve the educational opportunities of others. A rumor was heard that our state, like all other states, was passing legislation that would provide block grants for universities to improve the knowledge and teaching skills of the state's high school teachers of mathematics, chemistry, and physics. I quickly contacted our dean of arts and sciences. Because he was a chemist, I proposed that we collaborate on two grant proposals; he would take lead and be the principal investigator on a chemistry grant proposal and I would do the same on a physics proposal. Because each state was limited to one grant in each discipline, winning either grant would require writing the best proposal in the state. Our chemistry proposal was rejected, but our physics proposal was accepted.

Knowing that we could not directly improve the knowledge and skills of all physics teachers in the state, we focused on those teachers who had little or no background in physics. We proposed to identify ten very bright teachers with little or no coursework in physics and bring them to campus for sequential summer institutes in physics. Our goal was to improve their knowledge of physics and their pedagogical knowledge and skills.

Many individuals are so discouraged by their limitations that they are permanently dissuaded from writing grants. This chapter says that by looking at our limitations, often we can turn these limitations into strengths and then bring substantial strengths to our grant proposals. Reflect on your own background and identify some of your major limitations. Can you think of a way to use these limitations to strengthen your future grant proposals?

Choosing Language

The fact that money was being provided to improve science and math teaching skills at a time when the nation's math and science teachers were being criticized for students' low standardized test scores in science and math was no coincidence. The most common adjective found in the many education reform reports and articles was *rigor*. The writers were saying that our teacher education programs that prepared science and mathematics teachers lacked rigor. I used this knowledge and made our proposed program very *rigorous*. Each summer, each participant would take a full twelve semester hours of physics. This would be a heavy load, indeed, but these were especially gifted teachers. Instead of just "talking the talk" about rigor, this project turned the talk into real program improvements.

Unique Features

Through having had previous proposals funded, I knew that to be seriously considered for funding, a proposal has to get the attention of the evaluators, and gaining the evaluators' attention required a proposal to have one or more unique features. So, I reasoned that if one unique feature would help our proposal get funded, several unique features would almost make it a shoe-in. This proposal would definitely have several unique features including the following:

1. It would be highly rigorous.
2. It would have a special course taught by a special teacher.
3. It would have a weekly seminar that would be very nontraditional and motivating.
4. It would be loaded with laboratory experiences that required no expensive materials or equipment.
5. It would have a special evaluation system that occurred at a unique time.

A Special Course. Most of the coursework in this program would be standard physics courses, but the program would also have a very unique course on pedagogy for physics teachers. Instead of the common course on generic teaching methods or the common course on science methods, this course would be a special treat for teachers who were faced daily with challenging physics problems at the end of each chapter in their high school physics textbook. Even the textbook for this course would be special; unlike the books used in other college classes, it would not be a college text at all but would be the state-adopted textbook for high school physics classes. Once each week, the participants in this summer institute would have the unusual opportunity of seeing an expert work the end-of-chapter problems.

Our physics department had seventeen full-time faculty members and any could have worked these problems with little effort, but we decided to use none of them. The current literature had many articles on *master teachers.* To the layperson, and consequently to legislators, this term had a good ring. Of course, everyone should want all of our elementary and secondary classrooms staffed with master teachers. We took advantage of this knowledge and hired a local high school physics teacher who had earned the title, *master teacher.* Each week this teacher would leave her school for three hours to come over to the university and work the problems at the ends of the chapters in her high school physics text. What a treat for inadequately prepared teachers who were struggling with many of these problems. What a boost for a proposal!

As a sidebar, it is interesting that although the evaluators really liked the idea of our using a master teacher, and although this unique feature undoubtedly played a major role in their decision to fund this proposal, after one summer we decided to replace this highly competent master teacher because the program participants refused to give her the respect and cooperation that they gave to college professors. If we were starting all over from the beginning, would we include the high school master teacher? Indeed, we would. Another group of teachers might have responded differently. Anyhow, the first objective of grant writers must be to have a good idea and the second objective is always to sell this idea to the evaluators. We believe that the master teacher component was a major factor in getting this proposal accepted.

Though it is certainly true that too much ill advice is given to grant writers regarding the need to use jargon and other unfamiliar language, yet, like the previously discussed teacher burnout proposal, this proposal was aimed at getting funds that were established by legislators, and legislators pay an inordinate amount of attention to the language their constituents use. What we did that was different is that we didn't just use the language *master teacher;* we actually used a master teacher, and instead of just using the term *rigorous* to describe our program, we required each student to take a very heavy set of demanding courses.

A Weekly Seminar. As discussed in Chapter 12, effective grant writers learn to keep one eye on the RFP, being careful to respond to every part, while keeping the other eye on their own resources (what they have to offer that the competitors do not have or do not think about offering). Because our university was large and diverse, it was rich with resources, especially human resources. We wanted to bring all of these resources to the bargaining table, so we developed a weekly seminar.

Each Friday, the participants and the codirectors of the institute had lunch together in a dormitory cafeteria. After a leisurely hour-long period of eating and socializing, we would walk together to meet a special member of the university faculty who had volunteered to give us a special seminar. We were careful to invite professors who had topics that we knew would be of high interest to high school physics teachers. Among the many excellent speakers was a physics professor whose specialty was robotics. He brought a robot that he had designed and built and had it perform tasks at our commands. His presentation was unique in that through his work, the university had made the cover of *Time Magazine* twice by intervening to save a local multimillion dollar company that was scheduled for closing.

Another seminar was conducted by a member of the physics department whose specialty was quasars. That seminar had a segment that involved our going to the observatory at night to examine quasars. Since only a few physicists specialize in quasars, these teachers had an interesting story to share with their students the following fall.

Another fascinating seminar was conducted by a former member of the faculty who had been retired for seventeen years and who remained physically fit by working out at the university health center and by walking five miles a day, three days a week. This retired professor had spent his professional career teaching physics and researching the personal lives of famous physicists. He talked at ease for two hours, keeping us mesmerized with his fascinating stories, using a catalog drawer of 3″ × 5″ cards. Each card told a story about a particular physicist, and included personal information that was unknown to most people. Imagine the high school students' reactions to their teachers' personal encounters with robots, quasars, and stories on the personal lives of the physicists in their textbook. Imagine the influence that such a variety of unusual experiences would have on the proposal evaluators' ultimate decision.

> *Every grant proposal needs a unique feature to separate it from all of its competing proposals; and, as with this proposal, all grant writers bring this uniqueness to their projects by using their colleagues in the workplace or elsewhere and using their expertise. Make a list of professional colleagues and their respective areas of expertise. Include those colleagues who have unusual expertise and those who have unusually high levels of expertise.*

Other Unique Features. Other unique features included an abundance of inexpensive laboratory experiences and a special evaluation system. I asked my university to provide an automobile and gas so I could personally visit each participant *after* the summer ended and the participants returned to their schools. I wanted to see what they had found useful and what we might have done that would have helped even more. These evaluations showed an unexpected level of commitment and provided feedback, which I used to strengthen each subsequent proposal.

Lessons Learned from the Summer Physics Institute Grant

- Grant writers can garner support by studying the mission and goals of potential funders simply by closely examining the goals set forth in the RFP.
- All proposals can be strengthened by adding one or more unique features.
- Grant writers can strengthen their grant-writing programs by making a list of colleagues with unique expertise and colleagues with exceptionally high levels of expertise.
- Flexibility is an indispensable trait for all grant writing.
- Serious writers must never trust others to write their grants.

PROPOSAL THREE: A MILLION-DOLLAR TECHNOLOGY PROPOSAL

Apart from providing the means of improving programs and initiating new programs, perhaps the next greatest advantage to having a grant proposal funded is the opportunity it provides the authors to improve their grant-writing skills. Never has this been more obvious to me than the experience of writing a million-dollar technology proposal.

When I assumed responsibility for providing leadership at a very large college, I was shocked to learn that the college had no policy to ensure that the students left their program equipped with the technology skills that they would need throughout their careers. I was equally shocked to learn that this large college had only one computer lab and that that lab was woefully ill-equipped with dated computers. For years, the university, itself, had been slow to embrace technology. The president was unwilling to commit to any innovations that would require recurring expenses; he knew that technology is money and energy hungry. The more you spend on technology, the more you discover that you must spend to keep your investments from becoming dated.

I assembled a team of faculty members who indicated that they shared my concern, placed the director of our research and evaluation office in charge, and gave the team its assignment, which was to write a grant proposal that would correct our technology shortage. The team began meeting once a week to discuss this assignment. After a few weeks, the intervals between the meetings began to grow. I became concerned with the lack of progress and began nudging the team leader. My nudging turned to prodding. A year passed. It became clear to me that if a proposal was going to be written, I would have to write it.

Using Relationships with Potential Funders

I began by investigating possible funding sources, learning that in recent years, in order to avoid investing in equipment that required recurring expenditures, our university had resisted purchasing computers for its faculty and offices. It had, nevertheless, hired a major computer company to wire all of the dormitories to make computers available for students. With some 7,000 students living on campus, the running of cables to each room was an expensive project, so I wondered if the company who had gotten this large bid would be a good place to submit a proposal to meet our needs.

I asked my administrators if they might arrange for me to meet with one of this company's funding officers and was told that two officers would give me thirty minutes of their time in one joint session. I had only one shot, and I was determined to make the best of this unusual opportunity. I quickly researched the company's funding history and learned that it was a leader in funding distance education. So, I drafted a proposal that focused on distance education. We served some schools that were located in mountainous terrain. Each day, some of our students commuted over three hours each way to attend classes and another three hours to get back home, often after one A.M., only to have to get up and arrive at their schools by 7:30 the same morning. If anyone could benefit from a distance education grant, it was surely our institution. Distance education would enable us to take our classes to teachers who were having to teach all day, attend evening classes, and then drive home past midnight in time to get a few hours sleep before leaving for work the next morning. Clearly, nobody's need for distance education exceeded ours, and the company was a proven leader in distance education. It seemed a perfect match.

But here is where I believe many grant writers fail, and that is by putting all of their energy into one proposal and going for all or nothing. I was far too committed to improving our college to take that risk, so after drafting a distance education proposal, I drafted a second, very different proposal, then another and another until I had five rough drafts for five distinctly different proposals. I made two or three good color transparencies with graphs, charts, and tables for each proposal, enabling me to communicate my ideas clearly and quickly. After all, I had an average of only five minutes to present each proposal; that would leave five minutes, and I had special plans for those remaining five minutes.

I arrived early, set up the projector, and tested it. I ordered my transparencies so that I could give my presentations without notes and could stay within the allotted time for each. Twenty-five minutes had passed and I had given all five proposals. Now, it was time for a showdown, so I played my final trump card. I put one final transparency on the screen showing the title and a one-sentence description of all proposals and asked the officers to rate them. A zero would be given to any proposal that completely missed the target, one point to any that sparked an interest, and two points to any that the officers found especially intriguing.

Frankly, I believe that the evaluators considered my strategy a little excessive. They were reluctant to assign written numerical ratings to my proposals, but they were willing to discuss their reactions verbally, and the strategy paid off. I was shocked to learn that my favorite proposal, the distance learning proposal had sparked no interest. The officers' position was one of "We've done distance education, so let's move on to something new." Only one proposal aroused the interest of both of these evaluators. I was shocked to learn that it was the one proposal that focused on the topic that they knew nothing about, laboratory schools. But neither of these issues concerned me, for now I had my direction and I knew exactly what I had to do. I would target all of my energy in one direction.

As I carefully crafted this proposal, I proposed to replace our one, severely dated computer lab with twenty of the latest personal computers available and one server. Because our large special education department was located across campus, I proposed an identically equipped computer lab for that building. Since I had worked with the English department to establish university-wide writing requirements, I proposed a similar lab for the English department. Our large laboratory had separate wings for the elementary, middle, and high school; so I proposed the same type lab for each of these wings.

Using Your Strengths

Our laboratory school was an outstanding school in its own right. Although its students came from all socioeconomic levels of the community and two-thirds of the students had no other connection with the university, these students consistently scored among the highest of any in the state. The laboratory school was an intricate part of every education student's program. I proposed that all of these computer labs and all of the individual computers would be connected into one large network. This enabled our methods professors to introduce a piece of software and then take their students over to the lab school to see that same piece of software being applied in a classroom of students the same age as those the students planned to teach. This was a long-time dream of mine, and I knew of no college anywhere that had such an ideal system.

> *The success of this grant proposal can be attributed, at least in part, to the customer–client relationship of our university to the funder. Put frankly, we were a good customer. Think about your own workplace. Can you identify a company for which your company or institution has been a good customer? Now, try to identify a project that would benefit both you and this company.*

Using the Literature

When the proposal draft was completed, I researched the literature to find support for this program and to find data that would convince the potential funders that, although my ideas were without precedence, they were pedagogically sound. First, I defined *laboratory school* and then I reported research from the literature that showed the effectiveness of lab schools, and that, in spite of their effectiveness, all but one hundred lab schools in the country had been eliminated to save money. I then showed that the nation had only six lab schools that included all grades from nursery through high school and, of these, ours was the largest.

I made one point perfectly clear: by funding this proposal, the company would become an active partner with this great institution called *laboratory schools*. Even the father of the laboratory school, John Dewey, would have applauded this proposal.

In all, I had asked for a package of hardware and connections that cost $1.1 million. To my absolute astonishment, the company funded it in full; not one cent was negotiated. This, in itself was a victory, for it was the only proposal I had ever written that didn't require negotiation. With the letter of acceptance in hand, I asked my university to provide nice furniture for each of the 110 computers. This, too, was granted at a cost of $85,000.

Lessons Learned from the Technology Grant

The technology project taught me that successful grant writing requires serious commitment, determination, and tenacity. It reinforced my belief that if you have a good idea, you have the fortitude to investigate the market and carefully craft your proposal to make it fit the goals of a potential funder, and you are persistent, you can get your proposal funded. Our college had a number of good grant writers, and in fact each year our faculty consistently took second place among the nine colleges on our campus in the number of dollars generated through grant writing. As the senior officer in the college, I read, edited, and approved dozens of proposals each year. I already had learned that most fly-by-night proposals—that is, proposals that are quickly written to meet short deadlines—are rejected and, in contrast, proposals that are carefully written, and rewritten again and again are usually funded, if not on their first submission, then on a resubmission.

This proposal also taught me that if you are really serious about grant writing, never trust someone else to do your work. I was the one who felt this burning need to update our college's technology. My colleagues had gone along for years, comfortable without new equipment. They had adjusted well in the university's culture, which had no serious commitment to technology. Would I ever again collaborate on a proposal? Absolutely! But, from that time forward, I would make certain that each partner shared my level of commitment and passion for the proposal. Would I ever entrust the leadership for the writing of a proposal that I dreamed up to someone else? Absolutely not!

The proposal reinforced my belief that successful grant writers must remain flexible, acknowledging that the first and most important goal is to carefully design a proposal that will meet the funder's goals at a level promised by none of the competing proposals. It also reinforced my belief that while establishing need is an important factor in persuading funding agencies to support your proposal, it pales in comparison to the ability to convince the funder that you and your institution are winners. You must use your own unique strengths and the strengths of your institution and community to persuade your funder that you will do a better job than others would do at reaching the funder's goals.

SUMMARY

Grant writing is a highly competitive activity and a high level of success demands a well-structured approach. Yet, by choosing potential funders that have goals that parallel their own goals and by carefully crafting their proposals to make them meet the funder's goals, grant writers can succeed at the level that they are willing to work to achieve.

Serious grant writers have their own personal grant-writing programs. These programs are ongoing, as they continuously listen and look for opportunities and as they continue to build their grant-writing resources through staying current with the literature in their field, maintaining ongoing lists of data, including their own strengths and weaknesses. Although they may carefully select colleagues to collaborate with them, these grant writers do not trust their grant-writing programs to others; so when they do choose to collaborate, they select partners who are self-motivated self-starters—individuals who do not require prodding.

Excellent grant writers are flexible—so flexible that they always put the funder's goals ahead of their own, sometimes even changing the major thrust of their proposals.

Grant writers can give all of their proposals an advantage over competitors by including unique features in each proposal. Two additional advantages can be gained by (1) making lists of strengths and weaknesses and learning to use both their strengths and their weaknesses to strengthen their proposals and (2) seeking out grant proposal topics that can be advantageous to the potential funder in ways external to the goals stated in the RFPs.

RECAPPING THE MAJOR POINTS

The following guidelines can be used to strengthen grant writers' proposals:

- Always put the funder's needs first.
- Follow the RFP to a "t."
- Stay alert for new grant ideas and for new funding opportunities.
- Know your strengths and limitations.
- Don't be discouraged to learn that sometimes the best proposals are rejected.

- Always be flexible in both your thinking and your practices.
- Include unique features in each proposal.
- Disassociate yourself from those who would discourage you from writing grants.
- Never completely trust others to write your proposals.
- Keep up with current trends and developments in your field.
- Know your own professional and personal goals and use grant writing to reach them.
- Be persistent.

15

USING TECHNOLOGY TO WRITE GRANTS

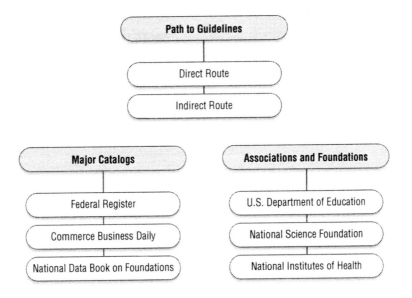

This chapter is about using technology to write grants. More specifically, it is about using the Internet. When computers first became accessible, courses were developed to teach students facts about the computer and to teach students how to write programs. Right away, students learned that using the computer was a very linear process. You either wrote your own program or you used an algorithm that someone else had written, following it step-by-step. But this chapter is not about program writing or algorithms. In fact, this chapter works with the Internet, and, of course, it works just opposite to program writing and algorithms. Instead of channeling their thoughts in one focused direction, use of the Web requires the user to think divergently; and instead of following the one-and-only path to the problem, the Web requires a lot of trial and error. This divergent nature of the Web makes it a perfect vehicle for grant writing because grant writing is not like an algorithm; there is no single correct method to follow. On the contrary, each grant writer, even the most experienced and most successful, has methodology that is somewhat unique. Effective grant writers develop generalizations that they use as guidelines, not hard and fast rules.

SURFING THE INTERNET

Each grant project begins by conducting a search. One grant writer may begin by using terms that seem logical. But, quickly, the writers ask themselves, "What other terms should I use?" Experienced surfers know that the slightest alteration can produce major differences in the results. For example, an investigator might begin by calling forth a favorite search engine and entering the term *grant writing*. Another grant writer might begin by typing in the same words, but enclosing them in parentheses, and this writer would get a different set of information. Or the investigator could get an even different set of information by typing in *requests for proposals* or *"requests for proposals."*

USING THE INTERNET TO VALIDATE

Once the investigator locates some guidelines, the next step is to decide what to do with them. When using the Web, a skeptical scientist's attitude is healthy. Instead of accepting the information as fact, it is far better to look up several guidelines and compare them. Chapter 13 discussed guidelines for writing a grant proposal. The Web can be used to validate the essential parts of a proposal. For example, I wanted some assurance that the views I shared in Chapter 13 about the parts of a proposal that I consider essential were shared by others who give advice on proposal writing. So, I typed in *grant proposal letters*. Then I scrolled until I found a heading that read *writing a grant proposal*. When I clicked on this option, I found an article by this same title written by Indiana Congressman Pete Visclosky, who explained that a proposal must be more than a report; it must be a convincing presentation.

I remembered reading on another website that grant writers must have passion. The congressman's article said that in addition to meeting all the requirements of the funding source, each proposal must have the following qualities:

- The proposal should have a clear and descriptive title.
- The proposal should be a cohesive whole, building logically with one section leading to another.
- Language should be clear and concise, devoid of jargon; explanations should be offered for acronyms and terms that may be unfamiliar to someone outside the field.
- Each part of the proposal should provide as brief a narrative as possible, with supporting data relegated to an appendix.

Reading this article made me feel confident because he was giving the same advice that I had given. The one additional piece of advice that he gave was to be cohesive and ensure that each part of your proposal flows logically to the next. Later, I added this tip to this book. So, the Web can be useful for discovering information to put into your grant proposals.

When using the Web, each source should be used to validate your previous understandings, and you should also look for additional information. Some surfers find this aspect of the Web irresistible; you never know what will be ahead.

I first used this article to validate my prior understandings. Incidentally, this article listed the components of a successful proposal. I felt somewhat reassured to see that the parts listed included the same parts that I had included when I wrote Chapter 13, namely, a cover letter, summary or abstract, introduction, problem statement or needs assessment, objectives, methods or procedures, evaluation, further funding (what happens to the project when the funding dries up?), budget, and appendix.

This article also gave the readers a hotline for the *Catalog of Federal Domestic Assistance,* which is *www.cfda.gov.* This site is composed of three sections: First-Time User's Guide, Browse the Catalog, and Find Assistance Programs. I was curious, so I checked out the First-Time User's Guide, and discovered a large database of federal programs for state and local governments. The site also had a list of answers to frequently asked questions (FAQ). At this site, I also learned how to apply for money to start a business. Under the heading "Where can I find assistance to start a business," I hit the hotline *small business* and found forty-one programs, shown in Figure 15.1. You can download application forms for these programs. Finding that this website also had a section titled, Developing and Writing Grant Proposals, I took that path.

FIGURE 15.1 Programs for functional area of small business—sample.

Programs For Functional Area Of Small Business
Your search returned 40 programs from the functional area of *Small Business*

CFDA #	Agency	Program Title
10.212	USDA	Small Business Innovation Research
10.406	FSA	Farm Operating Loans
10.767	RBS	Intermediary Relending Program
10.768	RBS	Business and Industry Loans
10.769	RBS	Rural Business Enterprise Grants
10.773	RBS	Rural Business Opportunity Grants
11.108	ITA	Commercial Service
11.110	ITA	Trade Development
11.150	BXA	Export Licensing Service and Information
11.313	EDA	Trade Adjustment Assistance
11.611	NIST	Manufacturing Extension Partnership
11.800	MBDA	Minority Business Development Centers
11.806	MBDA	Minority Business Opportunity Committee Development
14.412	FHEO	Employment Opportunities for Lower Income Persons and Businesses
15.124	BIA	Indian Loans_Economic Development

I continued to look for ideas that have not been addressed in this book, and I found a couple of excellent ones. To increase your organization's credibility, consider including the following:

- A brief biography of board members and key staff members
- The organization's goals, philosophy, track record with other grants, and any success stories
- Data that are relevant to the goals of the grantor and to the applicant's credibility

As keeping a grant-writing binder was suggested earlier, this source suggests, "Throughout the proposal writing stage, keep a notebook handy to write down ideas. Periodically, try to connect ideas by reviewing the notebook. Never throw away written ideas during the grant writing stage." I find this advice to be especially appropriate for when you are using the Web because once you leave a site, the chances of finding it again without a written reference are small.

Using the Yahoo search engine, I entered *grant writing* in quotes. Next, I went to EPA grant writing tutorial. Then, I saw EPA Purdue University.

By choosing Mock Grant Writing Activity, I found the following table of contents:

- Proposed summary
- Introduction to the organization
- Problem statement (or needs assessment)
- Project objectives
- Project methods or design
- Project budget
- Appendix

The site for EPA Purdue University listed the following tips to enhance grant proposal writing:

- Read the request for proposal (RFP) carefully.
- Organize your proposal according to the RFP.
- Pay attention to the point allocation before you begin writing.
- Explain things—don't declare them.
- Don't make assumptions of your reviewers.
- Avoid jargon and ACRONYMS.
- Don't simply reiterate buzzwords.
- Be innovative—new audiences, new techniques, and so forth.
- Be passionate.
- Be realistic.
- Be specific. "I would like this much in order to do this."
- Show the funder the return on its investment.
- Check grammar, spelling, and typos.
- Ask someone else to review it.
- Solicit partners.
- If the funder says, "No," ask why.
- Volunteer to be an evaluator.

This program is user friendly—written to help novice grant writers. By clicking on any one of the parts listed in the table of contents, you can get SOURCES. All serious grant writers should be familiar with some publications that provide funding agency sources. The Web can help you become acquainted with these and many other sources.

SOURCES AVAILABLE ON THE INTERNET

At a minimum, sources available on the Internet include (1) the *Federal Register*, (2) the *Catalog of Federal Domestic Assistance*, (3) the *Commerce Business Daily*, (4) the *National Data Book of Foundations*, (5) MedWeb, (6) GrantsNet, (7) the U.S. Department of Education, and (8) the National Science Foundation.

The **Federal Register**

The *Federal Register* is a daily government newspaper. As shown in Figure 15.2, this website includes information on applying for grants in each major U.S. government department.

FIGURE 15.2   **Federal Register**

December 12, 2002 (Volume 67, Number 239)

Table of Contents

ADMINISTRATION FOR CHILDREN AND FAMILIES

Notices

- Proposed Information Collection Activity; Comment Request 76409-76410
- Proposed Information Collection Activity; Comment Request 76408-76409
- Submission for OMB Review; Comment Request 76410-76411

BUREAU OF LAND MANAGEMENT

Notices

- Notice of Proposed Supplementary Rules on Public Lands Within all Arizona and California Long-Term Visitor Areas 76414-76417

CENTERS FOR DISEASE CONTROL AND PREVENTION

Notices

- Proposed Data Collections Submitted for Public Comment and Recommendations 76407-76408

DEPARTMENT OF AGRICULTURE

Notices

- Availability of an Environmental Assessment and Finding of No Significant Impact 76376
- Information Collection Activity; Comment Request 76376-76377

DEPARTMENT OF COMMERCE

Notices

- Amended Final Results of Antidumping Duty Administrative Review: Stainless Steel Plate in Coils from Italy 76381-76382
- Foreign-Trade Zone 122—Corpus Christi, TX Redesignation of Foreign-Trade Subzone 122A 76378
- Foreign-Trade Zone 15—Kansas City, MO Redesignation of Foreign-Trade Subzone 15D 76378
- Fresh Atlantic Salmon from Chile: Notice of Partial Rescission of Antidumping Duty Administrative Review 76378-76380

The Catalog of Federal Domestic Assistance

The *Catalog of Federal Domestic Assistance* is a must for many serious grant writers. This document lists over 1,400 different programs, tells who can apply for each, and gives the rules and regulations for applying. An aspect that is especially helpful and should be noted for each source is the range of dollars each program funds along with the average amount of dollars given per program. Hard copies of this document sell for about $70 each and can be obtained by writing to the following: Superintendent of Documents, U.S. Government Printing Office, Washington, DC 20402. Ask for stock # 922-014-00000-1.

The Commerce Business Daily

You may wish to check this document on the Web if your area is business rather than research. The U.S. government uses this publication to solicit bids from businesses.

National Data Book of Foundations

Because the federal government requires everyone who gives money to file an IRS form 990, you can look up any grant in the *National Data Book of Foundations* to learn what groups any party has funded and how much was awarded for each grant.

MedWeb

This public health website lists who is getting the grants in the field of health. You may wish to study the approaches of others who are writing successful proposals.

GrantsNet

This is the official website for the U.S. Department of Health and Human Services. This source lists many small and medium health grants.

U.S. Department of Education

This website gives information on funding opportunities and information on who is successful.

National Science Foundation

The National Science Foundation gives grants to support innovative programs in the sciences. The address is as follows: National Science Foundation, 4201 Wilson Boulevard, Arlington, VA 22230.

Another source that might be helpful to students who read this book is the Pell Grants. Using Yahoo, you can type in *grants* and scroll to Federal Pell Grants. This source provides undergraduates with funds that do not have to be repaid. The maximum per year is about $3,000 per student. Of course, this varies each year depending on the appropriations.

While visiting Yahoo, you might also want to check out the National Institutes of Health (NIH) grants. Simply, do the following:

Enter in quotes, *NIH Grants.*

Scroll to NIH Guide for Grants & Contracts.

Click this header and get a list of comprehensive archives of published NIH guide articles, listed by year over the past eleven years.

Choose a year and a weekly list.

Choose a week and scroll to Requests for Applications.

SUMMARY

The Internet has unlimited potential for those grant writers who learn how to use it effectively. In contrast to the use of algorithms, which are commonly used to write computer programs and require convergent thinking, successful internet use requires the user to get out of the box and think divergently. As all surfers know, this is fun, but it has some limitations. Because much of the information on the Internet is not clearly attributed, its quality is always suspect; therefore, the user must view it with suspicion, paying close attention to the sources. Secondly, as all internet surfers know, it is easy to waste a lot of time without making any progress, unless you identify some clear goals and keep them in focus. Two common uses that grant writers make of the Internet are (1) the gathering of information to expand their knowledge and (2) the gathering of information to verify or validate their understanding. The writing of this chapter was a good example of both of these uses.

This chapter provides examples of the diversity of paths an investigator can take when searching for topics and the totally different results that can occur from such minor changes as using or not using quotes, changing only one word, or changing search engines. The chapter also identifies major grant directories and grant sources, and provides directions and internet addresses for the same.

RECAPPING THE MAJOR POINTS

- The Web has a vast amount of information, but some of it is inaccurate.
- Successful Internet use requires much trial-and-error exploring.
- The Internet can be used to verify or validate information.

16

USING WRITING TO GAIN A TENURE-TRACK POSITION AND TENURE

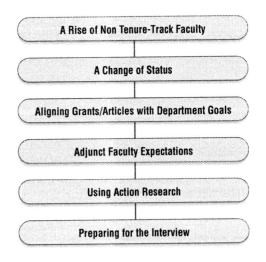

A Rise of Non Tenure-Track Faculty

A Change of Status

Aligning Grants/Articles with Department Goals

Adjunct Faculty Expectations

Using Action Research

Preparing for the Interview

THE RISE OF NON TENURE-TRACK FACULTY

As early as the beginning of the 1980s, the increasing demands for accountability placed on higher education institutions, and the failure of states to increase the budgets of their higher education institutions to support these increased demands, caused administrators to begin looking for ways to meet the increased demands without the help of increased budgets. Because salaries are the largest part of any institution's budget, it is only natural that administrators began to look first at the faculty for ways to cut their expenses. Clearly, the fastest solution to the increasing financial challenge was to hire more non tenure-track faculty.

The number of non tenure-track faculty immediately increased. A common question quickly surfaced. How many non tenure-track faculty members can an institution use without seriously damaging the quality of instruction at the institution? For, even when excellent non tenure-track faculty are used, the presence of more non tenure-track faculty reduces the number of tenure-track faculty, automatically forcing the remaining tenured and tenure-track faculty to serve on more committees and perform an increasing number of other noninstructional responsibilities. By the 1990s, an unwritten rule of thumb as to the number of non tenure-track faculty that should be used had become widespread. This rule said that institutions should not have non tenure-track faculty members teaching more than twenty percent of their courses. But by the end of the 1990s, more than a decade of continuous reductions in higher education budgets, coupled with constantly increasing demands for accountability, made it clear that most institutions across the country must exceed the twenty percent rule, just to survive economically.

WHAT THE CHANGE IN STATUS OF NON TENURE-TRACK FACULTY MEANS TO YOU

The trend that has just been discussed brings good news to adjunct faculty members who teach only because they enjoying teaching. It guarantees employment. Rest assured that if you do a good job and you hold a terminal degree in your teaching field, your chances of being offered the opportunity to continue as a non tenure-track faculty member are dramatically increased. However, this increased use of non tenure-track faculty brings bad news to teachers who seek to enter a tenure-track position and also to those who are already in tenure-track positions and are working to earn tenure. Remember that the sole purpose for using more non tenure-track faculty is to eliminate some of the tenure-track positions. This, in turn, raises the level of expectations placed on candidates for tenure-track positions and it also raises expectations placed on those who are teaching in tenure-track positions and are working to earn tenure. But the problem is not insurmountable; it just requires some strategy, a well-thought-out plan. The following suggestions are offered to help you use grant writing and article writing to garner a tenure-track position and eventually earn tenure.

ALIGN YOUR GRANTS AND ARTICLES WITH YOUR DEPARTMENT'S GOALS

Each department, school, and college's success depends on the service the unit provides to the institution; therefore, it seems logical that each unit would align its goals with the institution's mission. Learn the institution's mission and the goals of the department and school (or college) where you wish to earn a tenure-track position or gain tenure. Offer to start a discussion group on one of the unit's major goals, with the idea of planning a survey to gather more data on this goal, and ultimately writing a grant or article, or both, describing the group's work.

Today, institutions everywhere are claiming to be "teaching institutions." If asked what this means, administrators are likely to say that they value good teaching, which, no doubt, is true. But if asked what system they have in place to ensure the continuous improvement of teaching of their non tenure-track faculty members, most would not respond so readily. Couple this increased emphasis on quality teaching with increased use of adjunct faculty, and you will quickly see that at most institutions something is missing: Many, if not most, institutions have no plan for ensuring and increasing the quality of non tenure-track faculty's teaching.

Because the time for such a plan is overdue, why not develop one? Begin by reflecting on your own teaching experience. Make a list of the insights you have gained from your own experience teaching as a non tenure-track teacher, insights that beginning teachers should know. Next, make another list of teaching responsibilities that continue to give you the most problems. These two lists can become the outline for your plan. Talk to a few tenured faculty about your idea for studying this problem. The mere act of discussing it informs your colleagues of your seriousness about becoming a lifelong teacher/learner, and it informs your colleagues or future colleagues that you are dedicated to continue improving your teaching skills. If your institution does not have an orientation program for non tenure-track faculty, this might be a major part of your plan. Most adjunct faculty members would like to have a good orientation program designed for adjunct faculty. Figure 16.1 lists, in order of importance, the items that non tenure-track faculty members want most from their institution. The items in Figure 16.1 show the results of a national study of what adjunct faculty perceive as their greatest needs. Notice that the one thing that adjunct faculty members want most is to be involved in an orientation program. Notice, also, that several of the items listed in Figure 16.1 express a desire to be linked more closely to their colleagues.

FIGURE 16.1 Items that adjunct faculty want most from their institutions.

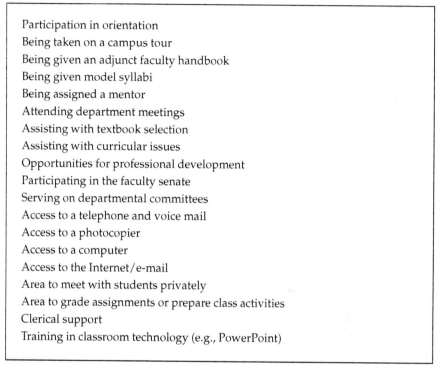

Participation in orientation
Being taken on a campus tour
Being given an adjunct faculty handbook
Being given model syllabi
Being assigned a mentor
Attending department meetings
Assisting with textbook selection
Assisting with curricular issues
Opportunities for professional development
Participating in the faculty senate
Serving on departmental committees
Access to a telephone and voice mail
Access to a photocopier
Access to a computer
Access to the Internet/e-mail
Area to meet with students privately
Area to grade assignments or prepare class activities
Clerical support
Training in classroom technology (e.g., PowerPoint)

Once your draft is complete, consider asking your department chair to give you some time at a future faculty meeting to share this plan. Let the faculty members know that you are searching for others who would like to join you in this quest. Let them know that once the plan is refined it will be presented to the department for consideration for adoption. Once adopted, you will have an excellent, timely topic for your next grant proposal, journal article, or both. Let your colleagues know that you want those who join you in developing this plan to also join you in using the new program to write grants and articles, for which they will be co-authors. Few faculty members could afford to refuse an opportunity to publish in a national, refereed journal.

ACTION RESEARCH

Action research is a generic term that is given to short-term, small studies conducted to answer questions the researcher has that will improve the researcher's daily work. Action research is attractive because it is fast, easy, and practical. Talk to a researcher on your faculty or to another researcher outside the department. Explain your plan and ask for topics and approaches you and your colleagues can use to learn new ways to enhance the teaching quality among non tenure-track faculty members at your institution. Direct involvement in action research has the following important benefits, among others:

- Helps solve classroom problems
- Encourages effective change
- Revitalizes teachers
- Empowers teachers to make decisions
- Identifies effective teaching and learning methods
- Promotes reflective teaching
- Promotes ownership of effective practices
- Verifies what methods work
- Widens the range of teachers' professional skills
- Provides a connection between instructional methods and results
- Helps teachers apply research findings to their own classrooms
- Enables teachers to become change agents

Combining action research, article writing, and grant writing can pave the way to earning a tenure track position and then to earning tenure. These approaches provide non-tenured faculty ways of gathering expertise and building credibility, qualities enjoyed by tenured faculty. Consider the tenured faculty members' perspective. Most of them have worked hard to write and publish articles in their professional journals. Many of them have worked even harder to write books. Many have worked for years conducting research and presenting their findings at professional conferences and in professional journals and books. These accomplishments have brought credibility to them and to their departments, and they may feel an obligation to protect the reputation and image of their department by ensuring that they screen out applicants who have not achieved academically. Furthermore, the increased demand for accountability, as alluded to earlier, has made the hiring process in higher education a buyer's market. Start building your own research library by keeping a research binder, gathering data and quotes that will ensure search committees that you have the expertise that they demand. This personal research library can facilitate your professional growth and advancement.

The oversupply of applicants for every vacancy enables search committees to be much more demanding of their applicants. In fact, in many fields the market is so flooded that every job announcement brings forth not only dozens, but hundreds of applications. This introduces another question; How about the "good old boy" and "good old girl" networks? The answer is that these are still alive and, indeed, in many searches they determine who among many highly qualified applicants are invited to campus for an interview. Serious candidates must also use this resource. Let's consider, for example, that you hold a terminal degree in the fine arts or the humanities. Who do you know who can help you land a tenure-track position? You might want to start with your friends who have been successful in landing positions at various colleges and universities. Prepare an outstanding resume and make sure that each of these friends has a copy.

In addition to using your former classmates as professional contacts, also consider your former professors. Perhaps you have already contacted some of these professors and asked them to provide professional references. These professors will be excellent individuals to receive copies of your resume. Not only is it possible that unexpected vacancies may appear on their campuses, but they also have many contacts on other campuses. You might want to send them extra copies of your resume to share with some of their colleagues on other campuses.

A common source that tenured and tenure-track faculty members use to locate vacancies and make contacts is professional conventions. Consider investing in the expenses required to attend the annual convention of your discipline. There, you can distribute your resumes and arrange for personal interviews. While you are there, attend the sessions led by keynote speakers and major panels. Take copious notes. Learn the issues of the day. This knowledge will be invaluable for use in future interviews, and in identifying topics to research and write about. These keynote speakers are shaping the future in your field. Some of them may sit on your professional board, some on the professional journal committee, and others on the planning committee for future conventions. Each keynote speaker or panel will ensure that the subject it addresses will be a significant issue a year or two from now. By focusing your research and writing on these topics, you will be engaging in work that your local tenured faculty and your prospective employers will consider important.

PREPARING FOR THE INTERVIEW

Let's face it; people hire those candidates who appear confident and relaxed. The problem here is that with so much of your future weighing on the outcome of each interview, you are likely to appear anything but confident and relaxed. This means that you must plan to be relaxed. You can do this by sorting out the accomplishments that you value most. If you have a good Power-Point presentation, with colored bar graphs and pie graphs, this will focus the audience's attention away from you and on your presentation. The good news is that it redirects your own attention away from yourself and toward your presentation. If you cannot prepare a PowerPoint presentation, transparencies or photos can become good substitutes. The secret here is to engage your audience in the presentation so that it becomes a discussion.

Now let's recap the strategy this chapter has offered non tenure-track faculty and tenure-seeking faculty for advancing professionally.

RECAPPING THE MAJOR POINTS

- Non tenure-track faculty who seek tenure-track positions, and tenure-track faculty who seek tenure, need a strategy, a plan to attain these goals.
- Grant writing and article writing can be used to gain both tenure-track positions and tenure. A logical way to plan to advance academically is to identify goals of the department in which you seek a tenure-track position or tenure.
- One goal for any department is to have a program to help non tenure-track faculty improve the quality of instruction and learning in their classes.
- Action research can be a powerful tool for gaining tenure-track positions and tenure.
- A research binder can be used to facilitate the use of grant writing and article writing to advance academically.
- A good grant writing library can facilitate professional advancement.
- Use PowerPoint or transparencies to show your accomplishments during interviews.

FINAL NOTE

You have much reason to be optimistic about your writing. Throughout this book, I have said that you can set your own goals and reach them. As I reflect on my two and a half decades of writing for publication, my first thought is that I wouldn't trade a moment that I've spent writing. Yes, I've spent a lot of my life writing, but I have also had time for my family, church, sports, and exercise. I've rarely even had to give up a game or show to write. All is relative, and the time I've spent writing has been more enjoyable than most of the leisure activities, to say nothing of the immense pleasure I derived from the end product.

If you remember only one thing from this book, let it be this: You can succeed at writing at the level that you choose to succeed. Reach for your own personal and professional goals, and use writing to achieve them. Oscar Wilde was right: "We are all lying in the gutter but some of us are looking up at the stars."

REFERENCES

Henson, K. T. (1996). Chapter Four: Teachers as researchers. In J. Sikula, T. Buttery, and E. Guyton (Eds.), *Handbook of research on teacher education*, 2nd ed. New York: Macmillan.

Henson, K. T. (2004). *Grant writing in higher education: A step-by-step guide*. Boston: Allyn & Bacon.

Reading/Language in Secondary Schools Subcommittee of the International Reading Association (IR). 1989. Classroom action research: The teacher as a researcher, *Journal of Reading, 33*(3), 216–218.

Appendix A

PREFERENCES OF JOURNALS IN VARIOUS DISCIPLINES

Kenneth T. Henson

This appendix contains a number of detailed tables (Tables A.1 through A.6) listing characteristics of journals in several disciplines, including business, education, health and physical education, nursing, librarianship, social and behavioral sciences, and technology education. Readers who may know of similar studies of characteristics of journals in other disciplines or who wish to conduct a study can contact me. I would be glad to consider including your data in future publications, giving you proper recognition.

Writing for Publication: Some Perennial Mistakes

Some people write for publication to give back to their profession, some to improve their profession, some to improve their teaching, and some to advance their own careers through securing tenure, promotions, and merit pay. Whatever the reason, both beginners and experts can improve their publishing success by increasing their knowledge of the journals to which they send their manuscripts.

For a decade and a half I have been surveying journal editors to get information to help writers select appropriate journals for their work and shape their manuscripts to meet the needs of those journals. The results of the most recent survey (1996–1997) are shown in Table A.1.[a] The return rate was

---

[a]I have compiled similar information on journals in other disciplines. This additional research appears in Tables A.2 through A.6.

90.7%. The diversity of these journals is reflected in the wide range in circulation, which varies from 200 to 200,000 subscribers. One of the most common mistakes writers make is failing to resist the urge to send their manuscripts to the most prestigious and best-known journals, ignoring the less widely circulated journals. This is unwise because it limits one's potential target audiences. The average readership for the journals I surveyed is only about 19,500, and more than half (53.8%) have fewer than 5,000 subscribers.

ACCEPTANCE RATES

Perhaps the single characteristic of journals that most captures the attention of writers is the acceptance rate. While this statistic is usually the first bit of information sought by writers, it is also, ironically, the one they most frequently ignore. Like moths drawn to a flame, few beginning writers seem able to resist the temptation to send their manuscripts to the journals with the lowest acceptance rates. The acceptance rates of the journals I surveyed range from 4% to 80%. More than one-fifth (21.3%) of these journals accept less than 10% of the manuscripts they receive. But a closer look at Table A.1 reveals that 38.3% of these journals accept at least 30% of the manuscripts received. Writers under pressure to earn tenure might be wise to avoid journals with very low acceptance rates.

REFEREED STATUS

Another characteristic that has overwhelming appeal for writers is the journal's refereed status. Yet, to put it mildly, professionals disagree on the meaning of *referee*. Because there is so little agreement on the meaning of the term, several years ago I developed a system to evaluate the refereed status of journals, awarding one point for sending manuscripts away to be judged, one point for sending a rating form to the referees, and one point for keeping the process anonymous. More than three-fourths (81.3%) of the journals I surveyed this year meet at least one of these criteria, and 56.3% scored three points. A common mistake is assuming that all refereed journals are better than all nonrefereed journals. In fact, some of the most prestigious journals are not refereed, in part because they invite the contributions of authors they want to have write for them. Unless your institution gives credit only for publishing in refereed journals, purposefully avoiding nonrefereed journals needlessly limits the audiences you can reach and reduces your number of publications.

RESEARCH FORMAT

An important decision that all education writers must make is whether to write research-based articles. Ninety-eight percent of the journals I surveyed report research in one form or another. About 42% of all the articles that appeared in these journals last year reported research. Intimidated by or disgusted with the rigor and demands they faced when writing their dissertations, some professors are determined to avoid all journals that publish articles that resemble dissertation style. These writers should realize that, by targeting journals that do not follow a research format, they can simply report data without adhering to the traditional dissertation/research format. A brief, well-designed, one-page questionnaire can gather enough good data to write one or more articles for journals aimed at practitioners. Most professors can expand their audience—and their publishing opportunities—by submitting to both research journals and to journals that do not follow a strict research-reporting format.

THEMED ISSUES

Only 7.5% of these journals print only manuscripts that fit their published themes, and almost one-third of the journals (30%) never publish themed issues. Yet authors have much to gain from writing in response to announced themes. Almost one-third (31.4%) of the articles that do appear in these journals are part of themed issues or sections. The primary advantage that comes from writing on a theme is that in most themed issues there is far less competition than in nonthemed issues. Why? Simply because many writers shun themed issues. The competitive difference can be seen clearly in those journals that publish both themed and nonthemed issues. For example, one quarterly journal included in this survey publishes two themed issues and two nonthemed issues each year. Its editor reported that 4.5 times as many manuscripts submitted for themed issues were published as for nonthemed issues.

The message here is clear: by targeting your manuscript to a theme you can reduce the competition and thus increase your chances of acceptance by as much as 450%. To accrue this benefit you must meet the manuscript deadline set for the particular themed issue. Most journals that publish themed issues announce themes for the coming year well in advance. By perusing a bound volume of your target journal in the library, you can discover which issue contains this useful information.

TURNAROUND TIME

Some mistakes occur through omission. Many writers who wish to publish fail to consider the effect of a journal's record for handling manuscripts promptly. Authors should consider the time journals require to make a decision about accepting or rejecting a manuscript. On average, the journals surveyed take about 2½ months to make this decision. Some take up to a year to decide, while about one-fourth will give their decision within one month.

More important than the time required for a decision is the time required to publish the manuscript. Once a manuscript is accepted, these journals require an average of 6.7 months to publish. But the range is wide. Some journals will publish your manuscript in a month, while others take as long as two years. Because the number of publications can affect decisions about professors' tenure, promotion, and merit pay, prospective authors should consider each journal's turnaround time before choosing a journal. Professors who need to amass publications to earn tenure might find that this single characteristic eliminates some journals from consideration.

REFERENCE STYLE

Most journals rigidly adhere to a specific reference style. Authors are responsible for knowing the style of their chosen journal and for preparing their manuscript to meet all requirements of that style. Editors sometimes look on errors in style as reflecting an author's carelessness, and excessive errors can lead to rejection. This survey found that writers generally fail to give a journal's chosen style the attention that it warrants. In my view, following a journal's reference style is second only to targeting its audience.

About two-thirds of these journals (64.6%) use APA (American Psychological Association) style. About one-third of them (29.2%) use Chicago style. Most successful writers choose a few journals and become highly familiar with their editors' expectations. A writer can save a good deal of time in the galley correction stage by choosing journals that use the same reference style.

RESUBMISSIONS

Writers often tell me that they have been asked to make revisions in their manuscripts and resubmit them. They ask whether they should comply with this request. My gut feeling is that they should. Most editors are very busy and receive far more manuscripts than they can use. Why would they choose to add to this work, unless they saw strong potential in a manuscript? But to be sure, I asked those editors who said that they sometimes request rewrites to specify what percentage of these corrected manuscripts they accept. The average acceptance rate for revisions is 84.8%. Ironically, many writers say that they never take editors up on requests to revise and resubmit. One editor said that she could not give me the percentage who resubmit because so few do.

Declining requests to correct, alter, and resubmit your manuscripts is a *big* mistake. In addition to getting your article in the journal of your choice, rewriting almost always improves your manuscript. I don't understand why a writer would turn down an editor's help in improving a manuscript, for it is through editing and rewriting that we continue learning how to produce ever-better manuscripts.

COMMUNICATING WITH EDITORS

This is the sixth article of its kind that has appeared in the *Kappan*. I altered each successive survey to gather information missed by the previous ones. Two new questions were added to this survey to determine editors' expectations with regard to contributors' use of technology as a means of communicating with them. One question asked whether the editors are ready to evaluate manuscripts on disk rather than in hard copy. The response was mixed. Few editors are ready to accept disks instead of hard copy, but, by phoning several of these editors, I learned that most of them want to receive a copy of the disk *after* the manuscript has been accepted. I also asked about electronic submissions. And editors are definitely moving in this direction. Almost two-thirds (65.1%) are willing to consider on-line submissions.

Writers often ask what they should do when months pass and they have not heard from an editor. Should they continue waiting, or should they write or phone the editor? I tell them that they should first learn the average turnaround time for the journal, and they shouldn't contact the editor until this time has passed. Your librarians can help you locate this information in such books as *The Art of Writing for Publication, Cabell's Directory of Publishing Opportunities in Education,* and *The Writer's Market.*[b]

Once the average turnaround time for your target journal has passed, you might consider contacting the editor to inquire about the status of your manuscript. About one-fourth (23.9%) of these editors say they prefer phone calls over letters. However, 34.8% prefer letters over calls, and the rest say that they are happy to receive either calls or letters. Whether you choose to call or write, though, remember that editors are busy; keep your communications brief and to the point.

Your ultimate choice of a journal should begin with a consideration of your purposes for wanting to publish and should take account of the information provided here. Once you have chosen a journal, read an issue from cover to cover to get a feel for the audience (the topics covered, the problems dealt with, and so on) and for the journal's style (writing style, reference style, and mix of research, philosophy, and practical information). If the journal has guidelines for authors, get a copy and follow it to the letter. By following these suggestions, you improve your writing while you increase your chances of acceptance.

---

[b]Kenneth T. Henson, *The Art of Writing for Publication* (Boston: Allyn and Bacon, 1995); David Cabell, ed., *Cabell's Directory of Publishing Opportunities in Education,* Vols. 1 and 2 (Beaumont, TX: Cabell Publishers, 1992); and *The Writer's Market* (Cincinnati: A & W Publishers, 1997).

TABLE A.1   Characteristics of a selected sample of education journals.

Journal	Number of Readers	Refereed	Research Articles (%)	Themed Issues per Year (%)	Acceptance Rate (%)	Weeks Required for Decision (Avg.)	Months Required for Publication (Avg.)	Preferred Length (in Ms. Pages)	Min./Max. Pages	Number of Additional Copies	Required Style	Electronic Submissions	Send Disk	Prefer Letter (L), Phone Call (P), Either (E)
Action in Teacher Education	3,000	3	20	—	20	16-24	1	20	1-20	2	APA	No	No	P
American Biology Teacher	11,000	3	60	0	55	8	5	16	1-16	2	Other	No	No	L
American Secondary Education	420	2	40	0	25	9	1-2	10-16	—	3	APA	Yes	No	L
Child Development	9,000	3	80	8	20	12	8	25	1-60	4	APA	No	No	E
Clearing House	3,000	3	50	20	20	16	5	—	—	1	Chicago	Yes	No	P
Comparative Education Review	2,400	2	80	—	15	—	10	30	20-40	3	Chicago	Yes	Yes	—
Contemporary Education	2,200	3	5	80	40	2	2	—	8-12	2	APA	No	No	L
Creative Child & Adult Quarterly	—	2	30	25	70	4	4	10	6-18	—	APA	Yes	No	L
College Student Journal	450	2	50	0	50	4	9-15	12-18	—	2	APA	Yes	No	L
Current Issues in Middle Education	200	3	50	—	80	4-6	6-8	10-15	6-10	4	APA	No	No	P
Eastern Education Journal	1,500	3	85	—	35	6	2	8-10	—	1	APA	Yes	No	E
Education	5,000	1	25	20	20	4	6	16	—	4	Chicago II	Yes	Yes	E
Education Forum	7,000	3	40	80	20	16	9	15	10-20	2	Chicago	Yes	Yes	L
Educational Horizons	12,000	3	30	95	5	12-52	6	8	3-20	1	Chicago	No	—	L
Educational Leadership	200,000	0	20	95	—	3-4	3-12	10-15	1-20	—	Chicago	Yes	No	P
Educational Perspectives	1,000	—	50	100	15	—	3-24	12	10-12	1	Chicago	No	No	L
Educational Record	10,000	3	2	100	20	6-8	3-5	12	5-15	1	Chicago	Yes	No	P
Educational Technology	5,600	0	20	—	9	2	3-6	10-40	6-25	3	APA	Yes	Yes	E
Elementary School Journal	4,327	3	99	40	5	8-12	6-12	30-40	—	2	APA	No	—	E
Harvard Educational Review	10,000	0	40	25	25	12-24	18	1-45	—	2	APA	No	No	L
High School Journal	2,000	3	60	12	30	12	3-6	12	5-18	2	APA	No	No	P
Journal of At-Risk Students	3,000	3	65	0	50	12	12	20	5-25	3	APA	Yes	Yes	P
Journal of Educational Relations	1,000	3	25	—	30	4	12	10	5-25	2	APA	Yes	No	L
Journal of Experimental Education	1,500	3	—	10	65	8-20	3-6	10-14	—	3	APA	—	—	P
Journal of Instructional Psychology	400	2	75	0	30	4	5	10	—	1	APA	Yes	No	E
Journal of Physical Education, Recreation, and Dance	28,000	3	10	10	30	8	6	—	—	3	APA	—	—	E
Journal of Res. in Science Teaching	3,000	3	80	0	20	16-20	9	40	—	3	APA	Yes	No	L
Journal of Staff Development	8,500	3	10	50	34	10	6	12	5-12	4	APA	Yes	No	P

	Number of Readers	Refereed	Research Articles (%)	Themed Issues per Year (%)	Acceptance Rate (%)	Weeks Required for Decision (Avg.)	Months Required for Publication (Avg.)	Preferred Length (in Ms. Pages)	Min./Max. Pages	Number of Additional Copies	Required Style	Electronic Submissions	Send Disk	Prefer Letter (L), Phone Call (P), Either (E)
Journal of Teacher Education	—	3	45	20	10	15-20	2	12-14	1-14	3	APA	Yes	No	E
Kappa Delta Pi Record	62,000	3	40	80	35	16	6	12	6-16	4	Chicago II	Yes	Yes	E
Learning and Leading with Technol.	11,000	3	10	—	49	16	6-12	6	3-9	1	APA	Yes	Yes	E
Middle School Journal	26,000	3	25	60	20	14	15	20	8-30	4	APA	No	No	P
NASSP Bulletin	42,000	0	40	25	10	2-4	2-24	7-10	—	0	Chicago	Yes	Yes	L
New Teacher Advocate	33,000	2	10	—	40	16	6	3	1-5	4	Chicago II	Yes	Yes	E
Perceptual and Motor Skills	2,000	1	90	0	33	3-4	1	—	—	9	APA	No	No	L
Phi Delta Kappan	150,000	0	50	50	5	8	9	15	1-25	0	Chicago	No	No	E
Planning & Changing[a]	558	3	80	25	10	5	24	—	1-10	15	APA	—	—	—
Principal	28,000	0	10	25	15	2-10	2-12	—	3-10	1	Chicago	Yes	No	L
Professional Educator	325	3	70	0	17	10	6	6-8	12-30	2	APA	No	No	E
Psychological Reports	1,900	1	90	0	33	3-4	1	—	—	4	APA	No	Yes	L
Reading Research Quarterly	11,000	3	90	0	10	8-12	6-9	25	—	6	APA	Yes	No	E
Reading Teacher	70,000	3	90	0	8	10-12	12	15-20	—	4	APA	Yes	—	E
Review of Educational Research[a]	17,000	3	100	0	12	8	3-6	40	1-18	2	APA	—	—	—
School Administrator	16,000	0	20	66	25	8	6	6	2-12	0	Assoc. Press	Yes	Yes	E
School Science and Mathematics	3,500	3	40	15	40	8-16	4-12	10-12	5-15	3	APA	Yes	No	P
Social Education[a]	20,000	3	40	60	30	2	20	—	6-20	4	APA	—	—	P
Social Studies	2,800	2	10	5	48	10	4-8	10-15	10-20	1	APA	Yes	No	E
Teacher Educator	1,000	3	70	25	15	10	4	20	—	2	APA	Yes	No	E
Teachers College Record	3,500	3	50	15	10	30	6	35	10-50	4	Chicago	—	—	—
Teaching & Learning[a]	250	2	50	0	40	6-8	3-4	20	6-30	—	Any Style	Yes	—	L
Techniques	40,000	0	10	0	5-10	6-16	—	—	—	0	Assoc. Press	—	—	E
Theory Into Practice	2,500	2	—	100	5-25	4-12	6-8	15	10-18	2-4	APA	Yes	No	E
Training and Development	40,000	3	5	0	10	4-6	6	15	10-25	1	Chicago	No	No	P
Vitae Scholasticae[a]	200	2	100	—	80	8	3-6	15-30	5-100	1	Chicago	—	Yes	L

[a]Data received from previous survey or after computation of figures reported in text had been completed.

TABLE A.2 Characteristics of a selected sample of other journals.

Journal	Number of Readers	Contributors Who Are University Personnel (%)	Refereed	Research Articles (%)	Themed Issues per Year (%)	Acceptance Rate (%)	Days to Answer Queries (Avg.)	Days to Acknowledge Receipt of Ms. (Avg.)	Weeks Required for Decision (Avg.)	Months Required for Publication (Avg.)	Preferred Length (in Ms. Pages)	Min./Max. Pages	Number of Additional Copies	Required Style	Effect of Photos on Acceptance (N=None, P=Possibly, D=Definitely, L=Likely)	Welcome Query Letters	Welcome Phone Calls	Prefer Letter (L), Phone Call (P), Either (E)
HEALTH & NURSING																		
Adapted Physical Activity Quarterly	800	80	3	70	—	40	—	10	13	6	20-25	—	3	APA	N	Y	Y	E
American Journal of Physiology	—	99	2	99	—	60	7	3	8	4	6-8	3-12	3	APS	L	Y	Y	L
Journal of Allied Health	1,500	100	3	95	—	25	5	8	7	5	12	—	1	AMA	N	Y	Y	L
Journal of American College Health	3,000	99	3	60	20	25	7	3	14	5	20	4+35	1	AMA	N	Y	Y	L
Journal of Applied Communication Research	2,000	95	3	90	20	20	2	2	8	12	25	—	2	APA	N	Y	Y	N
Journal of Health Education	10,000	75	3	75	30	20	18	14	8	11	10	1-12	3	APA	P	Y	Y	L
LIBRARIANSHIP/ INFORMATION SCIENCE																		
Journal of Education for Library and Information Science	1,600	95	3	95	25	—	11	11	9	16	—	—	2	Chicago	N	—	—	—
Library and Information Science Research	1,500	80	3	80	—	60	4	2	5	2	20	—	3	MLA	N	Y	Y	L
Library Quarterly	2,000	90	3	85	20	30	3	3	8	6	—	—	2	—	N	Y	Y	L
Wilson Library Bulletin	12,000	25	0	—	—	20	10	10	8	5	8-10	3-12	1	Chicago	P	Y	Y	L
SOCIAL AND BEHAVIORAL SCIENCES																		
The Counseling Psychologist	2,300	60	3	10	100	—	0	0	6	—	—	—	3	APA	N	Y	Y	L
Economics and Business Education	3,500	11	3	—	—	—	14	14	12	5	—	—	2	—	N	Y	N	L

	Number of Readers	Contributors Who Are University Personnel (%)	Refereed	Research Articles (%)	Themed Issues per Year (%)	Acceptance Rate (%)	Days to Answer Queries (Avg.)	Days to Acknowledge Receipt of Ms. (Avg.)	Weeks Required for Decision (Avg.)	Months Required for Publication (Avg.)	Preferred Length (in Ms. Pages)	Min./Max. Pages	Number of Additional Copies	Required Style	Effect of Photos on Acceptance (N=None, P=Possibly, D=Definitely, L=Likely)	Welcome Query Letters	Welcome Phone Calls	Prefer Letter (L), Phone Call (P), Either (E)
International Journal of Social Education	1,000	35	3	90	95	18	4	4	—	—	20-25	—	2	Chicago	P	Y	—	—
Journal for Specialists in Group Work	9,000	40	3	30	25	50	14	14	12	12	20	10-40	2	APA	N	Y	N	L
Journal of Child Psychology and Psychiatry	4,000	—	2	90	—	20	10	2	6	6	—	—	3	—	—	—	—	—
Journal of Counseling Psychology	4,000	—	3	90	—	25	7	7	6	6	20-30	—	4	APA	N	Y	Y	P
Journal of Humanistic Psychology	4,000	60	2	10	—	10	14	10	8	12	20	10-40	1	APA	N	N	N	L
Journal of Pediatric Psychology	1,000	—	3	95	15	20	3	2	6	9	25	—	3	APA	P	Y	Y	P
Journal of Youth and Adolescence	2,000	95	1	90	15	30	7	7	25	9	—	15-30	2	APA	N	Y	Y	L
Merrill-Palmer Quarterly	1,400	90	2	83	0	21	7	1	10	11	28	1-40	3	APA	—	Y	Y	L
Psychological Review	2,000	—	3	100	—	15	90	2	90	6	—	—	3	APA	N	N	N	N
Psychotherapy: Theory, Research, and Practice	7,000	—	3	98	—	20	7	7	14	11	15-20	1-20	3	APA	N	Y	Y	—
Social Education	26,000	10	3	10	15	18	3	3	9	7	3-8	3-20	4	Chicago	P	Y	N	L
Social Science Quarterly	3,600	—	3	—	—	14	0	0	8	9	23	1-30	3	Chicago	P	Y	N	L
The Social Studies	3,000	60	2	10	30	48	10	2	13	10	—	10-25	1	Chicago	P	Y	Y	L
Sociology of Education	2,500	90	3	100	25	10	7	2	12	9	30	1-50	3	ASA	N	N	Y	—
Theory and Research in Social Education	1,000	95	3	—	10	15	2	1	8	6	20	12+	4	APA	N	Y	Y	L

TABLE A.3   Characteristics of a selected sample of business journals.

BUSINESS	Acceptance Rate (%)	Refereed	Number of Subscribers	% of University Contributors	Prefer Query Letters	Welcome Phone Calls	Days to Answer Query Letters	Days to Acknowledge Ms. Receipt	Months Required for Publication
Academy of Management Journal	11	yes	8,900	95	no	yes	1	1	15
Academy of Management Review	12	yes	9,500	99	yes	yes	7	1	8
California Management Review	15	yes	5,500	85	no	no	7	1	8
Journal of Applied Behavioral Science	10	yes	3,000	80	yes	yes	7	7	11
Journal of Human Resource	15	yes	3,000	90	no	yes	14	7	12
Journal of Instructional Development	35	yes	1,500	83	yes	yes	14	3	4
Journal of Management	3	yes	1,300	95	no	yes	5	1	12
Journal of Management Development	35	yes	1,000	70	yes	yes	10	10	4
Organizational Dynamics	12	yes	9,500	99	yes	yes	7	1	8
Personnel Administrator	15	yes	5,500	85	no	no	7	1	6
Personnel Journal	10	yes	3,000	80	yes	yes	7	7	11
Psychology Today	15	yes	3,000	90	no	yes	14	7	12
Training & Development Journal	35	yes	1,500	83	yes	yes	14	3	4
Training	3	yes	1,300	95	no	yes	5	1	12

KEY: Descriptive: D   Action: A   Causal-Comparative: CC   Quasi-Experimental: Q   Developmental: V   Theoretical Model Building: T   Historical: H   Correlational: C   Experimental: E

Preferred Length of Mss. (# Pages)	Minimum/Maximum Pages	Theme Issues per Year (%)	Articles Reporting Research (%)	Types of Research (key below)	Number of Photocopies	Accept Letter-Quality Printouts	Accept Dot-Matrix Printouts	Effect of Photos on Acceptance
30	10/50	0	100	D, H, A, CC, Q, C, E	5	yes	yes	no
25	1/25	0	100	T	2	yes	no	—
25	15/30	20	50	D, H, CC, C, E, T	3	yes	yes	Psbl 8 × 10
20	10/30	25	95	D, H, A, CC, Q, V, C, E, T	5	yes	no	no
25	—	—	99	E, T, econ, emprcl	5	yes	yes	no
25	15/30	25	25	D, Q, V, T	4	yes	no	no
23	15/25	0	90	D, H, CC, Q, C, E, T	3	yes	yes	Psbl 5 × 7
—	—	50	50	D, H, A, V, T	—	yes	—	no
23	—	0	33	D, H, A, CC, V, T	2	yes	no	no
10	5/15	100	30	CC, V, C, T	3	yes	no	Lky 5 × 7
12	8/25	0	1	—	1	yes	yes	no
10	—	25	75	E	0	yes	yes	no
15	10/20	0	8	A, Q, E, T	1	yes	yes	no
10	1/5	0	6	D, A, CC, E, T	1	yes	no	Lky 5 × 7

TABLE A.4 Characteristics of selected HPERD journals.

Journals	Issues per Year	Total Circulation	Unsolicited Manuscripts Received Annually	Manuscripts Published Annually	Acceptance Rate (%)	% of Mss. Not Requiring Revisions	% of Revised Mss. Accepted	Status as Refereed Journal	Double-Blind Review of Ms.	Average Decision Time, Submission to Author Notification in Weeks	Average Time, Acceptance to Publication in Months	Preferred Length in Ms. Pages	Abstract Required	Letters of Inquiry Encouraged	Required Style
Adapted Physical Activity Quarterly	4	—	90	Varies	50	0	100	Yes	Yes	—	—	—	Yes	Yes	APA
Aethlon: The Journal of Sport Literature	2	550	75	10	15	0	75	Yes	Yes	16	12	15–25	No	Yes	PMLA
American Journal of Health Promotion	4	6,600	90	22	—	0	80	Yes	Yes	6	3	15–20	Yes	No	Chicago
American Journal of Public Health	12	35,000	1,000	150–200	15–20	0	20	Yes	Yes	6–8	6	15	Yes	Yes	AMA
Canadian AHPER Journal	6	1,800	30–40	36	55–60	65	90	Yes	Yes	8–12	6–12	8–10	Yes	Yes	APA
Canadian Journal of History of Sport	2	500	30	8	25	20	50	Yes	Yes	16	6	—	No	Yes	—
Clinical Kinesiology	4	1,500	40–48	16–20	65–70	10	85	Yes	Yes	20	9–12	8–10	Yes	No	APA
Health Education	6	9,000	350	70–80	20	60	80	Yes	Yes	6	8	10	Yes	No	APA
Health Education Journal	4	5,000	200	50	25	15	75	Yes	Yes	4	3	20	Yes	Yes	Harvard
Health Education Quarterly	4	2,500	—	—	—		—	Yes	Yes	12	8	20	Yes	Yes	AMA
Health Values: Achieving High Level Wellness	6	1,400	110	48	45	10	75–90	Yes	Yes	8	6	12–20	Yes	Yes	AMA
Hygie: Intl. Journal of Health Education	4	4,000	40	20	50	5	80	Yes	Yes	24	12	15	Yes	Yes	Similar to AMA
International Journal of Sport Biomechanics	4	850	60–70	32	49	12	60	Yes	Yes	8	2–3	20	No	Yes	APA
International Journal of Sport Psychology	4	1,000	60	26	30–40	7	30	Yes	Yes	24–32	2	15	Yes	Yes	APA
International Journal of Sports Medicine	6	1,200	150–200	80	55	5	50	Yes	Yes	4–8	5–12	9–15	Yes	Yes	Scientific English
Journal of American College Health	6	2,575	100	60	60	0	35–45	Yes	Yes	16	12	10–15	Yes	Yes	AMA
Journal of Applied Research in Coaching & Athletics	4	—	100	20	20	2	90	Yes	No	48	6	50	Yes	Yes	Chicago
Journal of Applied Sports Science Research	4	5,500	80–100	16–20	30–35	10	25	Yes	Yes	8	1–2	—	Yes	No	APA
Journal of Leisure Research	4	1,800	50+	20–25	20	0	90	Yes	Yes	14	10	20	Yes	No	APA
Journal of Motor Behavior	4	1,200	50–60	20	40	10	90–95	Yes	No	14	6	20–25	Yes	No	APA
Journal of Park and Recreation Administration	4	850	49	24	60	0	50	Yes	Yes	8	6	10	Yes	No	APA

Journals	Issues per Year	Total Circulation	Unsolicited Manuscripts Received Annually	Manuscripts Published Annually	Acceptance Rate (%)	% of Mss. Not Requiring Revisions	% of Revised Mss. Accepted	Status as Refereed Journal	Double-Blind Review of Ms.	Average Decision Time, Submission to Author Notification in Weeks	Average Time, Acceptance to Publication in Months	Preferred Length in Ms. Pages	Abstract Required	Letters of Inquiry Encouraged	Required Style
Journal of Physical Education, Recreation & Dance	9	28,000	235	153	25	10	90	Yes	Yes	16	12	7–12	No	Yes	APA
Journal of School Health	10	8,000	200	75	30	25	90	Yes	Yes	8–12	4–6	10–12	Yes	No	AMA
Journal of Sport and Exercise Psychology	4	2,042	120	27	25	1	80	Yes	Yes	9	6	25	Yes	No	APA
Journal of Sport Behavior	4	600	100	20–25	28	5	90	Yes	Yes	8	9	12	Yes	Yes	APA
Journal of Sport History	3	850	35	10	29	10	50	Yes	Yes	6–8	9	26	No	Yes	Chicago
Journal of Sport and Social Issues	2	425	39	8–10	18	50	80	Yes	Yes	12	10	20	Yes	Yes	APA
Journal of Sport Management	2	550	25–30	10–12	40–50	0	95	Yes	Yes	10–12	Varies	30	Yes	Yes	APA
Journal of Sport Sciences	3	600	100	20	25	1	80	Yes	No	10	4	5–40	Yes	No	Harvard
Journal of Swimming Research	4	3,000	75	16	20	0	100	Yes	Yes	4	1	4	Yes	No	APA
Journal of Teaching in Physical Education	4	700+	80+	20	20	0	60	Yes	Yes	12	6	30	Yes	No	APA
Journal of the International Council for HPER	4	2,000	—	—	—	—	—	Yes	Yes	6–8	—	6–20	No	Yes	No Set Style
Journal of the Philosophy of Sport	1	550	35	12	30	20	80	Yes	No	8	Varies	10–14	No	Yes	Chicago
Palaestra: The Forum of Sport, Physical Education and Recreation for the Disabled	4	5,000	50–60	45	60–70	5	85	Yes	—	4–12	3–12	6–8	Yes	Yes	APA
Parks and Recreation	12	22,000	36–50	60–65	55	1–5	85	No	No	8–24	3–8	8–12	No	Yes	Chicago
Perceptual and Motor Skills	6	2,000	1,500	350–400	25	2–5	30	Yes	No	3–4	2	—	No	No	APA
Physical Education Review	2	440	20–25	12–16	60	50	90	Yes	No	8–12	12	20–25	Yes	Yes	No Set Style
Play and Culture	4	300	40	30	56	0	92	Yes	Yes	8	5	20–30	Yes	No	APA
Quest	3	700	50	20–30	30–40	0	30–40	Yes	Yes	24–28	3	25–30	Yes	No	APA
Research Quarterly for Exercise and Sport	4	9,000+	300	40–60	25	0	25	Yes	Yes	2–12	8–11	24	Yes	Yes	APA
Sociology of Sport Journal	4	750+	110	24–28	20–25	1–3	20–25	Yes	Yes	6–8	6–9	16–30	Yes	Yes	APA
Strategies: A Journal for Sport and Physical Educators	6	6,000	100	48	50	—	—	Yes	Yes	8	3	10	No	Yes	No Set Style
The Physical Educator	4	5,000	80–85	40–44	50	75–80	75	Yes	Yes	6–8	10–12	10–18	Yes	Yes	APA
The Sport Psychologist	4	675	70	20–25	30	0	80	Yes	Yes	16	6	15–20	Yes	No	APA

TABLE A.5   Publishing requirements in educational communications, technology, and library science journals and magazines.

	Issues a Year	Theme Issues	Articles a Year	Theme Announced	% Research Based	Readership	Refereed
AI Magazine	4	1	16	Winter	80	17,000	L
Artificial Intelligence	12	2	50	1 Yr	98	5000	Na
Byte	12	12	150	6–12 M		500,000	N
Classroom Computer Learning	8		30–35	June		83,000	N
Collegiate Microcomputer	4		50–70		50	1500	Na
Communication Research	6	2	35	1–1½ Yr	85–90	2000	Na
Compute	12		70–80	1 Yr	80	110,000	In
Computers and Education: An International Journal	6	1	24–36	Selected from CAL Conference	100	1700	Na/In
Computers in the Schools	4	1	40	3 M		2000	Na
Distance Education	2	1 in 4	10	18 M	60	100,000	In
EDUCOM Bulletin Review	4	1–2	30	Not announced	25	15,000	Y
Education and Computing	4	V	40–50	Not announced	50		In
Educational and Training Technology International	4		10–12	1 Yr	30–50	2500	L
Educational Horizons	4	4	50	Every two years		15,000	Y
Educational Leadership	8	8	150	Mar., Apr., May	15	135,000	Na
Educational Researcher	9	1	25–30	On occasion	10	16,000	Na
Educational Technology	12	V	100	On occasion	V	50,000	N
Educational Technology Research and Development	4		40		50	4000	Na
Electronic Learning	8		80		10	85,000	N
IBM Journal of Research and Development	6	4	64	1½ Yr	80	50,000	Na
InCider	12		36			200,000	N
Information Technology and Libraries	4		12		60	7000	Na
Journal of Academic Librarianship	6		36		40	12,000	Na
Journal of Artificial Intelligence in Education	4		48		38	5000	Y
Journal of Broadcasting and Electronic Media	4	V	27	1 Yr	80	2500	Na
Journal of Communication	4	2–3	30–35	1 Yr	100	4000	Na
Journal of Computer Assisted Learning	4	V	20		80	1000	Na
Journal of Computer Based Instruction	4	V	20–25	Not announced	70	2300	Na/In
Journal of Computers in Mathematics and Science Teaching	4		48		38	5000	Y
Journal of Computing in Childhood Education	4		48		38	5000	Y
Journal of Education for Library and Information Science	5	V	16	Not announced	16	1800	Na
Journal of Educational Psychology	4					4300	Y
Journal of Educational Research	6		48		100	3500	Na
Journal of Educational Techniques and Technologies	4	1	6+	Winter	10–15	1000	In

Refereed Anonymous	Rating Scale	Query Letter	Query Phone	Publication Style	Page Length**	Copies to Submit	Receipt of Paper	% Accepted	Decision Time	Publication Time
Y	N	Y	Y		10–15	1	1–2 W	25	1–10 M	6 M
Y	Y	N	N	House	30	3	1 M	30	6 M	6 M
		Y	N	House	3000 Wds	1	2 W	1–2	6–8 W	2–6 M
		Y	Y	House	1000–3000 Wds	1	6 W	50	6 W	V
Y	N	Y	Y	House	None	3	1 W	60	12–14 W	3–6 M
*	Y	Y	Y	APA	25–30	3	2 W	10	8 W	5–6 M
Y	Y	Y	Y	Chicago	25–35	8	2 W	20	2–3 M	3–6 M
Y	Y	Y	Y	House	None	3	2 W	25–50	3–4 M	6 M
Y	Y	N	N	APA	15–20	3	3 W	30	3 M	12 M
Y	Y		Y	APA	10,000 Wds	2	1 M	50	9 M	3 M
Y	Y	Y	Y	Chicago	3000 Wds	1	1–9 W	20	1–9 M	4–6 M
Y	Y	N	Y	House	10	4	S		2–3 M	3–6 M
Y	N	Y	Y		300 Wds	2	1–3 W	50	2–3 M	2–6 M
Y	Y	Y	Y	Chicago	10	3	1 W	5	3–6 M	3–18 M
Y	Y	N	Y	Chicago	8–10	2	1 W	15	2 W–mths	6 M
Y	Y	N	Y	APA	15–20	4	1–2 W	10–15	6 W	2 M
N	N	N	Y	House	10–15	2	1 W	33	2 W	3–6 M
Y	Y	N	Y	APA	10–25	4	1 W	20	2–4 M	3–4 M
		Y	Y	House	5–6	2	1–2 M	5	1–2 M	1–3 M
Y	Y				V	2	S	50	1–2 M	5 M
		Y	Y	AP	10	1	1 W	10	1–3 M	6 M
Y	N	Y	Y	Chicago	20	2	1 W	60	6 W	3 M
Y	N	Y	Y	Chicago	12–25	2	1 W	35	1–3 M	2–12 M
Y	Y	N	Y	Chicago	10–25	3	2 W	20	2 M	8–12 M
Y	N	N	Y	APA	25–30	4	5 D	10–15	3 M	3–6 M
Y	N	N	N	Chicago	25–30	3	2 W	15	3–6 M	6 M
Y	Y	N	Y		3000 Wds	2	S	40	2 M	6 M
*	Y	N	Y	House	21	4	None	18	8 W	9 M
Y	Y	N	Y	Chicago	10–15	3	2 W	20	2 M	8–12 W
Y	Y	N	Y	Chicago	10–15	3	2 W	20	2 M	8–12 M
Y	Y	N	Y	Chicago	20	3	1 D	60	2–4 M	1½ Y
Y				APA	6	4		24	7 M	5–6 M
N	Y		Y	APA		2	2 W	33	2–3 M	2–6 M
Y	Y	N	Y	APA	12–15	3	2 D	10–15	1–2 M	1–2 M

Continued

TABLE A.5   *Continued*

	Issues a Year	Theme Issues	Articles a Year	Theme Announced	% Research Based	Readership	Refereed
Journal of Film and Video	4	V	12–18	V	90–10	2000	Na
Journal of Information Science	6		36		75	3500	In
Journal of Photographic Science	6		50+		100	2000	Na
Journal of Special Education Technology	4					1800	Na
Library and Information Science Research	4		20		95	514	Na/In
Library Resources and Technical Services	4		20+		16+	9000	Na
Mathematics and Computer Education	3		30		None	3000	Na
Media and Methods	5	2	40	6 M	None	41,000	N
New Directions for Continuing Education	4	4	35–40	Invited	20		N
Online Magazine	6		130		75	5800	N
Online Review	6	V	24		50		In
Optical Information Systems	6	3	60	Middle of year	50	2500	L
Performance and Instruction	10		120		10	6000	Na
Personal Computing	12	1	60	Not announced	100	525,000	
Phi Delta Kappan	10		150		75	150,000	N
Research in Science and Technology Education	2		18		100		Na/In
School Library Media Activities Monthly	10		30–40		20	8000	N
School Library Media Quarterly	4	V	12–16	Invited	50	8000	Na
Simulation and Games	4	V	25	6–12 M	75	1500+	Na/In
TechTrends for Leaders in Education and Training	6	6	40–45	April	10	10,000	Na
Technology and Culture	4		12–16		100	3000	Na/In
The American Journal of Distance Education	3	1–3	15–18	3–6 M	50	1000	Na
The Computing Teacher	9	4–5	100+	Fall	50	12,000	In
The Library Quarterly	4		12–15		75	3000	Na
Training and Development Journal	12		120		20	30,000	Na

Key:

D = Day	N = No	V = Varies	Y = Yes	** = Double spaced pages
In = International	Na = National	W = Week(s)	Yr = Year(s)	
M = Month(s)	S = Sent same day	Wds = Words	* = Upon request	

Refereed Anonymous	Rating Scale	Query Letter	Query Phone	Publication Style	Page Length**	Copies to Submit	Receipt of Paper	% Accepted	Decision Time	Publication Time
Y	N	Y	Y	MLA	None	3	V		V	2–5 M
Y	Y	Y	N	House	25	3	5 D	50–60	1 M	4–6 M
N	N	N	Y			3	2–3 D	98	2 W–6 M	2 M
Y	Y			APA		4			3.5–4.5 M	
Y	N	N	Y	APA	None	3	1 W	70	5–7 W	3–6 M
Y	Y	N	Y	Chicago	10–15	3	1 W	50	2 M	V
Y	N	N	N	House	2–10	6	Several W	30	6–8 M	3 M
		Y	Y		4–5	1	2 M	5		2 M
		Y	Y	House	12–25	2				
		Y	Y	House	5–10	3	1 W	85	2–3 W	3 M
Y	Y	N	Y	House		3	2 W	35–45	3–4 M	6 M
Y	N	Y	Y	APA	15–20	2	1–2 W	75	2 W	3 M
N	N	N	Y	APA	10	3	2–4 W	60	2–3 M	3–6 M
		Y	N		2500 W	1	1–3 W	5	1–3 W	4 M
		N	Y	Chicago	15	1	3 D	5	8 W	1–12 M
Y	Y	Y	Y		11–12	2	1 D	50	2–3 M	6–12 M
		N	Y	Chicago		2	1–4 W	0	1–6 W	2–8 M
Y	Y	Y	N	House	12–20	2	2 W	20	2–3 M	2–6 M
Y	Y	Y	Y	House	30	3	2 W	40	6–8 W	6 M
Y	N	Y	Y		5–20	3	2 W	25	2–3 M	4–6 M
Y	Y	N	Y	Chicago	40	3	1 W	30	6 M	15 M
Y		Y	Y	Chicago	8	3	1–2 W	50	3–6 M	3–6 M
Y	Y	Y	Y	APA	1200 W	2	1–3 W	45–50	3–6 M	1–3 M
Y	Y	N	Y	Chicago	40	3	2 W	25	6–8 W	7–10 M
Y	Y	Y	Y	Chicago	10–20	2	1 W	20	2 M	3–6 M

TABLE A.6   Fields of interest and publishers' suggestions.

Journals	Fields of Interest	Publishers' Suggestions
AI Magazine	Artificial Intelligence	*R
Artificial Intelligence	Artificial Intelligence	
Byte	Personal computers, hardware, software, and new technology	*R, *G
Classroom Computer Learning	Technology in K–12 education	Keep in mind that Classroom Computer Learning is for K–12 teachers and administrators who are already quite familiar and comfortable using technology.
Collegiate Microcomputer	Use of microcomputers in all areas of higher education	*R
Communication Research	Communication processes across all human social systems, including political, international, mass, organization, family, interpersonal and other communication systems	Acceptance Criteria: 1. Contribution to theory, 2. Research tests theory, 3. New development in method, 4. Quality of writing
Computer	Computer science and engineering	*R
Computers and Education: An International Journal	Use of computers in all levels of education	*G
Computers in the Schools	Educational computing K–12, Higher education	*I
Distance Education	Distance education, external studies, independent learning, adult education, correspondence education, and off-campus education	Present manuscript in journal style. Show evidence of wide knowledge of literature and comparative experience with other institutions and cultures. Voluminous citations are not necessarily evidence of the above qualities.
EDUCOM Bulletin Review	Computing policy making and planning, telecommunication	*C
Education and Computing	Education; computing	*C
Educational and Training Technology International	Educational technology; learning; new technologies	*C
Educational Horizons	Education	Read journal. Write to practicing teachers. Use only as many citations as really necessary, no more than 25.
Educational Leadership	Curriculum, supervision, instruction, and leadership	
Educational Researcher	Educational research	*R
Educational Technology	The complete field of educational technology	*R
Educational Technology Research and Development	Instructional development, effective instruction, computer applications, IAV, media selection and utilization	
Electronic Learning	K–12, college, all curriculum areas	*C, We do not accept many unsolicited articles, but please try anyway—you never know! Jon Goodspeed, Editor, (212) 505-3051
IBM Journal of Research and Development	Math, engineering, physics, computers	*G
InCider	Apple II computers	*C
Information Technology and Libraries	Library automation; advanced technology in libraries	Try to take a research orientation.

Journals	Fields of Interest	Publishers' Suggestions
Journal of Academic Librarianship		Double-space manuscripts and follow the Chicago format for references.
Journal of Artificial Intelligence in Education	Computing educators in general	
Journal of Broadcasting and Electronic Media	Mass communication; broadcasting	
Journal of Communication	Communication media; new technologies	*R
Journal of Computer Assisted Learning	Research; evaluation; use of computers to support learning	Do not make unjustified claims.
Journal of Computer Based Instruction	Computer use for direct instruction in all areas of education, and subject areas	*G, send self-addressed stamped envelope.
Journal of Computers in Mathematics and Science Teaching	Science and math educators	
Journal of Computing in Childhood Education	Childhood education	
Journal of Education for Library and Information Science	Library and information science education	All manuscripts are to be sent to the editor: Rosemary Ruhig DuMont, School of Library Science, Kent State University, Kent, OH, 44242.
Journal of Educational Psychology	Learning and cognition; psychological development relationships and individual related to instruction	
Journal of Educational Research	Research in elementary and secondary schools	Follow APA style; focus on variables that can be manipulated in educational settings.
Journal of Educational Techniques and Technologies	Native, foreign, second language teaching and learning; technology in language teaching and learning	Please use the APA style manual or Pergamon Press's Manuscript Manager—APA software.
Journal of Film and Video	Film and video media	
Journal of Information Science	Information science	
Journal of Photographic Science	Imaging, science, physics, chemistry, photography	*R
Journal of Special Education Technology	Research and theory, applied technology, product reports, and brief reports of technology projects	*G
Library and Information Science Research	Citation analysis, research in public, academic schools, and special libraries	
Library Resources and Technical Services	Cataloging, preservation, collection development, and reproduction of library materials	*I, Write clearly and directly; acknowledge the work of others appropriately; be original.
Mathematics and Computer Education	Mathematics and computer education in colleges	
Media and Methods	Technology in education	We are an application oriented magazine. No academic articles; straightforward journalistic style

Continued

TABLE A.6   *Continued*

Journals	Fields of Interest	Publishers' Suggestions
New Directions for Continuing Education	This is a sourcebook. Current trends and innovative practices in the broad field of adult and continuing education	Chapters are commissioned, not accepted.
Online Magazine	Online database searching	*C
Online Review	Information science, information retrieval, library science	
Optical Information Systems	CD-I, interactive videodisc, CD-ROM, WORM and rewritable disks, R & D, applications and integration	Prefer thoughtful essays as related to various optical technologies rather than an article which offers no insight into efforts.
Performance and Instruction	Performance technology and instructional technology	*R, * G, send self-addressed stamped envelope; write well. Good, readable prose impresses us all out of proportion to its importance.
Personal Computing	Using PCs as a tool in the business environment	
Phi Delta Kappan	Policy issues, research findings, trends in U.S. education, K–12 and postsecondary	*R
Research in Science and Technology Education	Science education; science teaching curriculum evaluation; technological education	Articles must be of an empirical nature. We will consider both quantitative and ethnographic types of research.
School Library Media Activities Monthly	School library media, K–8, curriculum and instruction	
School Library Media Quarterly	School library media programs, information skills	*G, 1. Writing should be lively and readable. 2. If research based, the research should be solid and it should be written up so that it is understandable to nonresearchers as well as other researchers. 3. Articles are welcomed which are theory, issue, or research based, but which demonstrate how to put the ideas into practice in a school library media program.

Journals	Fields of Interest	Publishers' Suggestions
Simulation and Games	Academic and applied issues in simulation, computerized simulation, gaming, modeling, role-playing, etc.	*G, New ideas and interdisciplinary endeavors are particularly welcome.
TechTrends for Leaders in Education and Training	Educational applications of the newest technologies to the learning process	Write in clear, conversational style about practical things you are thinking and doing. TechTrends features articles of popular interest.
Technology and Culture	History of technology as it relates to politics, economics, labor, business, the environment, public policy, etc.	*I, *G
The American Journal of Distance Education	Distance eduction	*R, *G
The Computing Teacher	Practical ideas a computer using educator can utilize right now for a subject area in the classroom or lab	*G
The Library Quarterly	Research and discussion in library science and related fields including communication, service to children	*I
Training and Development Journal	Current training and human resource practices, new theories and application, controversial issues and business trends affecting HRD	We are a magazine, not an academic journal. Write in an interesting, readable style. Academic research and theories are O.K., but only if described in a compelling way and related to practical, concrete, and specific application in the HRD field. Always keep the reader in mind, and give them information that will help them on the job. No footnotes! If you must use references, incorporate them into the text.

Key: *C = Contact journal first
   *G = Send for publishing guide
    *I = Publishing criteria in journal
   *R = Become familiar with the style of the journal

Appendix B

SAMPLE CALL FOR MANUSCRIPTS

The editors of *Educational Leadership* invite manuscripts on the following:

Themes for 1991–1992

Educating Today's Children and Youth
(September 1991)
Values, goals, and interests of today's youth. Arrangements by schools to work with parents and community agencies.
Deadline: March 1, 1991

Curriculum Integration (October 1991)
Interdisciplinary programs, forms of literacy (scientific, musical, and so on), multiple intelligences.
Deadline: April 1, 1991

Teacher Education and Professional Development (November 1991)
Preservice and inservice teacher education. Career development and professionalization.
Deadline: May 1, 1991

Transforming Leadership
(February 1992)
Shared leadership, teacher leadership, leader training.
Deadline: August 1, 1991

Schooling and Work (March 1992)
Vocational education, involvement of business and industry, tracking, proposals for national testing and certification.
Deadline: September 1, 1991

Beyond Effective Teaching (April 1992)
Current research on teaching and learning and its relation to practice.
Deadline: October 1, 1991

Whose Culture? (December 1991–January 1992) Multicultural education, culture-centered programs, humanities. *Deadline:* June 1, 1991

Assessment (May 1992) Reports on current efforts to develop measures more suitable than multiple-choice tests by which to evaluate students and schools. *Deadline:* November 1, 1991

What we look for . . .

The editors look for *brief* (1,500–2,000 words) manuscripts that are helpful to practicing K–12 educators. We are *not* looking for term papers or reviews of literature, and we rarely publish conventional research reports. We prefer articles in which the writer speaks directly to the reader in an informal, conversational style and the treatment of the topic is interesting, insightful, and based on the writer's experience. We usually don't find query letters helpful; we prefer to read the manuscript. Check each issue for an expanded notice about a specific theme.

How to prepare your manuscript . . .

To prepare your manuscript, double space *all* copy; number *all* pages; and show your name, address, phone number, and fax number on the cover sheet only. On page one, just above the title, indicate the number of words in the manuscript, including references, figures, and the like. Cite references in the text like this (Jones 1978), and list them in bibliographic form at the end of the article; or use citations in the form of numbered endnotes. See a recent issue of *Educational Leadership* for examples of citations. For other matters of style, refer to *The Chicago Manual of Style* and *Webster's Collegiate Dictionary.*

How to submit your manuscript . . .

Send two copies, and include a self-addressed stamped 9 × 12 envelope if you want them returned. It is not necessary to send unsolicited manuscripts by overnight mail—our deadlines are target dates, not factors in selection. You can expect to receive a postcard telling you that the manuscript has arrived; a response from an editor should arrive within eight weeks. If you discover a small error after mailing your manuscript, please do not send a correction; small errors can be corrected in the editing process.

What happens next . . .

If your manuscript is accepted, even provisionally, we will ask you to send a letter-quality original *or* an IBM-compatible diskette. Then your manuscript enters the pool of manuscripts on hand for a particular theme issue (or for use in "Other Topics"). When the editors assemble a particular issue, they review all manuscripts, both solicited and unsolicited, in order to make selections for the table of contents. All unsolicited manuscript selections are tentative until we go to press.

How to survive the editing process . . .

If your manuscript becomes a contender for the final table of contents, it is assigned to a staff editor, who shepherds it through all the editing and layout processes. Once your manuscript is edited, you will receive an edited version for your review, correction, and approval. At this time you will have a chance to correct errors, answer our queries, and update any outdated information. The style requirements of *Educational Leadership* dictate heavy editing, and we appreciate collaboration with the authors at any time in the process.

About artwork and photographs . . .

The editors like to have photographs and artwork related to the manuscripts, but these do not influence editorial selection. We appreciate having the opportunity to see your artwork—photos (black and white are best for us), book covers, student papers, and the like. Send them when you are notified that your manuscript has been accepted or when we have begun the editing process.

Send manuscripts to:

Dr. Anne Meek, Managing Editor
Educational Leadership
ASCD
1250 North Pitt Street
Alexandria, VA 22314-1403

Appendix C

SAMPLE ANNOUNCEMENT OF COMING THEMES AND REQUESTS FOR MANUSCRIPTS

March–April:
Teacher Education and the Academic Disciplines
Criticism of the teaching of the core subjects in the nation's schools is widespread. The remainder of the 1990s and the first decade of the twenty-first century will see continued discourse and debate about the teaching of the academic disciplines in the nation's secondary schools and perhaps in the upper levels of elementary schooling. Both thoughtful and ill-conceived solutions will appear in Sunday newspaper supplements, op ed pieces, and quasi-scholarly "reports."

   The editors welcome substantive manuscripts that go beyond the conventional rhetoric often accompanying discussion of this highly charged topic. What is the role of teacher education in this matter? What does research in the teaching of the academic subjects tell us? How do we move from exhortations for improvement to demonstrably improved pedagogy in the subject matter domains? What are the implications of the current attempts to develop subject matter pedagogy? How can teacher education faculty function more effectively with colleagues in the academic disciplines? Are there extant, potent examples of teacher education and the academic discipline faculties working effectively on a long-term basis? If there are, what characterizes these efforts? Can they be replicated? Can teacher educators assist in bringing improvements in the teaching of the academic disciplines to those currently in the schools?

   Manuscript submission deadline: June 1.

May–June:
The Changing Role of Teacher Educators

Economists forecast gloomy scenarios for the nation's economy; demographics continue to change dramatically; cries for accountability in higher education including teacher education abound; matters such as choice and site-based management promise an altered environment in the schools; partnerships between schools and industry, schools and business, schools and higher education grow. Teacher educators are in the midst of these and other far-reaching issues suggesting change in their roles.

The editors welcome both theory and practice manuscripts dealing with the complexities accompanying the changing environment. What are the policy implications of the reduced economy for teacher education in higher education? What changes in role are both explicit and implicit for teacher educators as local districts move more toward providing their own inservice programs? Can teacher education restructure itself to work more effectively with the schools? What does research suggest about these issues? What kind of leadership is needed in this changing world of higher education in which teacher education exists? What are the professional development issues for teacher education?

Manuscript submission deadline: August 1.

September–October:
Professional School Reform and Public School Renewal

Reform movements in SCDEs and public schools frequently operate separately from one another with little shared dialogue or purpose. An SCDE faculty may, for example, make dramatic shifts in the preparation of teachers and administrators and never relate those changes to their work with the schools. Similarly, a school may dramatically alter its class schedule and its pupil placement practices without talking with the institutions which send them student teachers.

The editors are interested in manuscripts that take in-depth looks at the issues related to the linkage between professional school reform and public school renewal, including scholarly debunking of the whole process. We especially desire manuscripts exploring the research implications or, preferably, reporting on research dealing with the problem. Questions authors might consider include: What evidence is there that programs uniting professional school actions and public school efforts have value? What kind of value? Are more highly qualified teachers the result? Do children learn better? What implications are there for the preparation of teachers? In instances where such activities are ongoing, what are teacher education students reading and doing that is different from a "conventional" program? What are the research problems? What are the fiscal implications?

Manuscript submission deadline: October 1.

November–December:
Teacher Education Faculty in the Twenty-first Century

SCDE faculty and teacher education faculty have been the subject of considerable writing and research in the past decade. The RATE studies and a work by numerous authors have described the work, demographics, productivity, and views and attitudes of the current faculty The question of the type of faculty requisite for the next century is of interest in this theme.

The editors recognize that manuscripts addressing this issue will tend to be speculative and theoretical rather than heavily research-based, but they hope that authors will attend to social and technological trends, changes and constants as they develop their theses. They urge authors to consider the past as they project towards the future in this necessarily complex topic. Questions pertaining to this theme include: Do changes in schooling suggest necessary changes in teacher education faculty? How can a historically conservative body of individuals such as teacher education faculty change? Is change, in fact, necessary? What are teacher education faculty likely to be doing in the twenty-first century? What impact will projected advances in technology and media have on teacher education faculty? Will Dewey and other major figures still be relevant? If so, how are the teacher education faculty likely to present them and their ideas?

Manuscript submission deadline: December 1.

Appendix D

ATTENDING WRITING WORKSHOPS

Kenneth T. Henson

I believe in attending workshops to learn how to improve your writing skills. While it's true I might be just a little prejudiced since I give writing workshops, I also try to attend each one that comes to town. Others are as hooked as I am. One dedicated writer, a teacher who lives in Hollywood, has driven her car to attend my workshops in Anaheim, Los Angeles, Las Vegas, and a week-long workshop in San Diego. I am telling you about her because she has taught me some things about attending workshops.

First, she sees the sacrifice of driving for a few hundred miles as acceptable because she perceives this expense as a professional investment. I think this is important because, when you invest in something, you expect a return—you plan a strategy to recoup your money. This participant arrives at each workshop with a list of questions. She doesn't dominate the workshop by asking all of them. Instead, she catches me during coffee breaks, and she joins my table at lunch. The topic of discussion is always "writing for publication," and she always gets in a few questions which she reads right off of her notepad.

Smart participants also sit up front and take notes. I once taught a course on radioactive fallout to a class of space scientists. As a young college graduate, I was more than a little intimidated to begin this class. But because of their level of interest and learning strategies, it was the easiest workshop I had ever taught. Since then I have given my two-day writing for publication workshop to over 100 audiences and have always been pleased with the participants. Most of them arrive determined to get specific information, and they don't leave without it. Just remember, whether you bring questions and get them answered or just sit and take whatever comes your way, the cost is the same. Most speakers enjoy determined audiences because they are able to give their very best when the audience is actively pursuing their topics.

I always welcome participants to bring along a piece of their work. Some bring books they have written; others bring only a few sentences of a first draft on an article they hope to complete. The fact that they have something, however small, is a reminder that they are on their way toward a chosen destination. If nothing more, at least take a tentative topic or title or two. You may ditch these for better ones but only because these served as stepping stones enabling you to reach the preferred ones.

To recap these ideas (thank goodness I no longer feel compelled to say recapitulate), here are some steps that I recommend you take before, during, and following your next writing workshop.

Before the workshop:

1. Write at least three or four questions that you want answered.
2. Jot down two or three possible topics.
3. Try to transform each topic into a tentative title.
4. Write down a goal or two that you hope to reach through writing for publication. These can be professional goals, private goals, or both.

During the writing workshop:

1. Ask at least one question during every segment of the workshop.
2. Arrive early and sit down front.
3. During each break, catch the speaker and ask one quick question.
4. If possible join the speaker for lunch, taking your written list of questions with you.

Following the writing workshop:

1. Review the answers you accumulated at the workshop and consider their implications for your writing program.
2. Review your goals and relate these to your workshop notes. What have you learned that can help you reach your goals?
3. Go home and write. Otherwise everything you have learned will gradually fade. Use the new information as if it were fresh vegetables that cost top dollar and will quickly spoil in the summer heat.
4. Give yourself a pat on the back. You have just done something for yourself that can help you grow.

Appendix E

UNIVERSITY PRESSES

Columbia University Press, 562 W. 113th St., New York, NY 10025 Literature, philosophy, fine arts, Oriental studies, history, social sciences, science, and law.

Duquesne University Press, 600 Forbes Ave., Pittsburgh, PA 15282 Humanities, social sciences for academics, libraries, and college bookstores.

Fairleigh Dickenson University Press, 285 Madison Ave., Madison, NJ 07940 Art, business and economics, history, music, philosophy, politics, psychology, and sociology.

Howard University Press, 2900 Van Ness St., N.W., Washington, DC 20008 Americana, art, business and economics, health, history, music, philosophy, photography, politics, psychology, religion, sociology, sports, science, and literary criticism.

Indiana University Press, 10th and Morton Sts., Bloomington, IN 47405 Humanities, history, philosophy, translations, semiotics, public policy, film, music, linguistics, social sciences, regional materials, African studies, and women's studies.

Iowa State University Press, 2121 S. State Ave., Ames, IA 50010 Biography, history, scientific/technical textbooks, the arts and sciences, statistics and mathematics, and medical and veterinary sciences.

Johns Hopkins University Press, Baltimore, MD 21218 Biomedical sciences, history, literary theory and criticism, wildlife biology and management, psychology, political science, regional material, and economics.

Kent State University Press, Kent State University, Kent, OH 44242 History, regional Ohio, scholarly biographies, literary studies, archaeological research, the arts, and general nonfiction.

Louisiana State University Press, Baton Rouge, LA 70803 Humanities, social sciences, Southern studies, French studies, political philosophy, and music.

New York University Press, Washington Square, New York, NY 10003 Art history, history, New York City regional history, philosophy, politics, and literary criticism.

Northern Illinois University Press, DeKalb, IL 60115 History, literary criticism.

Ohio State University Press, 150 Carmack Rd., Columbus, OH 43210   History, biography, science, philosophy, the arts, political science, law, literature, economics, education, sociology, anthropology, and geography.

Ohio University Press, Scott Quad, Ohio University, Athens, OH 45701   Nineteenth century literature and culture, history, social sciences, philosophy, business, and western regional works.

Oregon State University Press, 101 Waldo Hall, Corvallis, OR 97331   Americana, biography, economics, history, nature, philosophy, energy, and recreation, reference, scientific (biological sciences only), technical (energy), and American criticism.

Oxford University Press, 200 Madison Ave., New York, NY 10016   American history, music, political science, and reference.

The Pennsylvania State University Press, 215 Wagner Bldg., University Park, PA 16802   Agriculture, art, business, economics, history, medicine and psychology, music, nature, philosophy, politics, psychology, religion, science, sociology, technology, women's studies, and black studies.

Purdue University Press, South Campus Courts, Lafayette, IN 47907   Agriculture, Americana, art, biography, communication, economics, engineering, history, horticulture, literature, philosophy, political science, psychology, scientific, sociology, and literary criticism.

Rutgers University Press, 30 College Ave., New Brunswick, NJ 68903   History, literary criticism, anthropology, sociology, women's studies, and criminal justice.

Southern Illinois University Press, Box 3697, Carbondale, IL 62901   Humanities, social sciences, and contemporary material.

Stanford University Press, Stanford, CA 94305   European history, history of China and Japan, anthropology, psychology, taxonomy, literature, and Latin American studies.

Syracuse University Press, 1600 Jamesville Ave., Syracuse, NY 13210   Education, all levels classroom practices, teacher training, special education, trends and issues, administration and supervision, curriculum, and sociology of education.

Teachers College Press, 1234 Amsterdam Ave., New York, NY 10027   Education, all levels classroom practices, teacher training, special education, trends and issues, administration and supervision, curriculum, and sociology of education.

Temple University Press, Broad and Oxford Sts., Philadelphia, PA 19122   American history, public policy, and regional (Philadelphia area).

Texas A&M University Press, Drawer C, College Station, TX 77843   History, natural history, environmental history, economics, agriculture, and regional studies.

Texas Christian University Press, Box 30783, Fort Worth, TX 76129   American studies, Texana, theology, and literature and criticism.

University of Alabama Press, Box 2877, University, AL 35486   Biography, business and economics, history, music, philosophy, politics, religion, and sociology.

University of Alberta Press, 450 Athebasca Hall, Edmonton, Alberta T6G 2E8   Biography, how-to, reference, technical textbooks, and scholarly.

University of Arizona Press, 1615 E. Speedway, Tucson, AZ 85719   Regional Arizona, the Southwest, Mexico, anthropology, space sciences, Asian studies, Southeast Native Americans, and Mexico.

University of California Press, 2120 Berkeley Way, Berkeley, CA 94720   Art, literary studies, social sciences, and natural sciences.

University of Iowa Press, Graphic Services Building, Iowa City, IA 52242   Art, economics, history, music, philosophy, reference, and scientific books.

University of Massachusetts Press, Box 429, Amherst, MA 01004   Afro-American studies, art and architecture, biography, criticism, history, natural history, philosophy, poetry, psychology, public policy, sociology, and women's studies.

University of Michigan Press, 839 Green St., Ann Arbor, MI 48106   Americana, animals, art, biography, business/economics, health, history, music, nature, philosophy, photography, psychology, recreation, reference, religion, science, sociology, technical, textbooks, and travel.

University of Missouri Press, 200 Lewis Hall, Columbia, MO 65211   History, literary criticism, political science, social science, music, art history, and original poetry.

University of Nebraska Press, 901 N. 17th St., Lincoln, NE 68588-0520   Americana, biography, nature, photography, psychology, sports, literature, agriculture, and Native Americans.

University of Nevada Press, Reno, NV 89557   Regional history, natural history, anthropology, biographic, and Basque studies.

University of North Carolina Press, Box 2288, Chapel Hill, NC 27514   American and European history, Americana, classics, oral history, political science, urban studies, religious studies, psychology, sociology, nature books on Southeast.

University of Notre Dame Press, Notre Dame, IN 46556   Philosophy, theology, history, sociology, English literature, government, international relations, and Mexican-American studies.

University of Oklahoma Press, 1005 Asp Ave., Norman, OK 73019   North American Native American studies, Western history, Americana and art, Mesoamerican studies, and Oklahoma.

University of Pittsburgh Press, 127 N. Bellefield Ave., Pittsburgh, PA 15260   Scholarly nonfiction. No textbooks.

University of Tennessee Press, 293 Communications Bldg., Knoxville, TN 37996   Regional: Tennessee, Appalachia, and the South. American history, political science, film studies, sports studies, literary criticism, anthropology, and folklore.

University of Texas Press, Box 7819, Austin, TX 78712   Astronomy, natural history, economics, Latin American and Middle East studies, native Americans, classics, films, medical, biology, health, sciences, international relations, linguistics, photography, twentieth-century and women's literature.

University of Utah Press, 101 University Services Bldg., Salt Lake City, UT 84112   Western history, philosophy, anthropology, Mesoamerican studies, folklore, and Middle Eastern studies.

University of Wisconsin Press, 114 N. Murray St., Madison, WI 53715   Regional: geographical and environmental emphasis.

University Press of Kansas, 303 Carruth, Lawrence, KS 66045   Biography, history, psychology, philosophy, politics, and regional subjects.

University Press of Kentucky, 102 Lafferty Hall, Lexington, KY 40506-0024   History, political science, literary criticism and history, politics, anthropology, law, philosophy, medical history, and nature.

University Press of Mississippi, 3825 Ridgewood Rd., Jackson, MS 39211   Americana, art, biography, business and economics, history, philosophy, politics, psychology, sociology, literary criticism, and folklore.

Utah State University Press, Logan, UT 84332   Biography, reference and textbooks on Americana, history, politics, and science.

Wayne State University Press, 5959 Woodward Ave., Detroit, MI 48202   Americana, biography, economics, history, law, medicine and psychiatry, music, philosophy, politics, psychology, and literature.

Appendix F

SAMPLE PROPOSAL FOR FUNDING

Proposal to the State Department of Education
ECIA, Chapter 2
Mathematics and Science Improvement Program
Closing Date: February 15

NAME OF APPLICANT INSTITUTION The University of	

NAME AND ADDRESS OF OPERATING UNIT

TITLE OF PROPOSED PROJECT Summer Institute for Precollege Teachers of Physics	SUBJECT AREA Physics

BUDGET TOTAL $30,245.00	DESIRED STARTING DATE June 10	DURATION 10 week

Certification and assurances:

The applicant institution has a State-approved teacher education program in the subject area of the proposed project. The person whose signature appears as project director is authorized by the applicant institution to make this proposal. If funded, the institute will be implemented as approved. The applicant institution will accept responsibility for complying with all applicable State and federal requirements including the resolution of any audit exceptions.

Endorsements for the applicant institution:

Signature _____

Name and Title _____

SECOND SIGNATURE, IF APPLICABLE:

Signature _____

Name and Title _____

Physics Teachers Summer Institute Proposal
Table of Contents

I.	PROJECT SUMMARY	Page	1
II.	PROJECT DESCRIPTION		2
	A. Objectives		2
	B. Participant Selection		4
	1. Number of participants		4
	2. Policy for admission		4
	3. Selection procedure		5
	C. Program Content		6
	1. Physics 110		6
	2. Physics electives		7
	3. Integrated laboratory		8
	4. Seminar		9
	D. Additional Components		9
	1. Follow-up activities		9
	2. Evaluation		9
III.	STAFF		10
IV.	FACILITIES		11
	A. Instructional Facilities		
	B. Housing Facilities		12
V.	INSTITUTIONAL SUPPORT		12
VI.	BUDGET		14

Proposal for Summer Institute
for Precollege Teachers of Physics

II. PROJECT DESCRIPTION

    A. Objectives

Physics is the study of the laws of nature at the most fundamental level. As a result, all of modern science and technology derives much of its success from physics. It is because of scientific discoveries and applications that we live in such a technologically advanced world. For decades the United States has been the world leader in science and technology, and as a result, it is the most economically and militarily powerful nation on earth. These past developments are strongly tied to the successful education of our citizenry, and education will continue to be the key in the development of our nation.

Education in the sciences and mathematics is not only important in terms of training future scientists, engineers, and technicians, it is equally important for those who opt for other careers. We live in a highly complex country in which the results of science and technology affect us on a daily basis. We benefit from advances in communications, entertainment, and medicine, and at the same time, we must contend with unwanted results such as pollution and the danger of nuclear annihilation. As consumers and as voting citizens, both scientists and nonscientists must be prepared to make intelligent decisions regarding science and technology.

Recent studies, such as *A Nation at Risk* by the National Commission on Excellence in Education, have shown that the United States has fallen behind many other industrialized countries in educating its citizens. In addressing the reasons for this decline, the Commission has pointed out a severe shortage of qualified science and mathematics teachers almost everywhere in the country. A recent survey of all the school superintendents in this state has documented the shortage of qualified physics teachers (see Attachment). While this study clearly identified secondary schools where inadequately prepared teachers are teaching physics, it did not include the many small, rural secondary schools throughout the state which do not offer physics at all because of the lack of a properly trained teacher. Both of these situations are of major concern.

Of the many alternatives which could prove to be effective solutions to this dilemma, the most immediate would seem to be to retrain secondary teachers who are already certified in other fields. It is for this reason that the university enthusiastically accepts the state department of education's call for proposals for summer physics institutes. The university proposes an institute which is planned to meet the following objectives. The program will provide 15 teachers from throughout the state opportunities to:

1. Develop the knowledge and understanding which is expected in basic university physics courses.
2. Develop the understandings and skills needed to effectively teach the most commonly used physics textbook in this state's schools at this time. An experienced secondary school physics teacher will provide specific training to help participants use this text in the classroom and in the laboratory.
3. Develop laboratory skills associated with basic physics courses, including the use of computers in the laboratory. Emphasis will be placed on

designing low-cost experiments which can be used in all secondary schools, including those with the least facilities, equipment, and supplies.
4. Enable each participant to earn 12 semester hours of credit toward Class B certification in physics. It will be communicated, however, in the announcement of this program, that this benefit to the participants is secondary in significance, that the actual number of hours it will reduce certification attainment will vary among the participants, and that neither the university nor the state department of education will be obligated to provide further grants to those students to help them complete their certification requirements. Indeed, the participants, themselves, will be encouraged to assume this responsibility.

The program will provide for follow-up reinforcement and evaluation during the coming school year.

B. Participant Selection

1. Number of participants.

Fifteen participants will be provided total support. Up to three additional certified secondary teachers who wish to gain certification in the area of physics will be allowed to participate in the program without support. The university will provide tuition grants for these teachers.

2. Policy for admission.

Of particular concern is that some teachers are now teaching physics in the state's secondary schools without having been certified. Hence, the selection of participants for this institute will give first priority to noncertified teachers who are already teaching physics in our secondary schools.

Other secondary teachers who teach courses in other fields have been offered opportunities to teach physics as replacements for retiring teachers and noncertified teachers. These teachers who also have positions awaiting them next fall will receive secondary priority in the screening of applicants for this institute.

If there are other teachers who hold secondary teaching certificates who wish to achieve certification in the area of physics, they will receive the next priority in the selection process.

Candidates within each of these groups will be rated on the basis of letters from their employers, previous scholarships as evidenced by their academic records, and their personal commitment to teaching physics as expressed in a letter which they will be required to write. An attempt will be made to select applicants from small rural high schools over a broad geographic area.

3. Selection procedure.

a. All teachers holding temporary certification in physics will be identified through state department of education records. Each will receive a notice of this institute. All superintendents and curriculum supervisors will also receive a copy of the announcement. An announcement will also be sent to the state department of education with a request for inclusion in the state newsletter.

b. To be considered for this institute, applications must include a participant information form, a letter(s) of testimony from an appropriate school administrator(s) which specifies the candidate's expected teaching assignment, an academic transcript, and, when available, test scores. Applications must be received by April 30, 1985.

c. The selection will be completed and notification will be sent by May 10. Participants will be asked to respond by May 22.

C. Program Content

The institute will begin on June 10, and run continuously until August 17. The three courses, tutorials, and seminars will require a total of 266 contact hours. The courses involved are as follows:

Course	Title	Credit (semester hours)	Contact Hours
PHYSICS 110*	Secondary Physics for Teachers[b]	4	60
PHYSICS[b]	Physics Electives[b]	8	88
PHYSICS[a]	Integrated Physics Lab[a]	0	78
PHYSICS[a]	Seminar for Teachers[a]	0	10
PHYSICS	Tutorial[a]	0	30

[a]New courses may be added specifically for summer institute.
[b]Participants may elect from the following:
    PH 101–102 General Physics   4 semester hours
    PH 105–106 General Physics with Calculus   4 semester hours
    PH 253 Modern Physics   3 semester hours

The major components of this program are as follows:

1. PHYSICS 110—Secondary School Physics for Teachers.

The most immediate impact the proposed program can have on the teaching of high school physics is to improve the effectiveness and confidence of the participating teachers in the use of a text and related materials in their classrooms in the coming year. The most widely used of the state approved textbooks is *Modern Physics* (Holt, Rinehart and Winston, 1976). This text will be the focus of a four-credit-hour course meeting throughout the ten weeks of the institute (60 total contact hours). This course will concentrate mostly on the content of the text; laboratory work will be covered in a separate phase of the institute. Although all the institute staff will participate in this course in appropriate ways, the lead instructor will be an experienced high school teacher. The survey of the text will be intensive and detailed. The rationale for the course is that the most important prerequisite for effective use of the text is a teacher who has a thorough competence in all the subject matter of the text and confidence in his/her ability to explain that subject material to students. Each concept in the text will be examined and developed to whatever depth is necessary in order to achieve that competence on the part of all participants.

This course will also cover methods for supplementing the high school physics text. Demonstrations will be used as an aid in teaching the textbook material, with an emphasis on the use of low-cost demonstrations for high school courses. Computer-aided instruction will also be covered. Many high schools are acquiring microcomputers which can be used as a tool to help teach physics, if adequate software is available. A part of the course will emphasize selecting and using software for computer-aided physics instruction.

2. Physics Electives

Each participant will select one appropriate undergraduate physics course during each session of the summer term. The courses that will be available are PH 101–102, General Physics; PHd 105–106, General Physics with Calculus; and PH 253, Modern Physics. The course selected by the participant will depend upon his/her prior experience. Participants who have not taken a physics course in recent years will be advised to enroll in PH 101. Because of the special needs of the participants, a special section of PH 101 will be offered during the first summer session which will be open only to the institute participants. Participants with a sufficiently strong background may choose instead to take PH 105 or PH 253, which are offered as regular classes during the summer session at the university. In addition to regular class attendance (44 contact hours), each participant will be scheduled for three hours per week (30 total hours) of tutorial meetings with the class instructor. The purpose of the tutorial meetings is to provide the extra in-depth explanations of course material that may be useful to participants who have been away from undergraduate study in the sciences for an extended period. Participants will be evaluated on their work in regular classroom activities as well as tutorial sessions.

3. Integrated Laboratory for Physics Elective and for Physics 110.

Laboratory experiences are important both for the physics elective and the survey of a secondary school physics text. In the proposed program, these laboratory experiences will be integrated into a single laboratory organized for the institute participants. The laboratory will meet for thirteen three-hour sessions each term (78 total contact hours). Experiments will be selected from the regular lab of the physics elective and, wherever possible, will be conducted in parallel with similar experiments scaled for use in a high school laboratory. The purpose of this approach is to give participants two types of experiences. First, they need knowledge of the type of experiments currently conducted in undergraduate college level courses. More importantly, however, they need practical experience in setting up laboratory experiments appropriate for the high school physics laboratory (high school laboratories are more limited in time schedule and frequently in available equipment than college laboratories). The content of the integrated lab will be planned on an individual basis by the instructor of the physics elective and the consulting high school teacher. A graduate student will assist in the laboratory.

Some of the laboratory meetings will also be devoted to using microcomputers in the physics laboratory. Some experiments will be performed in which the computer is used to assist with taking and analyzing data.

4. Seminar for Teachers.

In order that the separate components of the program may be brought together to form a more unified experience, a weekly seminar for participants in the institute will be held. The content of the seminar will, in part, be developed based on the perceived needs of participants. In part, however, the seminar will be directed toward supplemental material, such as articles from *Physics Today, Scientific American, Science Education, The Physics Teacher,* and other sources of information on topics of current interest, puzzles, and games that stimulate interest in physics.

D. Additional Components
1. Follow-Up Activities

During the second half of the fall semester the co-directors will make an on-site visit to each participant's school. This follow-up visit will serve two purposes: (1) it will provide an opportunity to assess the value of the institute and (2) it will provide each participant opportunities to clarify any misunderstandings and to fill in any knowledge gaps about the content or skills set forth in the objectives of this institute.

2. Evaluation

The proposed program will be subjected to two types of evaluation.

(a) *Evaluation by participants.* Participants will be asked to evaluate the program at two stages. The initial evaluation will be made by a questionnaire administered near the end of the summer session. The effectiveness of each component of the institute will be evaluated. A second evaluation will be conducted near the end of the school year after participants have had classroom experience in using skills developed in the institute.

(b) *Evaluation by an outside observer.* At an appropriate point in the institute an evaluation will be sought from one or more outside observers. For this evaluation an effort will be made to obtain the services of an individual with supervisory experience and special knowledge in secondary level science education, in a state school system, the state department of education, and/or another institution of higher education in the state.

III. STAFF

Professional staff for the proposed institute will be composed of one coordinator, two assistant coordinators, a consulting high school teacher, the instructors of the physics electives, and the lab instructor. Résumés of principal participating staff are included as an appendix.

A. The coordinator of the program will be Kenneth Henson, Head, Area of Curriculum Instruction, College of Education. Philip Coulter, Chairperson and Professor, Department of Physics and Astronomy, and J. W. Harrell, Associate Professor of Physics, will serve as assistant coordinators. Dr. Henson's responsibilities will include attaining publicity for the program, evaluating the program, and preparing an institute report. He will further provide assistance in announcing the program, selecting the participants, conducting the follow-up component, and participating in the weekly seminars. Dr. Harrell's responsibilities will include arranging the weekly seminars, correspondence related to selection and notification of participants, and paperwork associated with participant support. Dr. Coulter will coordinate the responsibilities of Physics faculty in the program, assist with the weekly seminars, and help with the paperwork associated with participant support.

B. Dr. Peggy Coulter, teacher of mathematics and physics at Central High School and Adjunct Associate Professor of Education, College of Education, is being asked to serve as lead instructor for PH 110 and as consultant for the integrated laboratory and the tutorial session for the physics electives. Dr. Harrell will assist in the instruction for PH 110 in the areas of computer-aided instruction and low-cost lecture demonstrations.

C. The instructors for the physics electives are as follows: PH 101—Professor J. W Harrell; PH 105—Professor Chester Alexander; PH 102—Professor Richard Tipping; PH 253 and PH 106—Professor William Walker. These individuals will participate as tutorial leaders for participants who are enrolled in their classes. They will also serve as consultants for PH 110, the integrated laboratory, and the seminar for teachers.

D. A physics graduate student with experience in physics laboratories will supervise the integrated laboratory. The content of the laboratory will be a joint responsibility of the consulting high school physics teacher and the instructors for the physics electives.

IV. FACILITIES
   A. Instructional Facilities.
   Participants in the program will make use of facilities of the Physics Building of the university for work associated with the physics elective course, PH 110, the integrated laboratory, and tutorials. The computer laboratory in the College of Education will be available for use by the participants at specified times. This computer lab serves as the statewide depository for hardware and software. Participants will have the opportunity to duplicate any of the available programs that are in the public domain. The Seminar for Teachers will be scheduled at a lunch period and will make use of a private dining area in the Continuing Education Center.

   B. Housing Facilities.
   Residential participants will be housed in _____ Hall, the Continuing Education Center of the university. Housing is available at the rate of $50 per week. Meal service is provided in the same building at the cost of $12.50 per day. Meal service is also available to commuting participants at the Continuing Education Center.

V.   INSTITUTIONAL SUPPORT AND MANAGEMENT
   The university is able to commit support to the proposed program in the following ways:
   Released time for co-coordinators and secretarial staff (estimated in-kind contributions)

K. Henson	25% for 12 weeks	$2,861.54
P. Coulter	15% for 12 weeks	1,759.50
Secretary	10% for 14 weeks	276.00

Supplies for curriculum development projects,
   correspondence, etc. (estimated cash contribution)   200.00
Travel for follow-up activities (estimated cash contribution)
   Per-diem for six days @ $40/day   240.00
Tuition grants will be provided by the university
   for up to three additional unsupported participants.
   3 participants @ $731.50   2,194.50
TOTAL IN-KIND CONTRIBUTION $7,531.54

VI. BUDGET
   TUITION AND FEES:

| Tuition | @ | $552.00 |
| University Fees | @ | 104.50 |

Lab Fees 3 @ 25.00	75.00	
	731.50 x 15 =	$10,972.50
FIRST-TIME APPLICANTS: 6 @	15.00 =	$120.00

PARTICIPANT SUPPORT:

Commuters (4)
Mileage (3000 @ .22)	$660.00
Meals (50 @ $4.25)	212.50
Lab kits/materials	40.00
Textbooks	25.00
	937.50
	x 4 = $3,750.00

Residents (11)
Room (10 weeks @ $50)	$500.00
Mileage	60.00
Meals	577.50
Lab kits/materials	40.00
Textbooks	25.00
	1,202.50
	x 11 = $13,227.50

TOTAL PARTICIPANT SUPPORT	$16,977.50
TRAVEL FOR FOLLOW-UP ACTIVITIES	400.00
INDIRECT COST REIMBURSEMENT (16% of $11,072.50)	1,775.00
PROJECT BUDGET TOTAL for 15	$30,245.00

Appendix G

SAMPLE PROPOSAL RATING FORM

ECIA, Chapter 2
Mathematics and Science Improvement Program

INSTRUCTIONS TO THE REVIEWER: Study entire proposal before beginning the rating process because information relevant to a single rating criterion may be found in several sections of the proposal. Respond to each item on the rating form by (1) commenting on the strengths or weaknesses of the proposed project and (2) indicating the earned point-value on the scale, 0 through 5. The highest composite scores will identify the meritorious proposals. It may be helpful to note in your comments where in the proposal you found the significant data.

Indicate the total number of points awarded to the proposal at the bottom of page 3. On page 4 suggest any revisions that would better meet the overall objective of improving statewide teacher qualification in mathematics, chemistry, and physics.

Complete the reviewer identification section below. Send two copies of each review, one signed and one unsigned, to _____

Reviewer Name: _____

Address: _____

Office
Telephone: _____ Hours: _____ Home
Telephone: _____

Reviewer Signature: _____
Date Signed: _____

A. Are the objectives to be achieved in the institute precisely stated and reasonable?
Comment(s): _____

_____

Points earned:	_____	_____	_____	_____	_____	_____
	(0)	(1)	(2)	(3)	(4)	(5)

B. Are the recruiting and selection procedures appropriate?
Comment(s): _____

_____

Points earned:	_____	_____	_____	_____	_____	_____
	(0)	(1)	(2)	(3)	(4)	(5)

C. Do the proposed courses give reasonable assurance of achieving the objectives of the institute?
Comment(s): _____

Points earned:	_____	_____	_____	_____	_____	_____
	(0)	(1)	(2)	(3)	(4)	(5)

D. Is the instructional staff appropriate to the successful implementation of the institute?
Comment(s): _____

Points earned:	_____	_____	_____	_____	_____	_____
	(0)	(1)	(2)	(3)	(4)	(5)

E. Have adequate provisions been made for management and support personnel?
Comment(s): _____

Points earned:	_____	_____	_____	_____	_____	_____
	(0)	(1)	(2)	(3)	(4)	(5)

F. Are sound evaluation procedures included that will assure obtaining usable information about the degree of attainment of project objectives?
Comment(s): _____

Points earned:	_____	_____	_____	_____	_____	_____
	(0)	(1)	(2)	(3)	(4)	(5)

G. Has the sponsoring institution committed the necessary facilities, including instructional equipment, to the institute?
Comment(s): _____

Points earned:	_____	_____	_____	_____	_____	_____
	(0)	(1)	(2)	(3)	(4)	(5)

H. Does the proposal indicate an adequate level of fiscal and in-kind support from the sponsoring institution?

Comment(s): _____

Points earned: ‾‾‾‾‾   ‾‾‾‾‾   ‾‾‾‾‾   ‾‾‾‾‾   ‾‾‾‾‾   ‾‾‾‾‾

                  (0)   (1)   (2)   (3)   (4)   (5)

I. Is the proposed budget consistent with the size and scope of the proposed institute?

Comment(s): _____

Points earned: ‾‾‾‾‾   ‾‾‾‾‾   ‾‾‾‾‾   ‾‾‾‾‾   ‾‾‾‾‾   ‾‾‾‾‾

                  (0)   (1)   (2)   (3)   (4)   (5)

TOTAL POINTS AWARDED _____

Appendix H

PROFILE OF AN ARTICLE

Several aspiring authors have asked for a trip through the life of an article, starting with the inception of the idea and ending with the article in print. Following is such a profile.

If you are one of those systematic left-brain individuals who starts reading a book on page 1 and reads it through from cover to cover, perhaps you will remember the account of the day of the iguana. However, if you are a free spirit who skips about from one topic of interest to the next, don't worry; you have missed nothing of great importance to the story that follows.

Some of our richest opportunities for writing books and articles come at the least expected times. It was during my first of a series of many satisfying visits to the islands of the Bahamas that I discovered out of the clear blue sky that without being aware of it I had taken along a fellow traveler. This silent companion appeared as unsuspectingly as my new friend, the iguana.

I have always believed that all professors of any status at all, regardless of their discipline or gender, possess at least three essential status symbols: their own coffee mug, a briefcase, and at least one jacket with patches on the elbows. The climate in the Bahamas doesn't call for a lot of coffee or a large wardrobe, but there's absolutely no excuse for anyone representing academia to show up without a briefcase. Having served on a year-long Fulbright assignment and having responded positively to several requests of the U.S. Embassy to deliver speeches, I was sensitive to the international laws of etiquette; I have never crossed customs without my briefcase in hand.

Upon my arrival at the modest motel in Nassau, I sought the shade of a large beach umbrella and the writing space provided by the table it covered. My intention was simple and honest: I wanted to grade several sets of student assignments. Just as the business of a writer is to write, the business of a professor is to drink gallons of coffee and grade millions of papers.

STEP 1: THE IDEA

By general reputation, all professors, present company included, are entitled to a few idiosyncrasies. I believe that every course, whether graduate or undergraduate, should make at least two requirements of all students: a research assignment and a writing assignment. Both of these demands were reflected in the briefcase full of carefully bound sets of 5" × 8" index cards, which belonged to my undergraduate science methods students. This course required each student to read ten articles on a given teaching method and type on each of ten cards the information shown in Figure H.1.

More specifically, each student was required to select one method, read ten articles on this method, complete an index card for each article, and bind this set of cards with a rubber band.

As I grouped the sets of cards, I noticed that several students had chosen to research the oldest and most enduring teaching method through the centuries, the lecture. Each student had selected and cited ten sources. At that moment, my traveling companion spoke to me, saying, "Wake up. You have in your hands an article just waiting to be written." It was crystal clear. My little muse companion had provided an excellent idea for an article, one that would make a unique contribution to my field, and one that I would enjoy writing.

FIGURE H.1   Science methods course index card assignment.

| Name of teaching method: |
| Definition: |
| Strengths: |
| Limitations: |
| The teacher's role: |
| Source: ___Author___ ___Article___ ___Journal___ ___Vol.___ ___Issue___ ___Date___ ___pp.___ |

STEP 2: THE TITLE

All that was left for me to do was to set this prewritten article to words. So I took these decks of cards that focused on the lecture method and began to think about a title. While living in England, I had delighted in discovering a new set of professional books, a new genre of books in my own discipline that excited me. I read Sir Richard Ackland's curriculum books, which postulated that some of our knowledge comes from other-worldly sources—quite a change for an American, especially for one whose background is in the sciences! I fell in love with a living history and a living philosophy as I attended seminars at the University of London's King's College with the renowned Professor R. S. Peters. My weekends were spent soaking up the rich culture of London. They included frequent trips to one of Europe's largest bookstores, Foyle's. There, I had found a book titled *What's the Use of Lecturing?* Modeling my British counterparts, who treasured books and read them repeatedly until they mastered the content, I seized upon this well-researched yet practical book and read it with intensity. Although my copy of this book was lost in moving or storage, the title and contents were locked in my memory. What a perfect title for a book! It was brief, descriptive, and unassuming. What a title for an article! So I borrowed his title. Even the title itself had already been written for me, years earlier.

STEP 3: THE STRUCTURE

So far, this article was all fun and no work! I wondered how long that would last. At this juncture, I had to make a decision. I could blast forward straight ahead and write the introduction, or I could take a step back and survey the entire article, getting an overall view from the introduction to the summary. Since half of the fun in writing is synthesizing or taking some existing parts and perhaps adding a few new ones and putting them together into a meaningful sequence, I chose to go for the Gestalt.

Once again I looked at the cards. And once again my little muse friend appeared, bringing me yet another present. A quick glance at the note card on top showed me the outline for the entire article. If that weren't enough, even the subheadings were staring me straight in the face.

I. Introduction (definition)
II. Strengths
III. Limitations
IV. Role of the teacher
V. Summary

Well, so far this had been so easy that I am without a cliché to express just how easy it was. But now it was time to work, and I remembered a time honored cliché that served me well: "Before putting the pen to the paper or your fingers to the keyboard, get a clear grip on your audience."

STEP 4: IDENTIFYING THE AUDIENCE

To identify my audience, I asked myself, who (or what group or groups) would have the most interest in an article titled "What's the Use of Lecturing?" I realized that this question had already been answered. It came several weeks earlier at the beginning of the semester when I offered this topic to my teacher education students. Teacher educators like me need to know more about lecturing. So, with this audience in mind, I needed to write the type of information that would answer the questions that teacher educators would have about this topic.

STEP 5: CHOOSING THE JOURNAL

Now that the audience was identified, selection of the journals for targeting this manuscript was my next job. It, too, was easy. I happened to know some journals written for these audiences. This is a fringe benefit that comes with writing in your own field of expertise. From these familiar teacher education journals, I selected one that offered practical advice to secondary teachers and one that resembled this intended structure. Had I not been familiar with such journals, I would have checked an index such as ERIC or the *Education Index,* looking up the topic *lecturing.* Then I would note the names and addresses of the editors and journals. Next I would retrieve a sample of each journal, and from the samples choose one that had articles that resembled my outline in both structure and content. For example, these cards gave practical advice (e.g., *how to strengthen the lecture* and *the teacher's role*); therefore, I wanted a journal that was more practical than theoretical.

STEP 6: WRITING THE DRAFT

Following my own well-worn advice to "put the audience's concern first," I rushed off the introduction, proceeding through each subheading by simply choosing from the index cards what I considered the most useful knowledge under each subheading. Even the summary was quick and easy. I just assembled one or two key sentences from each section.

STEP 7: THE BIBLIOGRAPHY, REFERENCES, OR SUGGESTED READINGS

By now I was more than comfortable with my new friend. In fact, I was developing a dependence on him. Like a genie, he responded to my call, showing me that my bibliography had already been selected. All I had to do was choose the best of these references from the index cards and list them. Of course, as a professional person, I had the responsibility of checking each of these student-generated cards for absolute accuracy. My main idiosyncrasy concerning the use of students' work is never to use secondhand information without checking the original source for accuracy.

My next chore was to give this part of my manuscript a title. I could title this last section "References." But if I did, I would have to limit these entries to those entries that I had actually referred to in my draft. Or, I could label this section "Bibliography." This would enable me to include the references plus additional resources. A third option was available. I could make both a "Reference" section and a "Suggested Readings" section. This would enable the reader to locate quickly those entries that were referred to in the script and would also permit me to suggest further readings that would encourage the audience to pursue the topic beyond my article.

Remembering that most journals are quite rigid, I decided it was time to consult my journal. If the articles in my target journal use a combination of these sections, I could choose. If not, I had better use what the journal used.

Throughout this process, I had felt a little guilty. First, I had let my little friend do all the work, and I was going to get the credit for what I knew would be a fine article. Second, as I once again caught myself looking over my shoulder, I wondered whether anyone had caught me in the act of following the advice of an imaginary character. If so, my behavior must seem a little strange to all those people who themselves haven't benefited from such a helping hand.

I looked over my shoulder again, but this time I wasn't looking for my new friend. Rather, I was reacting to a burning sensation on the back of my neck. The sun had shifted and I was no longer under the protection of the umbrella. I glanced at my watch. About two hours had passed. The time had passed so fast that I felt as though I had been robbed of this part of my life. But then I realized that these two hours had produced a full draft of a good article. Not bad, I thought, for creating a quality product that would serve many of my colleagues nationwide.

With the draft complete, I knew that I would have to rewrite it several times. But I also knew that each rewrite would bring some improvement to the manuscript and to my own thinking about this subject. Indeed, when this manuscript was complete, I would have improved my ability to lecture. I would be a better teacher, so I had every right to feel good.

Within the next few days, I revised the manuscript several times. I even had a colleague read it and provide some suggestions. All of this polishing paid off; it wasn't perfect, but it was beginning to sound pretty good. It was time to contact an editor.

STEP 8: PREPARING THE QUERY LETTER

I wanted to avoid that fatal trap that lies in wait for so many perfectionists. I knew that if I waited until the manuscript was perfect to contact an editor, the manuscript would never be mailed. A quick trip to the current periodicals section of the library provided me with a current copy of the target journal. In the front, I found the editor's name and address. Carefully copying this information, letter for letter, I wrote the query letter shown in Figure H.2.

FIGURE H.2   Sample query letter.

Dr. Gerald Unks, Editor
THE HIGH SCHOOL JOURNAL

Dear Dr. Unks:

As an associate professor who has taught methods courses and written articles and books on teaching methods, I conduct periodic reviews of the literature to learn more about this topic.

As you know, through the years lecturing has remained the dominant teaching method in high schools and universities. Would you be interested in seeing a ten-page manuscript titled "What's the Use of Lecturing?" This manuscript is a product of a recent extensive review of the literature. It reports both the strengths and the limitations of the lecture method and it suggests methods teachers can use to improve their lectures.

I will look forward to hearing whether or not you are interested in reviewing this manuscript. Thank you.

Sincerely,

Kenneth T. Henson, Associate Professor
College of Education

Enc: SASE

SOME CRITICISMS

By keeping the query letter brief and focused on the topic, I have attempted to provide just enough information to get the editor interested in seeing this manuscript. Remember, the goal is to whet the editor's interest—nothing more. My experience and writings, coupled with telling about the review of the literature, were used to establish author credibility. The word *recent* was used to establish currency, telling the author that this is not an old manuscript that may have been rejected by several other publishers. To make certain that the editor knows that I expected to receive a response, I told the editor that I was looking forward to receiving a response.

Of course this letter has plenty of room for improvement. For example, it fails to convey a lot of author enthusiasm. I remembered what one of the editors surveyed said, "If the author doesn't appear enthusiastic, how will the readers react to the article?" Removal of *or not* in this sentence could increase the level of enthusiasm.

STEP 9: PREPARING THE COVER LETTER

Having prepared the query letter, it was time to prepare a cover letter. Why wait until a response to the query letter was received? So as soon as the query letter was in the mail, I wrote the cover letter shown in Figure H.3.

FIGURE H.3   Sample cover letter.

Dear   :

   Thank you for your letter of _____ expressing interest in the enclosed manuscript, "What's the Use of Lecturing?" Thank you for your interest in this information, which has resulted from a recent review of the literature.

   I shall look forward to receiving your response to this manuscript.

Sincerely,

Kenneth T. Henson, Associate Professor
College of Education

Enc: SASE
       "What's the Use of Lecturing?"

This cover letter is short and to the point. Using the phrase *recent review of the literature* reestablished the manuscript's credibility and currency. By including the title of this manuscript, the cover letter further reacquaints the editor with this project.

This manuscript and query letter were mailed, producing the article "What's the Use of Lecturing?," which appeared in a national refereed journal.

REVIEW OF PROFILE STEPS

This process followed the following steps.

Step 1   The Idea
Step 2   The Title
Step 3   The Structure
Step 4   Identifying the Audience
Step 5   Choosing the Journal
Step 6   Writing the Draft
Step 7   The Bibliography
Step 8   The Query Letter
Step 9   The Cover Letter

These steps can serve as an algorithm for other article manuscripts; yet, variations of this sequence are possible. For example, suppose you don't happen to have in your possession a review of the literature. You could begin by reviewing the literature as described earlier. Or, suppose you have been lecturing for a long time and you have several suggestions to share with your reader! You might want to begin by drafting the manuscript, later visiting the library or your computer terminal to conduct a review of the literature, using your findings to buttress your suggestions, and finally compiling a bibliography.

Glossary

Advance   Money a writer receives prior to publication to help cover the expense associated with preparing a manuscript. These expenses are usually deducted from the first royalty check.

Agent, Literary   Writers' assistants who help get contracts, more pay, and more rights and who help improve manuscripts.

Agent's Commission   Fee agents charge for services. Usually 15 percent.

American Society of Journalists and Authors (ASJA)   A national association of over 600 nonfiction writers which works to enhance the quality of writing. Publishes a newsletter and holds conferences. Located at 1501 Broadway, Suite 1907, New York, NY 10036.

Anecdote   A brief account of an incident, often humorous and often used to illustrate a principle.

Annotation   A note that explains a text.

Anthology   A collection of writings by the same or different authors.

A.P.A. Style   American Psychological Association's guidelines and rules for referencing.

Assignment, Writing   Commissioned work usually with either a set guaranteed pay or a set kill fee.

Author's Guidelines   Instructions printed in a journal to help prospective contributors prepare article manuscripts for that journal.

Author's Page   A page that lists the author's name and institutional affiliation.

Book Clubs   A club that buys large numbers of books at a grossly discounted price. Author's royalty rate is also usually significantly reduced.

Book Contract   A written agreement that spells out the responsibilities and rights of the author and the publisher.

Book Index   A list of major topics in a book. The author can either make up the index or have the publisher hire someone in-house or outside to make the index, whereupon the publisher deducts the indexer's fee from the author's first royalties.

Book Review   A written assessment of a book, intended to help a prospective consumer quickly determine if the book is worth buying or reading.

Bottom Line Writing   A style of writing that is brief and to the point.

Call for Manuscripts   A journal's advertisement written to solicit article manuscripts.

Chicago Style   A set of referencing guidelines contained in *A Manual of Style* published by the University of Chicago Press. Also called the Taurabian style.

Chunking   Breaking complex numbers or other information into small parts to facilitate its comprehension or recall.

Cliché   An overused phrase. Authors are often advised to avoid their use because they are more damaging than helpful.

Collaboration   Two or more writers working on the same writing piece.

Content Comparison Chart   A matrix designed to facilitate the comparison of similar documents.

Copyedited Manuscript   A manuscript that has been edited to remove errors and improve its communication.

Copy Editor   A publishing company employee who edits a book or article manuscript, correcting errors in punctuation, spelling, and syntax.

Copyright   Legal protection against unfair use of an author's work.

Cover Letter   (Also called a covering letter.) A letter that accompanies a manuscript. Correctly designed, the cover letter reminds the editor of his or her expressed interest in the work, and reestablishes the author's credibility and the manuscript's currency.

Credibility, Author   Assurance that an author has the expertise required to write whatever that author is writing for publication.

Credit Line   The author's name and affiliation and sometimes information to capture the reader's interest.

Database   A collection of related information stored in a computer.

Deadline   A specified time by which the author promises to submit a complete manuscript to the editor.

Editing   Reading the manuscript and making improvements by changing the content and syntax or removing errors and excessive words.

Editor, Acquisitions   An editor who seeks authors and manuscripts that match the company's publishing needs. Often working through agents, the acquisitions editor designs contracts.

Fair Use   The amount of copyrighted material that can be used without breaking copyright law.

Filler   A short manuscript used to "fill out" a journal issue.

Finishing Out   Locating a short manuscript or other material needed to complete an issue of a journal.

Fog Index   A formula for determining a writing's level of reading difficulty.

Freelance Writer   A writer who sells work to more than one client.

Galley Proof A manuscript set into print type.

Genre A category of writings (for example, self-help, how-to, or mystery books).

Glossary A list of definitions belonging to the same subject.

Guest Editor A professional outside the journal's staff who is invited or permitted to plan and construct an issue of that journal.

How-to Books A genre of books designed to explain how to accomplish particular tasks.

Kill Fee Compensation paid to an author for working on a project that is later canceled.

Lead Sentence The first sentence in a paragraph.

Model Release A written document granting permission to use someone's photograph in a publication.

On Speculation (Also called "on spec.") Nonobligatory agreement to consider a manuscript.

Proactive Business Writing A style of writing that empowers businessmen and business women.

Professional Book A book written to enable individual professionals to improve their professional skills.

Proofreading Reading a manuscript to remove errors.

Prospectus, Book A package of material an author designs to convince an acquisitions editor to offer a contract for a new book. Usually includes acknowledgements, preface, contents, and sample chapters.

Pseudonym A fictitious name for an author, used to protect the author's identity.

Query Letter (Also called a query). A letter to an editor that precedes the sending of the manuscript. Query letters are used to get the editor's interest in a manuscript.

Quotations, Books of Collections of quotations often used by writers.

Rating Scale Guidelines supplied by a journal for referees to use when evaluating a manuscript's potential for publication.

Refereed Article An article judged acceptable by selected professionals who use a rating scale and examine a manuscript anonymously.

Reference Books Books that writers use when writing.

Rejection Slip A notification from an editor rejecting a manuscript.

RFP Request for proposals, usually containing specific instructions on the desired content and format of proposals, deadline for submission of proposals, and other requirements.

SASE Self-addressed stamped envelope which editors expect authors to provide for the possible return of their manuscripts.

Self-help Books A genre of books written to help individuals improve their lives.

Self-publishing An author's publishing his or her own manuscripts.

Support Group   A group of writers who meet regularly to improve their writing skills.

Theme Issue   An issue of a journal having all or most articles written on the same theme.

Trade Book   Fiction and nonfiction books written to be sold to a mass market.

Turnaround Time   The time an editor requires to reach a publishing decision.

University Press   A book publisher associated with and usually belonging to a university. Most university presses specialize in a narrow subject range.

Vanity Publisher   A publishing company that requires authors to pay part of the publishing expenses.

Writer's Market   A comprehensive reference book for authors produced annually by the *Writer's Digest*.

Writers' Workshops   Workshops designed to help novice writers and experienced writers improve their writing skills.

Name Index

Aburdene, P., 4
Astaire, Fred, 44

Baughman, M. D., 144
Berger, Allen, 138
Brazelton, T. Berry, 141
Brooks, Douglas, 14
Brown, K. L., 62–63
Burack, Sylvia, 16
Bush, President George, 48
Buttery, Thomas R., 40, 102–104

Caesar, J., 7
Cheyney, Arnold, 40–41
Cheyney, Jeanne, 40–41
Clark, Mary Higgins, 16
Clemens, Samuel, 100
Clemet, Mary C., 226–227
Clouse, B., 161–162

Daugherty, Greg, 122
Dewey, John, 219
Dickens, Charles, 8–9, 64–66
Dunn, Rita, 10, 93–94

Einstein, Albert, 179
Eisner, Elliot, 5–6, 224
Eller, Ben F., 21

Faulkner, William, 69, 95
Fitzgerald, F. Scott, 100
Francis, Dick, 16

Galloway, C., 116
Garcia, Jesus, 29–30, 122–123
Gay, John, 57
Gilman, David, 6
Good, Thomas L., 6
Goodlad, John I., 81
Gore, Tipper, 34
Graham, Toby, 132–133
Grey, Zane, 100

Halpin, Gerald, 95
Halpin, Glenelle, 95
Hemingway, Ernest, 100
Henson, Kenneth, T., 17–19, 21, 64–66, 68, 69, 83–84, 92–93, 96, 102–104, 104–105, 137, 146, 147, 153, 196, 237–243
Hitler, A., 7

Jackson, Andrew, 224–225
Jarchow, Elaine, 10
Joyce, James, 95

Kilpatrick, James J., 90, 144
King, Stephen, 16

Locke, John, 54

Maddox, Robert, 12–13, 137
Mandela, Nelson, 208–209
Maverick, Maury, 44
Meyer, L. A., 93
Monza, H., 131

Naisbitt, J., 4

Orlich, Donald C., 175–176

Perkins, Maxwell, 100
Peters, Tom, 141
Pickins, A. L., 99

Ramirez, Olga, 170–171
Ramon, J., 90
Rawlings, Marjorie, 100
Rogers, Ginger, 44

Samson, Joan, 9, 44
Sheldon, Sidney, 16
Skeele, R., 227–228

Steinbeck, John, 7–8
Stevenson, Robert Lewis, 170, 224
Street, James, 100
Strunk, William, Jr., 14, 46, 98

Toppins, A. D., 56–57

Van Gogh, 2
Van Til, William, 26
Vonnegut, Kurt, 120

Welty, Eudora, 100
White, E. B.,14, 46, 98
Wilde, Oscar, 21–22, 236

Zinsser, W., 90

Subject Index

Ability to write, 20, 60
Abstracts, grant proposal, 184, 193–194
Acceptance rates, 238
Action in Teacher Education, 79
Action research, 87
Adjunct faculty, 231–232
Advanced editing exercise, 50
Advances on book contracts, 153
Advancing the professions, through
    publishing, 4
Advantages of writing. *See* Nature
    of writing
Affecting the reader, 170, 224
American Sociological Society, 124
Annual Reference Index. *See* Index,
    Annual Record
APA style, 94
Application, using examples to show,
    100–104
Applied journals, 27
Article length, 72–73
Article profile 283–290
Article writing versus book writing, 126
Artistic nature of writing, 5–6
Assertiveness. *See* Forceful writing
Assets, using, 172
Assurance to readers. *See* Promise
    to readers
At-press. *See* In-press
Attention, need to capture. *See* Hooks
Attitudes

of authors, 101
of editors, 108
Auctioneer, The, 8
Audience, importance of knowing, 90–91
Author-editor relationships, 109
Authors
    boldness, 119
    pomposity, 119
    self-confidence, 25, 119

Bahamas, 283
Behavioral science journals, preferences
    of, 244–245
Benefits of writing. *See* Nature of writing
Bible, 10, 47, 57
Bibliographical information, recording,
    29–30
Binder, grant writing, 225
Book chapters, using articles to write, 166
Book contracts, getting, 140–155
Book outlines, 143–144
Book prospectus, 143–149
    author description, 149
    book description, 146–148
    competition, description of, 149–150
    content comparison chart, 150
    market description, 148
    schedule for completing, 149
Book publishers, selecting 149–152
Books in Print, 150
Book writing, 140–155

Brevity, need for, 46–47
Brown-bag seminar, 138–139
Budget, grant proposal, 198–200
Burma Shave, 34
Burning desire to write, 120
Business Guide, 79
Business Index, 79
Business journals, preferences of, 246–247
Business of a writer, 40, 120
Business Periodicals Index, 29
Buyer's market, 9–10

*Cabell's Directory of Publishing
      Opportunities in Education,* 241
Call for manuscripts, 75
   sample, Appendix B, 258–260
Catalog of Federal Domestic Assistance,
      223–224
Chapter outline for books, 143–144
Charts, 36
Chicago Manual of Style, The, 94
Chronicle of Higher Education, The, 38–39
Chunking, 39
Clarifying nature of writing, 5–6
Clarity
   need for, 46, 97
   effect on acceptance, 46
   exercises to develop, 47, 48
   techniques for achieving, 46–48, 97–98
Clichés, 133–134
Collaborating, 125–126
   long distance, 126
   with students, 84–87
Cold reading, 94
Colleagues, as manuscript reviewers, 94
Colloquialisms, 50, 133–134
Coming themes
   announcements of, 75,
   sample, Appendix C, 261–263
Commitment to readers, 34–35
Communicating with journal editors,
      108–117, 241
Communications journals,
      preferences, 250
Competitive nature of writing, 9–10
Compulsion to write, 119–120

Computers, use in writing, 137–138
Computer search, 29
Concepts, using 81–82
Concise writing, 46–47
Conditional acceptance, 76
Confidence, effect of, 25, 60
Conjunctions, 50
Consultants, as sources of topics, 30–31
Content comparison chart, 150
Contract negotiation, 152–153
Contracts. *See* Book contracts
Contributing
   to professions, 4
   to readers, 35
Conventions, using, 30–31
Copyright permission, 130–131
Corporation funding practices, 175
Cover letters
   definition of, 115
   samples of, 85, 115
   revised, 86
Craft, writing as a, 20
Creative nature of writing. *See* Nature
      of writing
Credibility, establishing author, 61
Critical analysis of topics, 29–30
Cross Creek, 100

Data, a plural word, 95
Database, use of, 225
Deadlines, 175
Direct writing. *See* Concise writing
Descriptive nature of titles, 35
Disruptions, avoiding, 11–12
Dissertations, 25–27, 135

Economics and publishing, 142, 148
Editing exercises
   advanced, 44
   for conciseness, 47
   for gender fairness, 52
   for positive writing, 49
Editing
   nature of, 47
   role in writing, 47–48
Editor-author relationship, 109–115

Editors
  communicating with, 109–115
  requests for changes from, 76–77
Education Index, 29, 79–80
Education journals, preferences of,
    242–243
Eisenhower grants, 170–171
Elements of Style, The, 14, 46, 98
Eleventh hour grant proposals, 175–176
Empowering nature of writing, 4, 7, 8
Enlightening nature of writing, 5–6
Errors, eliminating most common,
    89–107
Examples, use of, 100–101
Excuses for not writing, 19–20
Expenses charged to authors, 129
Experience as a source of topics, 27–28
Expertise, author's use of, 27–28

Familiarity, 90–93. *See* Audience,
    importance of knowing
Familiar words, use of, 97–98
Fancy words, list of, 54–55
Fear, writer's, 25
Federal Register, 224–226
Fees, authors', 129
"Finishing out" a journal issue, 73
First sentence. *See* Lead sentences
First paragraph. *See* Lead paragraph
First purpose of a writer, 40, 120
Fixed royalty rates, 153
Flat fee royalties, 153
Flowcharts, use of, 69
Following up on surveys, 82
Forced writing, 6
Forceful writing, 7–8, 39–40
Forecasting the future, 30–32
  using journal editors in, 31
  using professional association, 31–32
  using speakers in, 30–31,
    yearbooks, 31–32
Forge forward, need to, 40
Foundation proposals, 176–178
Foundations. *See* Grant proposal
    writing; *National Data Book
    Foundations*

Frye Readability Graph, 74
Fulbright appointment, 1–3

Gender exercise, 53
Genders, fair treatment of, 52–56
Generic journals, 130
Glossary, 291
Goals, writing, 22
"Go ahead and write," 40
Goals through writing, 60
Gobbledygook, 54
Government documents, 173
Graduate students as collaborators, 135
Grammatical errors, 94
Grant proposal parts, 188–201
  abstract, 193–194
  budget, 198–200
    be reasonable, 198–200
    make in-kind contributions,
      198–199
  checklist, 199–200
  evaluation, 197–198
  purposes, goals, and objectives
    194–195
  requests for proposals, 189
  sample table of contents, 195
  sample timetable, 196
  sample title page, 192
  sample transmittal letter, 191
  table of contents, 194
  title page, 190–193
  transmittal letter, 189–190
Grant proposals
  abstracts, 184, 193–194
  budgets in, 185–186
  competitive nature of, 170
  convincing commitment, making a,
    180–181
  creativity in, 170
  deadlines in, 175
  evaluation of, 185–186
  flexibility, need for, 181–182
  format for, 175–176
  funder's goals in, 174–175, 196
  in-kind contribution, 198–199
  letters for, 178

Grant proposals *(continued)*
  matching expertise with needs, 179
  needs statement in, 175–176
  project objectives in, 176
  rating form, Appendix G, 280–282
  reasons for writing, 170–171
  requests for proposals, 175, 189
  sample, Appendix F, 270–279
  selecting funding sources for, 182–183
  selecting topics for, 179
  shotgun approach, 174
  source of grant topics, 171–172
  timing of, 171
  unique angle in, 179
  writing style for, 183–184
Grant proposals, three winning, 202–221
  grant writing workshops, 203
  Project ESCAPE
    dealing with disagreement, 207
    disseminating the grant, 209–211
    purpose, 203–205
    putting the funder's goals first, 205
    sample flowchart, 210
    unique features, 205–206
    using the literature, 206–207
    using modules, 207–209
  Summer Physics Institute
    lessons learned, 216, 219–220
    role of passion, 211–212
    unique features, 213–215
    using relationships with potential
      funders, 216–218
    using the literature, 218–219
    using your strengths, 218
Grant proposal writing 169–87
  assets, using your, 172
  develop fresh ideas, 171–172
  Eisenhower grants, 170–171
  essential materials
    *Catalog of Federal Domestic
      Assistance,* 173, 228
    Federal Register, 173, 227
    matching your strengths with
      funders' goals, 174–175
    National Data Book of Foundations,
      174, 228
  Internet resources, 222–229

  format for proposals, 175–176
  foundation proposals, 176–178
  guidelines for grant writing
    add a unique angle, 179–180
    be flexible, 181–182
    develop a project evaluation
      process, 185
    follow the RFP guidelines precisely,
      184–185
    make a convincing commitment,
      180–181
    make the proposal easy to read,
      183–184
    make your request economically
      responsible, 183
    match your expertise with the
      audiences' needs, 179
    test the budget against the
      narrative, 185–186
    use opportunities to learn about
      available money, 182–183
  making proposals timely, 171
  purpose of writing grants, 170
  requests for proposals, 175
  sample model proposal letter, 178
  sample needs statement
    evaluation, 177
  sample proposal abstract, 184
  sample proposal rating form, 280–282
  Triangular method, 174
Grants as writing topic sources, 27
Grant writer's binder. *See* Binder, grant
  writing
Graphs, when to use, 134
Guest editing, 116–117
Guidelines. *See also* Axioms, Cheyeny's
  for authors, 73–75
  for grant proposal writing, 179
  for publication, 73–75
  for reviewers, 75–78

Habit of excellence, 54
Headings. *See* Sub-headings
Health and nursing journals, preferences
  of, 244
Hooks, using, 35
How to Work for a Jerk, 144

HPERD journals, preferences of, 248–249
Humanities Index, 29

Idle reading, 16
Impressing editors, 46
Index cards, use in paragraphing, 67–68
Index Medicus, 29
Indiana University Workshop, 5
Indispensable manuscript qualities, 76
Information science journals,
    preferences of, 250
Informing nature of writing, 44
Initial printing, size of, 152
Initiative, author, 3
In-kind contribution, 198–199
"In press," 138
Integrity, author, 34–35
Internet, 222–229
Interruptions, avoiding, 10
Invited submissions, 162

Jargon, 47
Job, as a source of topics, 27–28
Journal characteristics, using, 72–78
Journal editors as source of topics, 31
Journal preferences, Appendix A,
    237–257
Journal profile, 159
Journals
    need to know, 72
    use of to shape articles, 72–78
Joy of writing, 119–120
Jump-start words, 49–50

Knowledge base, contributing to, 4

Lead paragraphs, 99–100
Lead sentences, 37–39
Length, calculating manuscript, 72–73
Librarianship journals, preferences
    of, 250
Libraries
    choosing target journals, 78–79
    topic identification, 78–79
    use of, 132–133
Library, personal, 14–15
Life of manuscript, 82

Linear writing, 123–124
Lists, using, 35–36
Literary agents. *See* Agents
Literary Market Place, 150
Literature review, 26
Location for writing, the best, 15–16
Long-distance collaborating, 126
Longhand, writing in, 10
Long words, 54–57
Luck, 45, 157–158

Mama's hats, 15–16
Managing manuscripts, system for,
    158–161
Manual of Style, A (Chicago style), 94
Manuscript
    preparation, 72–78
    preparation guidelines, 73–75
    tracking form, 164
Marathons, writing, 10
Matching grant proposal writer's
    strengths with funder's goals, 174
Maxims for writing (Cheyneys'), 41
Medical Index, 78
Meeting authors and speakers, 30–31
Megatrends 2000, 4
Merit pay, 4
Mileage from research, 164–166
Mistakes, list of common writing, 90–98
MLA Bibliography, 29
Money, as a reason to write, 4
Money Magazine, 122
Monograph, 153
Mood, 20
Multiple behavior of successful authors,
    123–124
Multiple submissions, 124–125
Multiple tracking system, sample,
    163–164
Muse, 284
Music store experience, 16
Myths, 17–19

Names, role in acceptance, 45
Names, order of author, 134–135
National Businesswoman, The, 11
National Data Book of Foundations, 228

National Institutes of Health, 228
National Science Foundation
    website, 228
Nature of writing
    creativity, 40
    self-discipline, 90
    unnatural act, 90
Negatives, eliminating. *See* Positive
    writing
Negotiating book contracts, 152–153
Newspaper readers, 63
"Not right for our journal," 89
Numerals, use in titles, 64–66
Nursing journals, preferences of, 244

Obtuse writing, 54–55
Occupation as topic source, 27–28
Office, writing, 13–14
"One-Pulse Words," 56–57
"On inspection," 16
On-line submissions, 241
Open-ended questions, 83
Opening paragraphs, 97, 99–100. *See also*
    Lead paragraphs
Opportunities to publish, 21
Organizing articles, 59–70
Organizing writing sessions. *See*
    Support groups
Outlines, using, 40
Over-quoting a source, 95

Paradoxes and promises article, 64–66
Paragraphing, 39–40, 67–69
Paragraphing exercise, 68
Passive voice, avoiding, 97
Pedantic writing, 97
Perception, role of, 21–22
Perfectionist error, 40
Permission to reprint. *See* Copyright
    permission
Personalizing writing, 15
Perspective, role in writing, 21
Phi Delta Kappa, 153
Phi Delta Kappan, 79
Photo grants. *See* Grants for
    photographs
Photo story, 157–158

Photos, use with article, 157
Physics Institute. *See* University of
    Alabama physics institutes.
Places to write, 14–18
Placing subjects and verbs. *See* Forceful
    writing
Plain talk, 46–48
Planning for success, 156–168
Pompous writing, 97
Portable offices, 15
Positive writing, 48–52
Post-It tabs, 15
Power of writing, 7
Power writing. *See* Forceful writing
Predicting popular topics, strategies for,
    30–32
Preferences of several journals,
    Appendix A, 237–257
Preparing manuscripts, 73–75
Prestige through writing, 3–4
Prioritizing journals, 158–161
Proactive nature of writing, 21
Professional associations as source for
    article topics, 31
Professional books, writing, 141–142
Professional contribution through
    writing, 4
Professional societies, use to identify
    topics, 31–32
Profile, article, Appendix H, 283–290
Profile of Bonnidell Clouse, 161–162
Promises to readers, 35
Promotion, writing to earn, 2
Proofreading. *See* Cold reading
Proposal for funding, sample of, 270–279
Proposal rating form, 280
Prospectus, book, 143–149
Protect manuscripts, need to, 136
Provincialism, ways to avoid, 100–104
Psychological Abstracts, 29
Publication guidelines, 73–75
Publishing expenses, paying 129
Publishers, selecting book, 149–152
Publishers Chart, 151
Purdue University grant writing Web
    site, 226
Purpose of writer, first, 40

Query letters for articles, 111–115
   definition of, 111
   samples of, 112, 113
   techniques for writing, 111–115
Query letters for books, 152
   sample of, 154
Questionnaire
   cover letters for, 82–83
   sample of, 85
Questionnaires to editors. *See* Surveys,
   sample of, 83
Questions asked by writers, 118–139
Quotes
   overuse of, 95
   using, 15, 80, 81

Raising PG Kids in an X-Rated Society, 34
Rating scales
   definition of, 75–76,
   sample of, 77
   use of, 75–77
Readability graph. *See* Frye readability
   graph
Readability level, 73
Readers' Guide, 29
Reading fee, 129
Reading level, system for calculating, 73,
Reasons for not writing, 1–23,
Reasons for writing, 119–120,
Refereed journal, definition of, 127
Refereeing, table for, 127
Referee status, system to
   determine, 238
Reference books, use to identify topics,
   29–30
Reference style, 240
Referencing articles and books, 93–94
Rejection
   how to handle, 122–123
   rates of, Appendix A, 237–257
Relationships, *See* Author-editor
   relationship
Relaxing nature of writing, 10, 11
Relevance, need for, 109
Request for proposals, 175, 189
Request to rewrite, 76–77
Research, sharing of, 3, 81

Research journals, writing for, 95,
   238–239
Responsibilities of editors. *See* Editor-
   author relationships
Resubmissions, effect on acceptance,
   136–137, 240–241
Résumés, reporting publications on,
   138, 166
Return rate, 82
Reviewers' guidelines, 75–78
Review manuscripts, author's need to,
   101–102,
Rewards of writing, 21
Rewrite, editors' request to, 136–137
Rewriting
   for a different audience, 44
   by editors, 76
   effect of, on acceptance, 136–137
   need to, 16
RFP. *See* Request for proposals
Rifle approach to grant writing, 174
"Right for our journal," 89
Rigidity of journals, 93–94
Roles, need to define collaborators',
   86–87
Rostrum, The, 16
Royalty rates, 152

Sample book chapters, sending, 145–146
Sample first page, 62–63
Sample manuscript tracking form, 164
Sample student article, 56–57
Satire, 166
Schedules, writing, 10–14
Scientific method, style of, 27
Search engines, 223, 225, 229
Seasoning, manuscript, 41
Selecting a book publisher, 149
Selecting target journals, 79–80, 99
Selective nature of today's readers, 34
Self-addressed stamped envelope
   (SASE), 75
Self-confidence, of authors, 25, 60
Self-denial required of authors, 11
Self-development as a reason to write,
   3, 4
Self-discipline, 9

Self-improvement, 3
Self-publishing
    advantages of, 129
    disadvantages of, 128
Self-reflection, writing as a means of, 5
Sending manuscripts, 9. *See also*
    Manuscript preparation
Sentence construction, 90
Sequencing, paragraph, 67–69
Serious writers, 2
Sex discrimination. *See* Genders, fair
    treatment of
Sharing ideas, through writing, 3, 5, 6
Short words, list of, 54–55
Shotgun approach to grant proposal
    writing, 174
Simultaneous submissions. *See* Multiple
    submissions
"Six Myths That Haunt Writers," 17–19
Smokestack theory, 175
Social Science Citation Index, 29
Social Science Index, 29
Social science journals, preferences of,
    244–245
Speakers as sources of topics, 30–31
Specialist versus generalist, writing as,
    129–130
Stimulating nature of writing, 11
Straightforward writing, 97
Stream of consciousness, 95
Style, writing, 43–58
Subheadings, using, 98
Substantive writing
    importance of, 36–37, 95–97
    need for, 61
    techniques for, 36, 61–67
Successful behavior of writers, 123–124
Successful writers, characteristics of,
    123–124
Success story, favorite, 120–122
Suggestions of editors, 120
Superintendent of Documents, 173
Support groups, 138–139
Surveys
    increasing return rates of, 82
    sample of, 83
    using, 81–82,

Survey to editors
    results, Appendix A, 237–257
    sample, 83

Table of contents, grant proposal, 194
Tables, use of, 134
Tale of Two Cities, A, 8–9
Target journals, selecting, 78–80, 99
"Teachers in Residence Partnership
    Program," 102–105
Teachers, power of, 8
Technology journals, preferences of, 250
Telephoning editors, suggestions for,
    109–111
Tenure and tenure-track positions
    adjunct faculty, 231–232
    adjunct faculty needs, 233
    using action research, 233–235
    using department goals, 232–233
    using interviews, 235–236
    writing to earn, 230–236
Theft of manuscript, guarding
    against, 136
Themes, 75, 99, 239. *See also*
    Announcement of coming themes
Theory Into Practice, 79
Thesis. *See* Dissertations
Thinking, effect of writing on, 5, 6
Time for writing
    the best, 12–13
    finding, 10–14
Time management, 134
Titles, writing, 34–37
    descriptive, 35
    guide to writers, 37
    hooks, 35, 38–39
    importance, 99
    promises, 35–36
Tooling up for writing, 13–14
Topic-screening, 29–30
Topics, identifying, 24–32
    dissertation as source, 25–28
    forecasting the future, 30–32
    grant as source, 27
    job as source, 27–28
    other occupations as sources, 28
    reference books as sources, 29–30

Tracking system, manuscript, 163–164
Triangular System for grant writing, 174
Turnaround time, 239–240

Unique angle in grant proposals, 179, 205–206
University of Alabama physics institutes, 104–105
University presses, 142–143. *Also see* Appendix E, list of university presses, 266–269
Updating dissertations and theses, 25–27
USA Today, 63

Vanity publishing, 128–129. *See also* Self-publishing, definition of
Vocabulary, role of, 18–19

Walking the walk, 104
Wildlife writer's story, 120–122
Word processor, use in writing, 137
Wordy expressions, list of, 54–55
Working nature of writing, 20
Workshops on writing, 5, 119–120. *See also* Appendix D, 264–265

World Wide Web, using the, 222–229
Write about what you know, 121–122
Writer Magazine, The, 16
Writer's Art, The, 90
Writer's Handbook, 16
Writers' main task, 40
Writer's Market, 150, 241
Writing, nature of
a clarifying process, 5–6
a learned activity, 20
a self-disciplined act, 10
an unnatural act, 90
a way of learning, 6
a way of sharing, 6
a way of self-reflection, 6
Writing classes, 55–56
Writing environment, 14–18
Writing tablet, use in library, 80
Writing workshops. *See* Workshops, writing.

Yearbooks. *See* Forecasting the future, 31–32
Yearling, The, 100